A Centripetal Theory of Democratic Governance

This book sets forth a relatively novel theory of democratic governance, applicable to all political settings in which multiparty competition obtains. Against the prevailing decentralist theory (deriving from Madison and Montesquieu), John Gerring and Strom C. Thacker argue that good governance arises when political energies are focused toward the center. Two elements must be reconciled in order for this process of gathering together to occur: institutions must be inclusive, and they must be authoritative. The authors refer to this combination of attributes as "centripetal."

While the theory has many potential applications, this book is concerned primarily with national-level political institutions. Among these, the authors argue that three are of fundamental importance in securing a centripetal style of democratic governance: unitary (rather than federal) sovereignty, a parliamentary (rather than presidential) executive, and a closed-list PR electoral system (rather than a single-member district or preferential-vote system). These institutions are tested against a broad range of governance outcomes.

John Gerring received his Ph.D. from the University of California at Berkeley in 1993. He is currently Professor of Political Science at Boston University, where he teaches courses on methodology and comparative politics. His books include *Party Ideologies in America, 1828–1996* (1998), *Social Science Methodology: A Criterial Framework* (2001), and *Case Study Research: Principles and Practices* (Cambridge University Press, 2007). His articles have appeared in *American Journal of Political Science*, *American Political Science Review*, *British Journal of Political Science*, *Comparative Political Studies*, *International Organization*, *Journal of Policy History*, *Journal of Theoretical Politics*, *Party Politics*, *Political Research Quarterly*, *Polity*, *PS: Political Science and Politics*, *Social Science History*, *Studies in American Political Development*, and *World Politics*. He was a Fellow of the School of Social Science at the Institute for Advanced Study (2002–03) and is the current recipient of a grant from the National Science Foundation (2007–10). He is the former editor of *Qualitative Methods*, the newsletter of the American Political Science Association Organized Section on Qualitative and Multi Method Research, and current president of the section.

Strom C. Thacker received his Ph.D. in political science from the University of North Carolina, Chapel Hill, in 1996. He is currently Associate Professor of International Relations and Director of Latin American Studies at Boston University. His research and teaching focus broadly on questions of political economy, governance, and development, with a regional focus on Mexico and Latin America. His books include *Big Business, the State, and Free Trade: Constructing Coalitions in Mexico* (Cambridge University Press, 2000). He is currently working on a project on the politics of public health. He has published articles in *American Political Science Review*, *British Journal of Political Science*, *Business and Politics*, *International Organization*, *Journal of Interamerican Studies and World Affairs*, and *World Politics*. He also has an ongoing interest in the politics of foreign aid and lending and the International Monetary Fund. He is a Faculty Affiliate of the David Rockefeller Center for Latin American Studies at Harvard University and a Fellow at the Frederick S. Pardee Center for the Study of the Longer-Range Future at Boston University. He has been a Visiting Associate Professor of Government at Harvard University, a Susan Louise Dyer Peace Fellow at Stanford University's Hoover Institution, and a Fulbright Scholar.

A Centripetal Theory of Democratic Governance

JOHN GERRING

Boston University

STROM C. THACKER

Boston University

CAMBRIDGE UNIVERSITY PRESS
Cambridge, New York, Melbourne, Madrid, Cape Town, Singapore, São Paulo, Delhi

Cambridge University Press
32 Avenue of the Americas, New York, NY 10013-2473, USA

www.cambridge.org
Information on this title: www.cambridge.org/9780521710152

First published 2008

Printed in the United States of America

A catalog record for this publication is available from the British Library.

Library of Congress Cataloging in Publication Data

Gerring, John, 1962–
A Centripetal theory of democratic governance / John Gerring, Strom C. Thacker.
p. cm.
Includes bibliographical references and index.
ISBN 978-0-521-88394-8 (hardback) – ISBN 978-0-521-71015-2 (pbk.)
1. Democracy 2. Political science. I. Thacker, Strom Cronan. II. Title.
JC423.G375 2008
321.8 – dc22 2007030488

ISBN 978-0-521-88394-8 hardback
ISBN 978-0-521-71015-2 paperback

To Asli

J.G.

To Matthew, Caroline and William

S.C.T.

Of the many analogies that have been remarked between Law in the Physical and Law in the Moral World, none is more familiar than that derived from the Newtonian astronomy, which shows us two forces always operative in our solar system. One force draws the planets towards the sun as the centre of the system, the other disposes them to fly off from it into space. So in politics, we may call the tendency which draws men or groups of men together into one organized community and keeps them there a Centripetal force, and that which makes men, or groups, break away and disperse, a Centrifugal. A political Constitution or frame of government, as the complex totality of laws embodying the principles and rules whereby the community is organized, governed, and held together, is exposed to the action of both these forces. The centripetal force strengthens it, by inducing men (or groups of men) to maintain, and even to tighten, the bonds by which the members of the community are gathered into one organized body. The centrifugal assails it, by dragging men (or groups) apart, so that the bonds of connexion are strained, and possibly at last loosened or broken.... Accordingly the history of every community and every constitution may be regarded as a struggle between the action of these two forces, that which draws together and that which pushes apart, that which unites and that which dissevers.

– James Bryce (1905: 96–7)

Contents

Figures

Tables

Acknowledgments

For comments and suggestions on portions of the manuscript we are grateful to Pablo Baramendi, Dawn Brancati, Tom Burke, Kent Eaton, Neil Englehart, Archon Fung, Chappell Lawson, Evan Lieberman, Arend Lijphart, Howard Reiter, David Samuels, Peter Spiegler, and David Waldner. For helpful answers to specific queries, or for sharing their data, we owe thanks to Victor Aguirregabiria, Andre Blais, John Carey, Tulia Falletti, Kenneth Hill, Macartan Humphreys, Mark Jones, Daniel Kaufmann, Philip Keefer, Atul Kohli, Branko Milanovic, Nicolas van de Walle, and David Weakliem. Thanks especially to Matt Shugart, whom we continually harassed for information regarding the shape of political institutions around the world. His encyclopedic knowledge was indispensable. For his ongoing support, and indefatigable patience, we are grateful to our editor at Cambridge University Press, Lew Bateman.

Portions of this book were presented at the annual meetings of the American Political Science Association; the Department of Political Science, Brown University; the Center for the Study of Democratic Politics, Princeton University; the Institute for Advanced Study; the Comparative Politics Workshop, Princeton University; the Seminar on U.S. and World Affairs at the Hoover Institution, Stanford University; the Comparative Politics Workshop, Stanford University; the Workshop on the Economic Consequences of Democratic Institutions, Duke University; and the COMPASS research group, Louvain-la-Neuve, Belgium. We thank all of the organizers of and participants in these meetings for the opportunity to present our research and for their useful comments on it. Papers drawn from this project have been published in *American Political Science Review*, *British Journal of Political Science*, and *Comparative Political Studies*. We thank the publishers for permission to incorporate portions of those papers into the book.

During the 2002–03 academic year, the authors were fortunate to obtain fellowships from the Institute for Advanced Study (Gerring) and Stanford University's Hoover Institution (Thacker). We are grateful to these institutions for their support, their delightful environs, and good company. Our departments at Boston University continue to provide a stimulating, supportive atmosphere for our teaching and research.

The book could not have been written without generous research funding from the Frederick S. Pardee Center for the Study of the Longer-Range Future at Boston University. We wish, in particular, to thank Fred Pardee, David Fromkin, Maddie Goodwin, and Connie Cramer for their support of our research at the center.

We also want to express our deep gratitude to Carola Moreno and Rodrigo Alfaro, who patiently worked through countless revisions of the data analysis and provided stellar research assistance.

Finally, we thank our families for their unending support throughout the long process of writing this book.

A Centripetal Theory of Democratic Governance

1

Models of Governance

Why are some countries better governed than others? This venerable question has innumerable possible answers. Variation in the quality of governance may be attributed to geography, economics, class and ethnic group dynamics, social capital, and political culture. It is also presumably affected by geopolitical factors, by political leadership, and by diverse historical legacies.

In this book we focus on the role of political institutions – that is, *government* – in providing good governance. Other factors (societal, cultural, geopolitical, or contingent) lie in the background. Within the realm of polities, we focus on democratic regimes. We understand a country to be democratic when multiparty competition is in place. (We are *not* interested, therefore, in the role of political institutions in maintaining or undermining democracy, a subject that has received a good deal of attention from scholars.)[1]

Why are many democracies plagued by corruption and ineptitude, while others manage to implement policies effectively and efficiently? Why do some democracies suffer from inefficient markets and low levels of investment while others enjoy low transaction costs, high levels of capital investment, and strong economic growth? Why are rates of morbidity, mortality, illiteracy, and other aspects of human well-being depressingly high in some democracies and impressively low

[1] Cheibub (2007), Linz (1990, 1994), Linz and Stepan (1978), Stepan and Skach (1993).

in others? More specifically, what effect do various political institutions have on the quality of governance in a democracy?

In this introductory chapter we lay out the currently dominant view on this subject, which we call *decentralist*, and set forth our own contrasting view, which we call *centripetal*. We then proceed to elaborate the causal argument underlying the centripetal theory of governance.

DECENTRALISM

Most recent work on the question of democratic governance is implicitly or explicitly decentralist. Contemporary writers and commentators usually assume that government works best when political institutions diffuse power broadly among multiple, independent bodies. This is the model of good government that most Americans embrace. It is also the model that most academics, NGOs, and international organizations (such as the World Bank) have adopted in recent years.

The decentralist paradigm is by no means new. In Western thought, the idea may be traced back to early attempts to constrain the abuse of political authority. Commonly cited exemplars include Greece and Rome in the classical age and the Italian, Swiss, and Dutch polities in the early modern era.[2] But the theory of decentralism was not fully formed as a self-conscious theory of governance until the seventeenth and eighteenth centuries. In the wake of the English Revolution, a cavalcade of scribblers and activists including William Blackstone, Lord Bolingbroke, Major Cartwright, Edward Coke, William Godwin, James Harrington, John Locke, John Milton, Robert Molesworth, Joseph Priestley, Algernon Sidney, and John Trenchard – collectively referred to as the Old Whig, Country, Commonwealth, or Dissenting tradition – formulated various facets of the decentralist model.[3] It was the English state, as a matter of fact and a matter of principle, that supplied a primary touchstone for these writers – even those, like Montesquieu and Rousseau, who resided abroad.[4]

[2] Gordon (1999).

[3] Brewer (1976), Foord (1964), Gunn (1969), Kramnick (1968), Robbins (1959/1968), Vile (1967/1998).

[4] In principle, these writers were largely agreed. But there was some considerable difference of opinion as to how principle matched up with reality. Many of the aforementioned writers were highly critical of the actual workings of English government

All this began to change after the American Revolution, a revolution motivated by Old Whig principles. As the British polity became increasingly centralized throughout the course of the nineteenth century, a new democracy appeared, embodying the decentralist ideal in a more conspicuous fashion. The Constitution of the United States wrote decentralist principles into the country's fundamental law, and the *Federalist Papers* provided an interpretive catechism. If ever a country was founded self-consciously on the decentralist ideal, that country was the United States. Not surprisingly, in the subsequent centuries and up to the present time the normative ideal of a de-concentrated, decentralized polity has been associated with the theory and practice of the American Constitution.[5] So it was that the decentralist ideal, an inheritance of political thought in England, gained a new home in its former colony.[6]

Among Old Whigs perhaps the most revered writer of all was William Blackstone, whose *Commentaries on the Laws of England* educated generations of British jurists. Blackstone's interpretation of the English constitution would endure for several centuries (until Bagehot's *English Constitution*, to be discussed later). The key feature of this interpretation was the "mixed" constitution, an idea derived from Aristotle. Blackstone explains:

> The legislature of the kingdom is entrusted to three distinct powers entirely independent of each other, first, the King; secondly, the Lords Spiritual and Temporal, which is an aristocratical assembly of persons selected for their piety, their birth, their wisdom, their valour, or their property; and thirdly, the House of Commons, freely chosen by the people from among themselves, which makes it a kind of democracy; as this aggregate body, actuated by different springs, and attentive to different interests, composes the British Parliament, and has the supreme disposal of every thing; there can no inconvenience

in the post-Revolutionary era. The dominance of the Crown and of the "Court" party was thought to compromise the formal principles of balance, separation, and member independence. It was alleged by these writers that the Commons was controlled by corrupt factions, which extended royal munificence to those who obligingly supported its policies on the floor of the Commons, and whose insidious influence threatened to upset the delicate balance of center and periphery.

5 Switzerland, along with pre-modern polities in England, the Netherlands, and northern Italy, are also occasional reference points.

6 Bailyn (1967, 1968), Pocock (1975), Pole (1966), Shalhope (1972, 1982), Wood (1969).

be attempted by either of the three branches, but will be withstood by one of the other two; each branch being armed with a negative power sufficient to repel any innovation which it shall think inexpedient or dangerous.[7]

The theory of the mixed constitution, with all its parts in balance, was said to extend back to Anglo-Saxon England.[8]

This notion led directly to the theory of the separation of powers, as articulated initially by Montesquieu and somewhat later by Madison, in the famed Federalist Paper 51.[9]

The great security against a gradual concentration of the several powers in the same department, consists in giving to those who administer each department the necessary constitutional means and personal motives to resist encroachments of the others.... Ambition must be made to counteract ambition.... In republican government, the legislative authority necessarily predominates. The remedy for this inconveniency is to divide the legislature into different branches; and to render them, by different modes of election and different principles of action, as little connected with each other as the nature of their common functions and their common dependence on society will admit.[10]

Amalgamating the work of Montesquieu, Madison, and countless other constitutionalists from the eighteenth century to the present, M. J. Vile arrives at what he calls a "pure doctrine" of separate powers.

It is essential for the establishment and maintenance of political liberty that the government be divided into three branches or departments, the legislature, the executive, and the judiciary. To each of these three branches there is a corresponding identifiable function of government, legislative, executive, or judicial. Each branch of the government must be confined to the exercise of its own function and not allowed to encroach upon the functions of the

[7] Blackstone (1862: 36).

[8] Pocock (1957/1987).

[9] "When the legislative and executive powers are united in the same person, or in the same body of magistracy, there can be then no liberty; because apprehensions may arise, lest the same monarch or senate should enact tyrannical laws, to execute them in a tyrannical manner. Again, there is no liberty, if the power of judging be not separated from the legislative and executive powers. Were it joined with the legislative, the life and liberty of the subject would be exposed to arbitrary control; for the judge would be then the legislator. Were it joined to the executive power, the judge might behave with all the violence of an oppressor" (Montesquieu, quoted in Casper 1989: 214).

[10] Madison, Federalist 51 (Hamilton et al. 1787–88/1992: 266–7).

> other branches. Furthermore, the persons who compose these three agencies of government must be kept separate and distinct, no individual being allowed to be at the same time a member of more than one branch. In this way each of the branches will be a check to the others and no single group of people will be able to control the machinery of the State.[11]

Separate powers thus refers to a division of labor and diffusion of power at the national level (or indeed at any single level of government).

Federalism, the second theoretical component of decentralism, is also an ancient idea.[12] Broadly interpreted, the federal idea may be traced back to city-state confederations in classical Greece, the medieval Hanseatic League, and the equally venerable Swiss confederation. If we take a more restrictive view of what it means to be federal, the arrival of this form of government has a fairly precise date: the founding of the American republic. Indeed, the United States was the first polity to invoke federalism as an explicit theory of governance.

Thus, the theory of decentralism has two fundamental axioms, one pertaining to horizontal divisions (separate powers) and the other pertaining to vertical divisions (federalism). Both are enshrined in the U.S. Constitution. Potentially, the theory of decentralism extends to other political institutions as well, a matter we shall shortly explore. But first, it is important that we take note of two quite different perspectives on the virtues of decentralization.

The dominant strand, including Blackstone, Montesquieu, and Madison, sees in decentralized institutions a mechanism to prevent direct popular rule, or at least to moderate its effects. A majoritarian system, it is feared, is prey to manipulation by unscrupulous leaders and envious masses bent on the redistribution of wealth.[13] A second

[11] Vile (1967/1998: 14). See also Brennan and Hamlin (1994), Gwyn (1965), Marshall (1971: 100), and Tomkins (2001).

[12] "A constitution is federal," writes William Riker (1964: 11), "if 1) two levels of government rule the same land and people, and 2) each level has at least one area of action in which it is autonomous, and 3) there is some guarantee (even though merely a statement in the constitution) of the autonomy of each government in its own sphere." On the theory and intellectual history of federalism, see also Beer (1993), Davis (1978), and Mogi (1931).

[13] Riker (1982).

strand, associated with Paine, Rousseau, and others of a radical (in present parlance, left-wing) persuasion, sees in decentralized power a mechanism for bringing government closer to the people. Their assumption is that centralized power is usually controlled by elites, whose interests run contrary to those of the masses. The only hope for popular control of government is therefore to de-concentrate the locus of decision making.

Radicals share with their Establishment confreres a belief that government is mostly to be feared, rather than trusted. Both Madison and Paine see good government as equivalent to limited government. In the much-quoted words of Adam Smith:

> Every system which endeavors, either, by extraordinary encouragements, to draw towards a particular species of industry a greater share of the capital of the society than what would naturally go to it; or, by extraordinary restraints, to force from a particular species of industry some share of the capital which would otherwise be employed in it; is in reality subversive of the great purpose which it means to promote. It retards, instead of accelerating, the progress of the society towards real wealth and greatness; and diminishes, instead of increasing, the real value of the annual produce of its land and labour.
>
> All systems either of preference or of restraint, therefore, being thus completely taken away, the obvious and simple system of natural liberty establishes itself of its own accord. Every man, as long as he does not violate the laws of justice, is left perfectly free to pursue his own interest his own way, and to bring both his industry and capital into competition with those of any other man, or order of men. The sovereign is completely discharged from a duty, in the attempting to perform which he must always be exposed to innumerable delusions, and for the proper performance of which no human wisdom or knowledge could ever be sufficient; the duty of superintending the industry of private people, and of directing it towards the employments most suitable to the interest of the society. According to the system of natural liberty, the sovereign has only three duties to attend to; three duties of great importance, indeed, but plain and intelligible to common understandings: first, the duty of protecting the society from the violence and invasion of other independent societies; secondly, the duty of protecting, as far as possible, every member of the society from the injustice or oppression of every other member of it, or the duty of establishing an exact administration of justice; and, thirdly, the duty of erecting and maintaining certain public works and certain public institutions, which it can never be for the interest of any individual, or small number of individuals, to erect and maintain; because the profit could never

repay the expence to any individual or small number of individuals, though it may frequently do much more than repay it to a great society.[14]

In pithier, though perhaps overstated, terms, Thomas Paine opines,

Society is produced by our wants, and government by our wickedness. The former promotes our happiness *positively* by uniting our affections, the latter *negatively* by restraining our vices. The one encourages intercourse, the other creates distinctions. The first is a patron, the last a punisher. Society in every state is a blessing, but government even in its best state is but a necessary evil, in its worst state an intolerable one. . . . Government, like dress, is the badge of lost innocence; the palaces of kings are built on the ruins of the bowers of paradise.[15]

Among twentieth-century writers decentralism takes a number of different forms, each with its own terminology, theoretical framework, and policy concerns. This far-ranging camp includes early group theorists;[16] British pluralists;[17] American pluralists;[18] writers in the public choice tradition, especially as oriented around the intertwined ideas of separate powers, fiscal federalism, veto points, and insulation;[19] Guillermo O'Donnell's conception of horizontal accountability;[20] and certain renditions of principal-agency theory.[21] This set of views is for the most part consonant with modern conservatism (i.e., nineteenth-century liberalism), as articulated by A. V. Dicey, Milton Friedman,

[14] Smith (1776/1939: 650–1). Centuries later, the idea is reiterated in public choice work. "Rent-seeking activity," writes James Buchanan, "is directly related to the scope and range of government activity in the economy, to the relative size of the public sector" (Buchanan 1980: 9; see also Colander 1984: 5).

[15] Paine (1776/1953: 4). James Madison (1973: 525) concurred, though in more moderate tones: "It has been said that all Government is an evil. It would be more proper to say that the necessity of any Government is a misfortune."

[16] Bentley (1908/1967).

[17] Laski (1917, 1919, 1921). For writings by G. D. H. Cole and J. N. Figgis, see Hirst (1989).

[18] Dahl (1956, 1961, 1967), Herring (1940), Truman (1951).

[19] Aghion et al. (2004), Brennan and Hamlin (1994), Buchanan and Tullock (1962), Hammond and Miller (1987), Henisz (2000, 2002), Keefer and Stasavage (2002), Lake and Baum (2001), Mueller (1996), Niskanen (1971), North and Weingast (1989), Oates (1972, 1999), Persson et al. (1997), Rasmusen and Ramseyer (1992), Tiebout (1956), Weingast (1995). For skeptical discussion of these assumptions, on purely formal grounds, see Treisman (2003).

[20] O'Donnell (1999).

[21] Moreno, Crisp, and Shugart (2003).

Friedrich Hayek, Robert Nozick, Herbert Spencer, Wilhelm von Humboldt, and Ludwig von Mises.

Despite their evident differences, all twentieth-century decentralists agree on several core precepts: diffusion of power, broad political participation, and limits on governmental action. Fragmentation sets barriers against the abuse of power by minorities, against the overweening ambitions of individual leaders, against democratic tyrannies instituted by the majority, and against hasty and ill-considered public policies. Decentralist government is limited government. Each independent institution acts as a check against the others, establishing a high level of interbranch accountability. Bad laws have little chance of enactment in a system biased heavily against change, where multiple groups possess an effective veto power over public policy. The existence of multiple veto points forces a consensual style of decision making in which all organized groups are compelled to reach agreement on matters affecting the polity.[22] Limitations on central state authority preserve the strength and autonomy of the market and of civil society, which are viewed as separate and independent spheres. Decentralized authority structures may also lead to greater popular control over, as well as direct participation in, political decision making. Efficiency is enhanced by political bodies that lie close to the constituents they serve, by a flexible apparatus that adjusts to local and regional differences, and through competition that is set into motion among rival governmental units.

So much for the theory. What are the specific institutional embodiments of decentralism? Separate powers implies two elective lawmaking authorities as well as a strong and independent judiciary. Federalism presumes the shared sovereignty of territorial units within the nation-state. Both also suggest a bicameral legislature, to further divide power at the apex and to ensure regional representation. In addition, the decentralist model seems to imply a written constitution, perhaps with enumerated individual rights and explicit restrictions on the authority of the central state. Most decentralists embrace the single-member district as a principle of electoral law, maximizing

[22] Buchanan and Tullock (1962). Although this vision of politics is associated with the work of George Tsebelis (1995, 2000, 2002), Tsebelis himself does not present a normative argument for a multiple-veto-points constitution (see Appendix A).

local-level accountability. Some advocate preferential-vote options (within single- or multimember districts) or a system of open primaries, thus decentralizing the process of candidate selection. Taking the principle of decentralism seriously leads us toward several additional institutional features: multiple elective offices, frequent elections (short terms), staggered terms of office, nonconcurrent elections, fixed-term elections (thus removing the tool of parliamentary dissolution from party leaders), term limits, popular referenda, recall elections, and loose, decentralized party structures.

Although one might quibble over details, there is no denying the basic institutional embodiments of the decentralist political order, where power is diffused among multiple independent actors. This is the reigning paradigm of good governance at the turn of the twenty-first century.

CENTRIPETALISM

In contrast to the precepts of decentralism, we argue that good government arises from institutions that *create* power, enhancing the ability of a political community, through its chosen representatives, to deliberate, reach decisions, and implement those decisions. Following James Bryce (see the epigraph), we refer to such institutions as centripetal, signifying a gathering together of diverse elements.[23]

Centripetalism, as the term implies, is more centralist than decentralist. Accordingly, its intellectual lineage may be traced back to Thomas Hobbes, Jean Bodin, and the concept of sovereignty as it developed in the seventeenth century.[24] Arguably, the primordial theory of governance is Hobbesian. The first task of government is to prevent humans from killing each other. Keeping the peace is necessary if civil society is to persist, and is achievable only in a political system that monopolizes power in the hands of a single individual. Challenges to unitary sovereignty lead to discord and, at the limit, to civil war, as Hobbes himself witnessed. The sovereign's will to power is in fact the secret ally

[23] The term "centripetalism" has also been employed in the context of party competition (Cox 1990; Reilly 2001; Sartori 1976; Sisk 1995). Our usage is evidently much broader. Another important antecedent is the work of Arend Lijphart, discussed at some length in Appendix B.

[24] Merriam (1900).

of good government, for a successful assertion of sovereignty produces a reign of tranquility. The stronger the sovereign, the more durable the peace.

This is, to be sure, a rather limited vision of good governance. Hobbes did not expect the sovereign to perform good works, beyond suppressing rebellion. In later centuries, the centralist ideal became more expansive. By the end of the nineteenth century it was possible to envision a sovereign who was at once supreme (for a limited time) and accountable. Walter Bagehot, who perhaps more than any other writer deserves to be credited as the theorist of democratic centralism, identified this new model of government in his classic work, *The English Constitution*, where he contrasted the developing Westminster polity with the highly decentralized American polity:

> Hobbes told us long ago, and everybody now understands, that there must be a supreme authority, a conclusive power, in every State on every point somewhere....[25] The splitting of sovereignty into many parts amounts to there being no sovereign.... The Americans of 1787 thought they were copying the English Constitution, but they were contriving a contrast to it. Just as the American is the type of *composite* Governments, in which the supreme power is divided between many bodies and functionaries, so the English is the type of *simple* Constitutions, in which the ultimate power upon all questions is in the hands of the same persons.... The English Constitution, in a word, is framed on the principle of choosing a single sovereign, and making it good; the American, upon the principle of having many sovereign authorities, and hoping that their multitude may atone for their inferiority.... Parliamentary government is, in its essence, sectarian government, and is possible only when sects are cohesive.[26]

For reform Whigs, Tories, and nineteenth-century Liberals including Burke, Peel, Disraeli, Gladstone, and Bagehot, strong government – personified in the bureaucracy and the cabinet – was a mechanism to resist popular pressures, restrain corruption, and limit the extravagances of the monarch.

A quite different motivation could be found among social liberals such as T. H. Green, L. T. Hobhouse, Graham Wallas, and Sidney and

[25] Bagehot (1867/1963: 214–15).
[26] Ibid., 219–22.

Beatrice Webb.[27] For the Fabians, strong government was a vehicle for social progress – strong enough to deal with the complexities of a turbulent, industrializing society and to overcome the resistance of privileged classes. Thus, like decentralism, the centralist vision draws on two delicately counterposed perspectives. An aristocratic, conservative ("Whig") version of centralism sits beside an egalitarian, social-democratic ("Fabian") version. Both survive today.[28]

These are centralism's intellectual roots. What about its political-institutional forms? As a specific set of institutions, centralism is usually identified with the English polity as it developed in the nineteenth century. During this busy century the ancient English constitution underwent a slow but dramatic transformation. The unelective branches of the state – the monarchy and the House of Lords – became increasingly vestigial, while the effective electorate, focused on the House of Commons, grew to include a majority of adult males. Constituencies became primarily single-member. These factors were sufficient to cause a dramatic centralization of power in the hands of Liberal and Conservative party leaders. Britain was thus transformed in the course of a century from one of Europe's most decentralized polities to, arguably, its most centralized.[29]

Meanwhile the American polity, while undergoing some degree of centralization, did not evolve nearly so fast nor so far as the British polity – a fact noticed by Bagehot and by many American commentators.[30] With respect to their political institutions, Britain modernized while its former colony did not. Thus, by the turn of the century a divergence of political forms had occurred across the shores of the Atlantic, a divergence that became even more dramatic as the twentieth century progressed. For those critical of the American trajectory, the new Westminster model was a model of "responsible party government." The American polity, by contrast, was

[27] Freeden (1978).

[28] Samuel Huntington is an articulate exemplar of centralist conservatism (e.g., Huntington 1968, 1981; see also Crozier et al. 1975). Most contemporary social democrats are centralists in the Fabian tradition.

[29] Cox (1987), Harrison (1996).

[30] Ford (1898/1967), Goodnow (1900), Lowell (1889), Wilson (1879/1965, 1885/1956).

criticized for its divided government, weak parties, and consequent lack of accountability.[31]

Today the centralist model, although rarely articulated in a self-conscious fashion, is attractive to scholars in a wide range of research traditions including economics and rational choice;[32] new institutionalism;[33] the welfare state and the developmental state;[34] and various critiques of interest group liberalism, pork barrelling, side payments, and political rents, evils commonly attributed to a fragmented ("hyper-pluralist") political structure.[35] For these writers, the secret of good government is to be found in a consolidation of political power within the framework of multiparty democratic elections. Operationally, this is usually understood as unitary government (rather than federalism), parliamentarism (rather than presidentialism), a first-past-the-post electoral system, strong parties, two-party dominance, and an unwritten constitution.[36]

While the Fabians (and the increasingly scarce Whigs) championed Westminster centralism, others were nervous. Over the course of the

[31] American Political Science Association (1950), Burns (1963), Fiorina (1980), Ranney (1962), Schattschneider (1942).

[32] Downs (1957), Schumpeter (1942/1950).

[33] Moe and Caldwell (1994), Olson (1982, 1986).

[34] Evans et al. (1985), Immergut (1992), Katzenstein (1978), Krasner (1978).

[35] Fiorina (1977), Lowi (1969), McConnell (1966).

[36] For the most part, we use the terms "centralist" and "Westminster" interchangeably. However, one other model of democratic centralism has attracted the attention of scholars in recent years. Fifth Republic France, in a marked departure from previous French republics, has managed to centralize political authority in the hands of a directly elected president, whose powers include the selection of the prime minister and the dissolution of parliament. The French president thus has considerably greater powers than the American president, under normal circumstances. The caveat is that in order to achieve this centralization it is necessary that parties have a strong electoral presence, as well as a strong presence in the legislature, and party competition must also be reduced to two major parties or coalitions. Otherwise, the president and his appointed prime minister will be unable to muster consistent majorities in the legislature and thus will be forced into a situation not unlike that of presidents in other polities (e.g., in the United States). "Cohabitation" appears to be on the rise in recent decades; indeed, it may be a semipermanent feature of the Fifth Republic. If so, the latter no longer serves as a paradigm of centralism. And even if not, we may doubt whether other polities, in societies less advanced and with shorter lineages of party competition, could achieve the requisite levels of party organization to assure that majorities in parliament regularly complement presidential victories. In short, as a general system of constitutional design (leaving aside the French experience) it seems that the French model of semi-presidentialism combined with single-member districts is unlikely to be as centralist as the Westminster model.

nineteenth century, a small group of high-minded – and generally high-born – reformers began to wrestle with the implications of a political system that centralized power in the hands of two political parties and – more alarmingly, perhaps – in the hands of the person who happened to lead the majority party. Dissent gradually crystallized around a set of reforms of electoral system law. Proportional representation (PR) was the remedy sought by a group of vociferous campaigners across Europe and North America, including Leonard Courtney, Thomas Hare, Sir John Lubbock, and John Stuart Mill in England; Victor d'Hondt in Belgium; Carl Andrae in Denmark; Eduard Hagenbach-Bischoff in Switzerland; Victor Considerant and André Sainte-Lague in France; and Francis Fisher and Simon Sterne in the United States.[37] Their arguments were varied, and not all would stand the scrutiny of later generations. But three points deserve mention here. First, PR reformers objected to the localist tendencies of the British electoral system, centered as it was on small (one- and two-member) constituencies. A proper political system, they thought, should act in the general interest, not in the interests of narrow constituencies. PR reformers were also bothered by the vulnerability of such a political system to the vagaries of popular opinion. Since elections in a Westminster system often rested on the votes of a few electors in swing districts, party leaders had to test the current of public opinion carefully before taking the initiative. This led, it was charged, to a plebiscitarian style of leadership, one oriented more toward pleasing the electorate's whims than advancing its long-run interests.[38]

Third, and most important, PR reformers objected to a system of election that effectively represented only two groups in parliament, and only one group in government. "In a really equal democracy," wrote Mill, "every . . . section would be represented, not disproportionately, but proportionately. . . . Man for man [the minority] would be as fully represented as the majority. Unless they are, there is not equal government, but a government of inequality and privilege: one part of the

[37] This section draws on Barber (1995: chapter one), Carstairs (1980), Commons (1907), Droop (1869), Farrell (2001), Hart (1992), Mill (1865/1958), and Noiret (1990). Of the outpouring of literature in the late nineteenth and early twentieth century on the subject of electoral reform, Droop (1869) is perhaps the most impressive example of early thinking about the role of electoral systems in politics and policy making.

[38] Hart (1992), Mill (1865/1958).

people rule over the rest." Indeed, Mill continued, "Democracy, thus constituted, does not even attain its ostensible object, that of giving the powers of government in all cases to the numerical majority. It does something very different: it gives them to a majority of the majority, who may be, and often are, but a minority of the whole."[39]

In the wake of initiatives launched by Mill and other early protagonists, PR became a reform cause with global dimensions. Many arguments were added to the arsenal, and a few subtracted. Perhaps the most important change in perspective concerned reformers' views of the role of political parties. While early PR enthusiasts were leery of the "machine" elements associated with organized parties and the consequent loss of member independence, later PR boosters turned the argument on its head. PR would *magnify* the strength of political parties, and this would be a good thing for democratic governance, for it would achieve the insulation from popular pressures that Mill and his cohort desired. Indeed, the operation of political parties under a PR system is quite different from its operation in a first-past-the-post electoral system. In the latter, party leaders cater to the median voter; small shifts of public opinion typically lead to great shifts in party control, and party leaders are therefore vulnerable. Not only do they risk losing office, and with it virtually all policy-making influence, but they also risk losing their place at the head of the party, for party losses are quite naturally blamed on the leadership. In PR systems, by contrast, party leaders can more easily ride out bad electoral weather. Secure in their leadership posts (since intraparty selection is generally controlled from above), secure from rapid alterations in the public mood (since they need only please a small contingent of hard-core supporters whose electoral support tends to be consistent from election to election), and secure from the necessity of implementing an electoral mandate (since governments are formed after extensive periods of negotiation, and subsequent policy making obscures party responsibility), party leaders approximate Mill's ideal of an "instructed minority" with long time horizons.[40]

39 Mill (1865/1958: 103–4).

40 Ibid., chapter seven. John Commons was one of the first advocates of PR to recognize the positive role of political parties in the governance process. Proportional representation, he writes, "is based upon a frank recognition of parties as indispensable in free government. This very recognition, instead of making partisan government all-powerful, is the necessary condition for subordinating parties to the public good.

Today, the modal form of government in Continental Europe conforms to the constitutional template suggested by early PR reformers. It is unitary, parliamentary, and closed-list PR. This may be coincidental; certainly, it was spurred by forces beyond the reformers' high-minded ideals. But it is noteworthy. In any case, this form of government has not received comprehensive theoretical treatment.[41] From existing theoretical perspectives, it appears as a mishmash: part centralist, part decentralist.

We argue that there is a coherent theory of politics lurking behind the façade of Continental European governments and others like them around the world. We use the term *centripetalism* to capture the intellectual lineage of centralism along with the criticisms leveled by advocates of PR. Centripetalism is rightly regarded as a modification of the British Westminster model along Continental lines.

The theory builds on the fundamental premise that good government results when political energies are focused toward the center. Two elements must be reconciled in order for this process of gathering together to occur. Institutions must be *inclusive*: they must reach out to all interests, ideas, and identities (at least insofar as they are relevant to the issue at hand). And they must be *authoritative*: they must provide an effective mechanism for reaching agreement and implementing that agreement.[42] In Pascal's well-chosen words, "Plurality which does not reduce itself to unity is confusion. Unity which is not the result of plurality is tyranny."[43] Centripetalism thus implies both (a) broad-based inclusion and (b) centralized authority.[44]

To control social forces, as well as physical forces, we must acknowledge their existence and strength, must understand them, and then must shape our machinery in accordance with their laws. We conquer nature by obeying her" (Commons 1907: 134).

41 The electoral system debate, first broached by J. S. Mill and his contemporaries in the mid-nineteenth century, has drawn a good deal of academic attention in recent years. Yet the current debate is narrowly cast. It concerns electoral rules, not broader features of constitutional design, and tends to focus on the rather simple question of how electoral systems structure party competition (Baron and Diermeier 2001; Cox and Shugart 1996; Finer 1975; Hart 1992). Our theoretical interests are broader, and in this respect resonate with older, nineteenth-century debates.

42 We should note that the principle of authority does not in any way preclude the delegation of power so long as such powers remain accountable to the center and can be withdrawn or rearranged at any time (see chapter five).

43 Pensee 870 (Pascal 1958: 261).

44 This two-dimensional theory of governance conforms closely to Giovanni Sartori's (1987: 131) distinction between vertical and horizontal dimensions of democratic

This theory suggests the following organizational forms, modeled on the Continental European polity: a unitary (rather than federal) constitution; a parliamentary (rather than presidential) executive; a closed-list PR electoral system (rather than single-member district or preferential-vote systems); the power to dissolve parliament (no fixed terms); no incumbency limits; few elective offices; congruent election cycles; strong parties; multiparty (rather than two-party) competition; and popular referenda only at the instigation of the legislature (or not at all). Each of these institutional features serves to maximize – and, if possible, to reconcile – the twin goals of inclusion and centralization, thus focusing power toward the center and gathering together diverse elements into a single policy stream.

Although one hesitates to rest any theory this broad on the status of individual countries, it may be heuristically useful to observe that while the United States is the generally acknowledged avatar of decentralism, Scandinavia offers some of the best exemplars of centripetalism among the world's long-standing democracies. Denmark, Norway, and Sweden are all centripetal polities, as are a number of new or recently reformed democracies in Europe. Thus, the identification of centripetalism with the pattern of politics normal in Continental Europe is an appropriate theoretical and empirical point of departure.

CONTRASTS

We have now discussed a variety of different models of democratic governance. One method of summarizing these contrasts is suggested by the combination of two dimensions that we have already introduced, *inclusion* and *authority*. The first indicates the extent to which political institutions are designed to incorporate a diversity of interests, ideas, and identities in the process of governance. The second indicates the extent to which political institutions centralize constitutional sovereignty within a democratic framework. The intersection of these two dimensions provides a two-by-two matrix within which

polities. The first relates to "subordination, superordination, and coordination – in essence, with the hierarchical structuring of collectivities." The second relates to coordination and communication efforts across levels (see also O'Donnell 1999).

		AUTHORITY –	AUTHORITY +
INCLUSION	–	*1. Anarchy*	*2. Centralist*
INCLUSION	+	*3. Decentralist*	*4. Centripetal*

FIGURE 1.1. Models of governance in two dimensions.

a variety of influential models of governance may be parsimoniously arrayed, as illustrated in Figure 1.1.

The combination of low inclusion and low authority (cell 1) defines the condition of anarchy (minimal or no rule). The combination of centralized authority without inclusionary institutions (cell 2) is the definition of democratic centralism, as evidenced by the Westminster model. The combination of decentralized authority and inclusion (cell 3) is the hallmark of the decentralist model. Lastly, the combination of authority and inclusion (cell 4) defines the centripetal model we have just elaborated.

Our principal focus is on the contrast between decentralism and centripetalism, and it is this contrast that we develop in the remainder of the book. To review, decentralists envision political institutions that are separate and independent of one another, resulting in a decision-making process that is segmented and localized, and consequently requires broad consensus in order to achieve changes in the status quo. Centripetalism sees the source of good government in institutions that reconcile inclusion and authority, bringing interests, ideas, and identities toward the center into an authoritative decision-making process.

At a lower level of analysis, there are a number of dimensions upon which these two models may be usefully contrasted: *territorial sovereignty* (federal versus unitary); *the legislative branch* (bicameral, symmetrical, and incongruent versus unicameral, asymmetrical, or congruent); *the executive* (presidential versus parliamentary); *the electoral system* (single-member district or preferential-vote versus closed-list PR); *the constitution* (written and with explicit limits on sovereignty versus unwritten or ambiguous in nature, with no explicit limits on sovereignty); *dissolution* (fixed terms versus variable terms); *term limits* (yes or maybe versus no); *elective offices* (many versus few);

TABLE 1.1. *Contrasting models of democratic governance*

	Decentralism	Centripetalism
Territorial sovereignty	Federal	Unitary
Legislative branch	Bicameral, symmetrical, and incongruent	Unicameral, asymmetrical, or congruent
Executive	Presidential	Parliamentary
Electoral system	Single-member or preferential-vote	Party-list PR
Constitution	Written, with explicit limits on sovereignty	Unwritten or ambiguous; no explicit limits on sovereignty
Dissolution	No (fixed terms)	Yes
Term limits	Perhaps	No
Elective offices	Many	Few
Election cycles	Incongruent	Congruent
Candidate selection	Open, diffuse	Closed
Voting cues	Personal and party vote	Party vote
Party system	Two-party or multiparty	Multiparty
Political parties	Weak, decentralized, porous	Strong, centralized, bounded
Referenda	Possibly	No (or only at instigation of legislature)
Exemplars	Brazil, Switzerland, the United States	Denmark, Norway, Sweden

election cycles (incongruent versus congruent); *procedures for candidate selection* (open and diffuse versus closed to all but party members); *voting cues* (personal versus partisan); *political parties* (weak, decentralized, porous versus strong, centralized, bounded); and *referenda* (optional versus nonoptional or only at the instigation of the legislature). These stylized contrasts are presented in Table 1.1.[45] Note that the two models are different along all fifteen dimensions. (Of course, this list could easily be extended.) Sometimes the contrast is a matter of degree and sometimes it is categorical. In any case, it is clear that we are faced with quite opposing views of how to achieve good governance within a democratic framework.

[45] For other attempts to schematize centralist/decentralist models of governance, see Lijphart (1999), MacIntyre (2003), and Przeworski (2003).

THE ARGUMENT

Having contrasted two general models of democratic governance, we now turn to a more focused discussion of centripetalism, the theoretical basis for the rest of the book. Earlier, we stipulated that two elements must be reconciled in order for centripetal energy to be generated within a democratic polity. Institutions must be *inclusive*: they must reach out to all interests, ideas, and identities (at least insofar as they are relevant to the issue at hand). And they must be *authoritative*: they must provide an effective mechanism for reaching agreement and implementing that agreement.

This is a problematic claim on the face of it. These two principles seem so radically opposed to one another that it is difficult to envision how a single institution, or set of institutions, could satisfy one criterion without sacrificing the other. They evoke dichotomies: masses versus elites, the people versus the state, small government versus big government, democracy versus autocracy, Rousseau versus Hobbes. Granted, if governance is conceptualized in the usual way, as an arena in which interests are fixed and politics a zero-sum competition for goods, then the notion of reconciling inclusion and authority is Pollyannaish. It seems fanciful to suggest that an institution could empower leaders without, at the same time, disempowering citizens.

We suppose, however, that interests are to a certain degree endogenous, rather than primordial. Though interests can certainly shape institutions, institutions also condition the creation and reproduction of interests and identities. In particular, decentralist institutions establish a frame of reference in which identities and interests are conceptualized within a state/society dichotomy. In this context, citizens are primed to see the state as a threat and civil society as an arena of relative liberty, and to conceive of power in zero-sum terms. A stronger state means a weaker citizenry, a debilitated local community, or a "co-opted" interest group.

By contrast, centripetal institutions foster a positive-sum view of political power. Government is seen as *creating* power, enhancing the ability of a political community, through its chosen representatives, to deliberate, reach decisions, and implement those decisions. The authority of the centripetal state derives from its ability to bring diverse groups and diverse perspectives to a common meeting ground under conditions of voluntary choice, achieving the institutionalization of political conflict. The power of the centripetal state is thus gained through the strength of its popular legitimacy, its persuasive powers. Rather than representing a compromise position between inclusion and authority, we suggest that centripetal institutions actually reconcile these two principles, drawing the diverse strands of society together toward a single locus of sovereignty. The people rule, but they do so indirectly, through chosen representatives, and in a fashion that enhances rather than detracts from the authority of the state.

Let us explore this notion further. Centripetal institutions gather broadly; their roots are deep, that is, *embedded*. Through these institutions diverse interests, ideas, and identities ("interests," for short) are aggregated. Particularistic interests are converted into ideologies; ideologies are converted into general-interest appeals; parochial perspectives are nationalized. Centripetal institutions thus encourage a search for common ground. Centripetal institutions should culminate in an authoritative decision-making process, one not easily waylaid by minority objections. Institutions pull toward the center, offering incentives to participate and disincentives to defect. *Voice, not vetoes* is the motto of centripetalism.

Visually, we may imagine the centripetal polity in a pyramidal shape, broad at the bottom and narrow at the top, with myriad connecting routes leading up, down, and across. Centripetal institutions thus establish an interlocked set of representative bodies stretching from the electorate at the base to the cabinet and prime minister at the apex. The electorate is represented in a legislature, which is in turn divided into committees, subcommittees, party caucuses, a cabinet, and perhaps various cabinet committees and commissions. At each stage of this process, a delegation of power – a representational act – occurs. Tying all of these horizontal levels together is the vertical structure of the political party, the paradigmatic linkage mechanism.

This pyramidal structure fulfills the mandate of centripetalism. It gathers widely at the base, channeling interests, ideas, and identities upward to a single, authoritative policy-making venue. At each level, some narrowing of perspectives necessarily occurs. However, the pyramid encompasses a diversity of political parties as well as a variety of informal channels of communication. Through these channels (e.g., special commissions, corporatist-style consultations, constituent-MP communications, hearings, ombudspersons, and so forth), nonpartisan messages can be heard (i.e., interests, ideas, and identities that do not fit neatly into the parties' varied missions). In this manner, centralized political authority may be rendered compatible with the inclusion of diverse interests.

THE CAUSAL MODEL

How does this process work? How does a specific set of political institutions foster centripetal energy and, ultimately, influence the quality of governance in a polity? How do the pieces of the centripetal puzzle fit together?

Not all political institutions are of equal significance. Presumably, some of those listed in Table 1.1 have greater impact on policy making than others. And some are undoubtedly more "structural" (causally exogenous) than others. We refer to the most consequential and most structural factors as *constitutional.* They include (1) the nature of sovereignty, (2) the structure of the executive, and (3) the rules of electoral contestation. A fully centripetal system is unitary, parliamentary, and closed-list PR. (Accordingly, a fully decentralist polity is federalist, presidential, and either single-member-district or preferential-vote.) These three constitutional factors are the prime movers of the centripetal model as applied to national-level politics within a democratic framework. Since these factors are sometimes difficult to define and to operationalize, this section is devoted to an elaboration of key concepts. (Chapter five takes up further details.)

Unitarism refers to the location of constitutional authority within a nation-state. In a unitary system, sovereignty is vested in the central (national) government; in a federal system, it is vested in the regional governments or is shared between national and subnational units. (Note that subnational authorities refer specifically to *regional* governmental bodies – states, territories, provinces, *Laender* – not to local bodies.) To have a unitary system does not mean that all, or even most, decision making occurs at the center; considerable power may be delegated. (The Swedish state is a good example of this.) The crucial point is that in a unitary constitution this power may be retrieved without altering the fundamental rules of the game. In a federal system, by contrast, subnational authorities enjoy constitutional status; their power is inherent rather than delegated.

Parliamentarism is a system of government in which the executive (the prime minister and cabinet: collectively, "the government") is chosen by, and responsible to, an elective body (the legislature), thus creating a single locus of sovereignty at the national level. Presidentialism, its contrary, is understood as a system where policy-making power is divided between two separately elected bodies, the legislature and the president. The president's selection is usually by direct popular election, though it may be filtered through an electoral college (as in the United States), and the rules pertaining to victory (e.g., by relative or absolute majority) vary from country to country. His or her tenure cannot be foreshortened by parliament except in cases of gross malfeasance. He or she is actively engaged in the making of public policy, and in this sense plays a political (i.e., partisan) role.

Closed-list PR is a form of electoral system in which each district is multimember, each party nominates a slate of candidates (the list), and parties control the nominations process (it is "closed").[46] This may be contrasted with electoral systems where selection is by plurality (winner takes all) or preferential-vote (where voters are allowed to make choices within a party's list, either by an open-list provision or by a pre-election open primary, and where such choices determine the selection of candidates).

How do these constitutional institutions structure politics and policy making within a centripetal polity? We surmise that three causal mechanisms are critical: (a) party government, (b) conflict mediation, and (c) policy coordination. *Party government* refers to a democratic regime where parties are strong (relatively centralized and ideologically coherent), and where they effectively organize political behavior at mass and elite levels. *Conflict mediation* refers to the mechanisms

[46] If there is preferential voting this option does not determine the rank ordering of the candidates on a party's list, or is swamped by the number of party list votes. Note that when using the term "preferential-vote electoral system" we refer only to systems in which the voters have real – de facto – control over the ordering of candidates on a list or where nominations are handled by a direct primary on the American model. In most systems where preferential voting is an option, the preference votes are swamped by party votes. This sort of system has no, or very few, consequences for the structure of internal party control. For further discussion see chapter five.

FIGURE 1.2. Summary of the causal model.

by which diverse interests, identities, and ideas are institutionalized within a democratic polity. *Policy coordination* refers to the ways in which various political units (parties, interest groups, agencies, legislatures, executives, et al.) in a nation-state interact with one another, and the degree to which that interaction enhances the provision of public goods. The elaboration of these causal pathways consumes the first part of the book (chapters two through four). We argue that centripetal constitutions are more successful in achieving these goals than decentralist constitutions.

The second part of the book comprises an empirical test of the theory. Specifically, we attempt to test the relationship between centripetal constitutions and good governance, as captured by three broad policy areas: (a) political development, (b) economic development, and (c) human development. Within each area, we identify a number of specific factors intended to measure good or bad governmental performance along that dimension. Political development is measured by a country's aggregate public tax revenue, infrastructure development, political participation, and regime volatility. Economic development is tracked by indicators of trade openness, per capita income, and growth volatility. Human development is understood through infant mortality rates, public health expenditures, and total schooling attainment. Cross-national empirical tests probe the causal role of centripetal institutions in achieving positive outcomes across this wide range of indicators.

Figure 1.2 summarizes the causal model, including exogenous factors, causal mechanisms, and outcomes of interest. Granted, this is not an easy model to verify, or even to summarize. Since it is a comprehensive model of politics, it touches upon every causal mechanism that is presumed to influence politics and policy within a democratic setting. Students of politics have been chewing over these matters for centuries, and it may seem an act of extraordinary hubris to propose that they be covered in the space of a single volume. Complicating matters further, only a few of the links in this long causal chain can be accurately measured, and hence empirically tested. While inputs and outputs are measurable (with some important caveats, to be addressed), the intermediate factors in this causal story are virtually impossible to monitor over time and across countries in a systematic fashion. A degree of speculation is therefore inevitable.

In the face of such difficulties, our goals must be modest. In this short book, we aim to lay out a series of arguments linking centripetal democratic institutions with improved governance and to provide some tests of the empirical relationship implied between those institutions and specific governance outcomes. We believe that the demands of theory building, as well as the practical demands of policy makers and citizens, justify the exercise. Sometimes a synoptic view of politics is warranted. The reader will note that we make extensive use of references to the secondary literature on subjects that we can afford to pursue only in passing. In the concluding chapter of the book, we offer a qualified defense of "grand theory" in the social sciences.

PART ONE

CAUSAL MECHANISMS

How might unitarism, parliamentarism, and closed-list PR improve the quality of governance within democratic polities? Having outlined the broad theoretical parameters of the argument in chapter one, we now turn to a more detailed discussion of causal pathways. Chapter two focuses on the effects of these constitutional institutions on the creation and maintenance of a form of rule known as party government. Chapter three addresses the probable effects of these institutions in mediating extreme forms of political conflict, particularly conflict rooted in ethnic identities. And chapter four attempts to demonstrate why centripetal institutions may do a better job of coordinating diverse policies across the various levels and institutions of government.

Throughout this discussion, our narrative foil is the theory of decentralism, introduced in chapter one. At each stage, we attempt to show why centripetal institutions might be expected to produce better governance than decentralist institutions. Granted, many of our arguments must remain speculative, for we do not know – and are not in a position to test empirically – many of the stipulated causal pathways. Yet it is essential that we lay out in fairly detailed terms why centripetal institutions might lead to better governance, overall, within a democratic framework. The goal of this section of the book is to convince the reader that there is a strong prima facie case for the theory. This forms the background for our empirical tests of the theory, as laid out in the second section of the book.

2

Party Government

E. E. Schattschneider points out that every polity is biased in favor of some forms of popular participation, and against others. Political institutions can hardly play a neutral role in the organization of interests, ideas, and identities. Some activities will be "mobilized in" and others will be "mobilized out."[1] We argue that the bias of a polity with a centripetal constitution – that is, unitary, parliamentary, and closed-list PR – is toward strong parties. Conversely, decentralized constitutions should encourage weaker, more diffuse parties and issue- and sector-specific organizations.

A "strong" political party, let us say, is characterized by a high degree of internal unity, external differentiation, and centralized control.[2] If most parties in a polity are strong (in these senses), one may infer that parties are the dominant governing power in that polity. "Party government" obtains.[3] Operationally, this means that in this

[1] Schattschneider (1960).

[2] By "party" we mean an independent organization within civil society that nominates officials for public office. We assume that the party is differentiated from the formal institutions of government. Where party and government are indistinguishable, as they are in most authoritarian settings, we cannot say that a "strong" party exists, at least not as a distinct organization.

[3] Since the term "party government" often refers to government by a single party (rather than by a coalition) and appears to exclude the party's role in the electorate, some prefer the more general concept of party strength. However, in common usage these terms are quite similar and will occasionally be used synonymously in the following discussion. See Castles et al. (1988), Castles and Wildenmann (1986), Cox and McCubbins

polity nominating decisions stick; the party vote trumps the personal vote; issue space is broadly ideological rather than issue-specific; elective offices at the national level are effectively restricted to party members; ticket splitting is rare; the process of candidate selection is confined to party members; the system of campaign finance is centralized in the hands of the national party organization; legislative activity is partisan rather than individualistic; and national, regional, and local branches of a party are ideologically aligned with one another.

Naturally, these are matters of degree. Perhaps no polity in the world fully satisfies all these criteria. The concept of party government, like many concepts in social science, is best understood as an ideal type. As such, we argue that parties with the foregoing characteristics are more likely to develop from centripetal institutions than from decentralized institutions. Ceteris paribus, a centripetal polity will provide a closer approximation of the party government ideal. In succeeding sections of this chapter we show how each of the constitutional components of the centripetal polity – unitarism, parliamentarism, and closed-list PR – contribute to stronger parties within a democratic context.

UNITARISM

Federalist polities usually show a higher degree of party system disaggregation than one would anticipate under unitary circumstances, all other things being equal. The centrifugal effect of federalism on national and subnational party systems has been noted in Argentina, Belgium, Brazil, Canada, India, Mexico, Nigeria, Russia, Switzerland, the United States, and Venezuela.[4] Even Germany has struggled against

(1993), Eaton (2002), Fiorina (1980), Katz (1987), Mainwaring and Scully (1995), and Ranney (1962). Our notion of party strength does not refer, however, to the development of partisan subcultures; the density of grassroots organization; the colonization of formally nonpolitical arenas such as popular entertainment, business, and the bureaucracy; or the internal structure and workings of the party (with the exception of certain factors to be discussed).

[4] On Argentina, see Gibson (1997), Jones (1997), Remmer and Wibbels (2000), and Sawers (1998). On Belgium, see Martiniello (1997: 290) and O'Neill (2000: 119). On Brazil, see Samuels (2000a, 2000b, 2003) and Weyland (1996). On Canada, see Cairns (1988) and Wilson (1983). On India, see Chhibber (1999) and Ray (1987). On Mexico, see Cornelius et al. (1999), Rubin (1996), and Snyder (2001). On Nigeria, see Dent (2000). On Russia, see Ordeshook (1996). On Switzerland, see Steinberg (1996) and Church (2000). On the United States, see Bensel (1984), Elazar (1972),

the fissiparous tendencies of wayward states like Bavaria, with its nominally independent conservative party.[5] In each case, the constitutional recognition of center/periphery distinctions seems to preserve and entrench regional distinctions by making them more salient. Where regionally based elective bodies exist – legislatures and governors, with their attendant bureaucracies, budgets, and programs – it naturally behooves politicians to craft a regional identity side by side with (and perhaps even against) their national identity. Federalism highlights regions; regions enhance regionalism; and regionalism – the religion of section – challenges the authority of the center.

By contrast, unitarism nurtures party strength because it mandates the predominance of national power over regional power bases. Specifically, it mandates that there be only one supra-local level of elective power. This, of necessity, becomes the prize that all viable political parties must seek, and in the seeking these party organizations find it advantageous to achieve a higher level of coherence and consolidation than they otherwise might.

PARLIAMENTARISM

Parliamentarism also has important effects on party strength.[6] Recall that a parliamentary system is defined as one where the executive is chosen by and responsible to the parliament. This means that a legislative election in a parliamentary system is, in effect, a vote to choose a government. Indeed, the first order of business after any parliamentary election is the selection of a new government by the entering members of parliament (MPs). This is undoubtedly the most important vote that they will cast during their term of office. In this respect, parliaments function as electoral colleges. Precisely because a constituent's vote for an MP is also, at the same time, a vote for an elector, the constituent quite naturally wishes to know what sort of choice the MP is going to

Key (1949), Rae (1994), Schantz (1996), Scheiber (1975), Truman (1955), and Turner (1932). On Venezuela, see Penfold-Becerra (2004). For general treatments of this issue, see Brancati (2007), Chandler (1987), Geddes and Benton (1997), Riker (1964), and Stepan (2004).

5 See Urwin (1982).

6 Bagehot (1867/1963), Bowler et al. (1999), Carey (2002), Cox (1987), Epstein (1964), Janda (1992), Ozbudun (1970), Shugart and Carey (1992).

make and what the complexion of the resulting government is likely to be. She could, of course, simply choose the "best man" available as MP and leave it to him to determine the choice of government. This is how legislatures were originally envisioned in eras prior to party organization. That they did not remain in this protean state is testament to constituents' desires to have a hand in the choice of government. But in order to make this choice real – in order to understand the options available and to enforce the MP's pledge – party organization is necessary. To vote for a Labour member in Britain is to vote for an MP who is pledged to vote for the Labour Party leader as the next prime minister, and who will be punished if she fails to do so. We can think of parties in functional terms as a direct response to popular demands for accountability. They are also, of course, an attempt by elites to maximize power by centralizing authority in the hands of a majority.[7]

In a presidential system, things are different. Since the executive is chosen separately, the legislative election concerns only the selection of a legislator. Granted, control of the legislature may have important consequences for the allocation of committee seats, the conduct of legislative affairs, and the control of the overall political agenda. However, this pales by comparison to the choice of a government in a parliamentary system. Thus, it is logical for constituents to make their voting choice according to some combination of (a) national/party and (b) local/candidate cues. (For present purposes, party cues can be viewed as equivalent to national affairs and candidate cues as equivalent to local affairs.) While party cues predominate in parliamentary systems, candidate cues are relatively more prominent in presidential systems.

Thus, parliamentary systems encourage partisan voting, where parties usually have a national (or at least regional) identity, while presidential systems encourage nonpartisan (candidate-based), localistic voting. The underlying explanation for this fact is that legislative elections in parliamentary systems are more consequential, for they have the effect of determining the next government. A single act selects both a legislature and an electoral college. All sorts of repercussions,

[7] Aldrich (1995), Cox (1987), Schattschneider (1942).

including the allocation of campaign finances, the allocation of media attention, the degree and effectiveness of candidate activity, and the organization of the parties, flow from this central constitutional fact.[8]

CLOSED-LIST PR

The sheer diversity of electoral system types complicates any discussion of the role of electoral systems in structuring political parties (a problem that we face in all portions of this book). Recall that our theory contrasts closed-list PR electoral systems with two quite distinct types of electoral organization: preferential-vote systems and plurality systems. We begin with the former and proceed to the latter.[9]

In preferential-vote systems, members of the same party must vie against each other for the voters' affection. Wherever an electoral system fosters this sort of intraparty competition, we can expect fragmentary results at the national level – either well-established party factions, as in the Italian Christian Democratic Party and the Japanese Liberal Democratic Party, or a localistic orientation among backbenchers, as in Ireland. Preferential voting does not always result in party fragmentation, as the case of Australia illustrates; but there is a strong probabilistic relationship.[10]

Since preferential-voting electoral systems are relatively rare, the more consequential comparison is with electoral systems based on single-member districts (SMDs) without a preferential-vote option. (Recall that a PR system is, by definition, multimember [MMD].) Here, the implications of electoral-system design are subtler. Indeed, some SMD polities sustain parties that are as strong as any found in the world today. The United Kingdom in the twentieth century and France in the

[8] A historical explanation of this contrast between parliamentarism and presidentialism would emphasize the reciprocal behavior of masses and elites (Cox 1987). However, the bottom line remains the same. Where the executive is not separately elected, he or she will be chosen by parliament. And wherever the executive is chosen by parliament, it is natural for this fact to nationalize and partisanize behavior at elite and mass levels, for members of the electorate will want to ensure mechanisms of accountability, and members of the elite will want to maximize their power by constructing stable majorities.

[9] This discussion draws on Carey and Shugart (1995), Eaton (2002), and Katz (1980).

[10] On SNTV, see Bowler and Grofman (2000). On STV, see Bowler and Farrell (1991). On the distinction between effective and ineffective open-list systems, see Katz (1986).

Fifth Republic serve as prime examples. Even so, it seems likely that, ceteris paribus, closed-list PR systems foster stronger parties. Moreover, closed-list PR is most effective in fostering strong parties where barriers to party building are most severe, that is, in polities that are new, economically underdeveloped, or heterogeneous (divided along tribal, ethnic, religious, linguistic, or geographic lines). There are several reasons for this.

First, coherence is fostered by the ability of party leaders to determine, or at least to influence, the order of the party's list, and hence the selection of candidates to the legislature. A closed-party-list system usually results in a fairly centralized system of party nominations. To be sure, the construction of lists varies from polity to polity and from party to party. Sometimes it is regional leaders who construct the party's lists; sometimes lists are constructed by party leaders at the constituency level (which may be considerably smaller than a region); and sometimes national party leaders are able to determine party lists (as in Israel and the Netherlands, where the nation comprises a single electoral district). But in virtually all cases we anticipate a more centralized process of candidate selection where there are multimember districts with effectively closed party lists. In single-member districts, by contrast, candidate selection is almost always a constituency-level affair. These constituencies are, of course, smaller than they would be if that same country employed multimember districts, meaning that the decision unit is more localized.[11]

Of much greater importance is the way in which closed-list PR systems structure the vote, and hence the power of political parties vis-à-vis individual candidates. Single-member-district electoral systems tend to foster strong relationships between individual candidates and voters in the constituency. He is "their" man; they are "his" constituents. This means several things. First, it means that voting in an SMD system is likely to be more personalized, less partisan. Consequently, parties working within such electoral systems will have to devote greater effort to cultivating the constituency vote.[12] Second, and relatedly, it means that it will be more difficult, and more costly, for national party leaders

[11] Bowler et al. (1999: 7–8), Crepaz and Birchfield (2000), Epstein (1967/1980: 225–6), Katz and Mair (1992: Table D.5), Ranney (1965). But see Gallagher (1988: 259).

[12] Heitshusen et al. (2002).

to discipline recalcitrant MPs. The more entrenched is the MP in the district, the more likely it is that constituency associations will resist this pressure (remember that they may have considerable control over candidate selection), and the more votes it will cost the party at the next election. In a list-MMD system, by contrast, party leaders have more options, and those options are more palatable. They can discipline a member by moving that individual down a notch or two on the party's list instead of expelling her from office (the only option available in an SMD system). If they choose to remove the individual from the party's list (or place her so low as to effectively prevent her from gaining office), the electoral ramifications are minimal, since her identification with the constituency is likely to be peripheral. It is quite common for voters in a closed-list PR system to recognize *none* of the names on their party's local list. Even if a local notable (a person with fairly high name recognition in the locality) heads the list, her existence does not matter very much in the ultimate choice of most voters, because the voter is aware that she is electing a list rather than a set of discrete candidates. In sum, closed-list PR systems should encourage party voting, and party voting, in turn, enhances the power of party leaders.[13]

PR systems, finally, tend to foster party systems with more than two "effective" parties (parties whose participation in the government is essential to attaining a parliamentary majority).[14] This enhances the relative strength of each party within a polity, for a complex set of reasons. Consider that parties in a multiparty system are small houses, rather than big tents. As such, their ideological and social composition is apt to be more uniform. In this respect, closed-list PR systems foster a more coherent, more "ideological" set of parties. By this we do not mean that there will be greater distance between major parties in a multiparty system than between major parties in a duopoly. The SPD and the CDU, the major parties on the left and right of the German party system, are probably closer in policy and in rhetoric than the Democratic and Republican Parties in the United States, for example. Similarly, we do not expect parties in a closed-list PR system to behave in more adversarial, dogmatic ways than their counterparts in two-party systems. Sweden offers a good example of a pragmatic,

[13] Norris (2004: chapter ten).
[14] Taagepera and Shugart (1989).

consensual, nondogmatic party system, with upwards of five sizeable parties. The point is simply that the level of *internal cohesion*, both at elite levels and at mass levels, is apt to be greater where there are more options from which to choose. Voters and activists are likely to find a better "fit" between their preferences and the available partisan choices.[15] Sorting is easier; hence, there will be fewer renegades within the parties. And if dissidents become a significant force within a party, this dissension is likely to lead to a party split rather than to enduring intraparty factions, for PR systems erect lower entry barriers to new parties (at the national level). The result of this fission, although momentarily disturbing to party-system equilibrium, is in the long run re-equilibrating; both the old party and the new party can now claim a high level of internal coherence. When "voice" mechanisms fail, disagreement is managed through exit. The result is that the party label in a closed-list PR system is likely to be perceived as a highly useful cue for the voter, a coherent ordering device for conceptualizing politics at the electoral level. This, in turn, is likely to translate into higher levels of grassroots party loyalty. By contrast, within a two-party (or two-party-dominant) system, dissidents must remain within a party that they dislike or choose to wander in the wilderness. Greens in Germany were able to establish their own party, which has become a critical force in national politics over the past few decades; Greens in the United States are not so fortunate.

Party strength is, in important respects, the product of the loyalty a party inspires among party members and party voters. All other things being equal, we expect this loyalty to be greater where there are more choices and where each of the available (viable) choices is more coherent. Internal coherence and external differentiation tend to characterize party systems in PR polities. For all these reasons, we can expect stronger parties in a polity with party-list PR relative to the same polity under a preferential-vote or single-member-district electoral system.[16]

[15] Norris (2004: chapter six).

[16] Carlsson (1987: 201). Some of the strongest evidence for this proposition comes from studies that compare the behavior of legislators chosen under parallel list and district systems (Haspel et al. 1998; Lancaster 1986; Moser 2001: 117; Patzelt 2000: 38–9; Stoner-Weiss 2001: 401; Stratmann and Baur 2002).

CONCLUSIONS

We have argued that all three centripetal institutions enhance the strength of political parties in a democratic setting. Parties will experience greater unity, differentiation, and centralization if situated within a constitution that is unitary, parliamentary, and closed-list PR. Despite the difficulty of effectively measuring party "strength" across polities, this assertion is relatively uncontroversial.

It is much more difficult to demonstrate that strong parties lead to better governance. However, the claim has strong prima facie plausibility. Indeed, it has been the consensus view among political scientists since the founding of the discipline.[17] Beginning with the turn-of-the-century writings of Walter Bagehot, Henry Jones Ford, A. Lawrence Lowell, and Woodrow Wilson, poor governance has usually been associated with factionalism and with individualistic behavior on the part of party members, and good governance with party unity. We concur. But we must also clarify the reasoning behind this general assumption. In order to do so, we return to our principal foil, the decentralist theory of democratic governance.

From the decentralist perspective, strong parties have negative ramifications. They insulate elites from popular control, restrict the recruitment of new leaders, ossify intraparty competition, and prevent district-level accountability. Decentralized parties, by contrast, introduce competition within the party organization, competition that should have healthy effects, following the general idea that competition improves the quality of governance (see chapter one).

Decentralist logic is problematic, however, in the following respects. First, in opening up political parties to internal democracy one also usually decreases the unity of these parties. Thus fragmented, they cannot serve as instruments of aggregation and accountability. Nor can they effectively compete against one another, for they are no longer unitary entities. Note that *intra-* and *inter*party competition are inversely related. Given this fundamental fact of politics, one must make a choice about which sort of competition to privilege. The centripetal theory

[17] Castles et al. (1988), Castles and Wildenmann (1986), Cox and McCubbins (1993), Fiorina (1980), Katz (1987), Muller (2000), Ranney (1962), Schattschneider (1942, 1960), Ware (1987). Contrast Katz and Mair (1995), and Levitsky (2003). See Kitschelt (2000) for an important rejoinder to Katz and Mair (1995).

supposes, with Schattschneider, that competition is more conducive to good governance when it exists between parties, rather than within parties.[18]

One reason for this is that it is difficult for porous parties to aggregate interests effectively at the grassroots level. Because a divided party has the capacity to stand for many things, it may simply reproduce at the national level whatever disaggregation is apparent at the local level. Interest groups in a fragmented polity are even less likely to perform this function, since the organization of interest groups usually mirrors the fragmentation found at a constitutional level. (Fragmented institutions in the formal sector foster a parallel fragmentation in the informal sector.) If parochial interests and identities are not transformed into national ideologies, the quality of governance is likely to suffer, for political elites will find it difficult to resist parochial pressures if this is the predominant mode of interest organization in a polity. In this setting, clientelism may triumph over partisanship.

Indeed, weak political parties are usually associated with particularism. Over a century ago, Henry Jones Ford argued that partisanship and corruption are "fundamentally antagonistic principles. Partisanship tends to establish a connection based upon an avowed public obligation, while corruption consults private and individual interests which secrete themselves from view and avoid accountability of any kind. The weakness of party organization is the opportunity of corruption."[19] This makes sense if one considers that wherever parties are weak, policies are necessarily the product of ad hoc coalitions of individual politicians or of intraparty factions. Neither circumstance is conducive to good governance, for both sorts of ties subordinate the general interest to particular interests. And both weaken the ties between the party and its national electorate. Intraparty wrangling, as often noted, is usually damaging to the party's electoral prospects. Factional leaders sit adamantly on their hands until their demands are met, while the party's public image takes a beating. This is easily explainable, since factionalism by definition impairs the ability of a party to coordinate its members' activities. Organizational weakness thus loosens bonds of accountability that would otherwise exist

[18] Schattschneider (1942).
[19] Ford (1898/1967: 322–3).

between voters and politicians, because the party is not able to act as a unitary agent. Its principal, the electorate, can neither assign blame nor exact punishment.[20]

Our stress on the unitary nature of political parties should not give the impression that there is no disagreement within a ("strong") party's ranks. On the contrary, disagreement serves the party's long-run interests so long as these internal critiques have as their goal the ongoing success of the party. In order to be successful, a party must "think"; and in order to think, a party must discard its partisan ("ideological") hat and assume its thinking hat. Consider that a party's fate in the polls hinges largely on its ability to provide the goods, that is, to act in the public interest, rather than in the interest of narrow, "partisan" demands. Thus, the success of a political party rests on its ability to juggle both roles successfully, the partisan role and the nonpartisan role. Paradoxically, party strength may encourage nonpartisan puzzling. The stronger the party, the easier it may be to convince activists that the party's core mission is not being compromised when it engages in such nonpartisan puzzling and to convince the electorate that the general interest is not being compromised when it invokes the principles of party government. Successful party government is a masterful juggling act, an act made possible when key players agree to assume their assigned roles and to coordinate with one another, responding to leadership cues. The structure of the party synchronizes individual career goals with the party's quest for political power. Members cannot hope to move up the political ladder unless they walk in step with the party's directives (at least when in public view). Party loyalty is a prerequisite to personal advancement. But partisanship is also a prerequisite to nonpartisan puzzling over the nature of the public interest. Thus, political leaders climb a ladder of abstraction – from parochial interests, to party interests, to the public interest.

Parties are like cabinets and legislatures in this respect. To the extent that they provide a collegial environment for discussion of ideas, this should benefit the party's performance over the long haul. The fact

[20] For discussions of factionalism and governance in Brazil, see Amorim Neto and Santos (2001); in Italy, see Golden and Change (2000) and Zuckerman (1979); in the Philippines, see Lande (1965); in Thailand, see Ockey (1994); in Venezuela, see Coppedge (1994); more generally, see Belloni and Beller (1978), Hine (1982), and Schmidt et al. (1977).

that a good deal of nonpartisan behavior is tolerated, and perhaps even encouraged, in a system nominally described as "party government" is testament to the strength of parties as political organizations in a centripetal polity. They can afford to let their members stray, secure in the knowledge that they can be called back into the fold whenever it is necessary to stand shoulder to shoulder. The distinction between a "whipped vote" and a "free vote" is apropos. In the former, all members of a party vote together. In the latter, party leaders lift the whip in order to allow backbenchers to "vote their conscience" (or their constituencies). We do not feel that the existence of a free vote, even on important issues of public policy, compromises the strength of political parties. The important point is that party members would vote in unison if the party's recognized agenda and public standing required them to do so. Similarly, party members do not always wear their partisan hat when speaking and voting in committee. But they would if party leaders asked them to do so.

Thus, we do not view the existence of strong parties as a bar to deliberation – quite the opposite. The key to party government is the bending of parochial and partisan will to the service of the public interest. Precisely because strong parties vest power in party leaders rather than in rank-and-file members (or, for that matter, nonpartisan constituencies), the party is likely to prize winning office over satisfying member preferences. Under conditions of multiparty competition, this should result in better governance overall than one would expect from a candidate-centered or highly factionalized party system.

3

Conflict Mediation

A successful polity must institutionalize conflict, integrating diverse groups and competing interests. In the contemporary era, the most troubling species of conflict is the extreme sort often associated with "ethnic" struggles, that is, struggles based on ascriptive identities such as religion, language, race, region, and caste. It is this sort of struggle that seems to pose the greatest threat to social peace, good governance, and indeed to the integrity of the polity.[1] Consequently, it is this sort of struggle that we are primarily concerned with when discussing the topic of conflict mediation, though we imagine that whatever arguments might be advanced with respect to the role of political institutions in extreme conflicts would also be true, a fortiori, of conflict in its more moderate forms.

Some institutional forms seem to work to bring elite actors together, to act in union as part of a larger project. Other institutional forms work to accentuate the differences among elites, offering incentives to individuals to defect from group decisions and to pursue entrepreneurial strategies. We refer to the former as a *collegial* or

[1] We do not take a strong position on the relative "constructedness" of ethnic identity. We presume that ethnicity is not innate and to this extent must be socially constructed. We presume that ethnic identities are always to some extent in flux and that individuals have multiple identities, any one of which may be dominant at a given time. On the other hand, we also presume that ethnicity has a degree of "stickiness"; it is not entirely up for grabs. In this respect, ethnic identities are "institutions" and may be approached as causal factors in social action.

cooperative style of politics, and to the latter as an *adversarial* or *individualistic* political style.

Our argument, in brief, is that the most effective way to mediate conflict and foster consensus is through political institutions that are, at once, inclusive and authoritative. Conflicts are thereby channeled through representative bodies toward the center. They are broadened in scope (i.e., nationalized), institutionalized, and ultimately, if things go right, amicably settled. It is important to stress that the process of conflict mediation is regulated by a central authority ("the state"), an authority strong enough to enforce bargains and, if necessary, to enforce peace when agreements are broken. Centripetal institutions set in motion a dynamic in which elites inside and outside the government have strong incentives to establish national priorities and reach common ground on policy problems. Power attracts, and centripetal power usually creates centripetal incentives.

That centripetal institutions might serve as instruments of conflict mediation is not surprising if one considers the reigning theory of conflict arbitration. Lawrence Susskind and Jeffrey Cruikshank write:

> Consensus building requires informal, face-to-face interaction among specially chosen representatives of all 'stakeholding' groups; a voluntary effort to seek 'all-gain' rather than 'win-lose' solutions or watered-down political compromise; and, often, the assistance of a neutral facilitator or mediator. Such approaches must be treated as supplements – and not alternatives – to conventional decision making. Officials with statutory power must retain their authority in order to ensure accountability.[2]

In the opinion of this leading text, the combination of inclusion and authority is critical for successful conflict mediation at an individual

[2] Susskind and Cruikshank (1987: 11). The authors continue, "One obvious way to evaluate the fairness of a settlement is to judge the fairness of the process by which the resolution was reached. This suggests a number of questions, such as: Was the process open to public scrutiny? Were all the groups who wanted to participate given an adequate chance to do so? Were all parties given access to the technical information they needed? Was everyone given an opportunity to express his or her views? Were the people involved accountable to the constituencies they ostensibly represented? Was there a means whereby a due process complaint could be heard at the conclusion of the negotiations?" (Ibid., 21; see also Susskind et al. 1999).

level. It should not be surprising if the same dynamics also apply at a societal level.

Of course, we must keep in mind that social conflicts occur for many reasons. Of these reasons, we are concerned here only with those that might be linked to political institutions within democratic polities. This is in keeping with our general theoretical framework, as introduced in chapter one. More specifically, we are concerned with the role of key centripetal institutions – unitarism, parliamentarism, and closed-list PR – in achieving consensus, or at least containing conflict within lawful bounds.

UNITARISM

Federalism is commonly looked upon as a mechanism for mitigating hostilities, particularly those grounded in ethnic identities. Granting a regionally concentrated group control of a subnational government, according to proponents of federalism, is thought to co-opt demands for complete autonomy, giving politicians a bailiwick to call their own and an incentive to support the regime (or at least not destroy it). At the same time, it should assuage fears of ethnic cleansing and/or ethnic assimilation. Even if they cannot control the national government, minority groups will have a "home" of their own, with some constitutional protection against possible depredations emanating from the center. Finally, federal units may offer an effective veto against legislation and/or constitutional changes running counter to an ethnic group's perceived self-interest.[3]

We readily acknowledge that, sometimes, the assignment of regional autonomy moderates extreme sentiments, allowing for the survival of the nation-state and for its successful governance under a federalist constitution. Switzerland, for example, seems to offer a relatively successful case of ethnic conflict assuaged by federal institutions. However, in many other cases – for example, Belgium, Bolivia, Canada, Ethiopia, India, Nigeria, and Russia – the role of federalism in

[3] Bermeo (2004), Brancati (2006), Cohen (1997), Gurr (2000), Kaufman (1996), Lijphart (1968, 1977, 1984b, 1999), Tsebelis (1990).

mediating ethnic conflict is open to debate.[4] Thus, on balance, the empirical record is equivocal.[5]

Indeed, the recognition of regional autonomy (i.e., federalism) often has unintended effects and may actually exacerbate conflicts, particularly those of an ethnic nature. Begin with the fact that in a federal system regions possess their own elective legislatures, perhaps an elective chief executive (e.g., a governor), and a regional bureaucracy. These regional governments are important policy-making bodies. As such, they tend to structure politics at the regional level (as well as at the national level). Because regional governments offer a prize worth fighting for, we can expect that they will lead to subnational political systems, each with its own more or less independent dynamic. This creates incentives for regional parties (parties that are not competitive nationally) or national parties with semi-independent branches at the regional level.[6]

Alan Cairns notes with reference to Canada that "the structure of federalism has generated a pronounced trend toward the separation of federal and provincial party systems. This is manifested in tendencies toward distinct political careers at both levels, separate national and provincial organizations, and separate sources of party finance."[7] Even within the same political party, regional and national perspectives often diverge. Across different parties, many of which are strong only in one or two regions, there is the potential for even greater conflict. Cairns concludes, "The parties at different levels of the federal system exist in different socio-economic environments, respond to different competitive situations, and are products of particular patterns

[4] A third class of federal countries has no significant ethnic differences of a "bounded" nature (such that one group may be effectively distinguished from another) and therefore is less prone to extreme ethnic-based conflict (e.g., Argentina, Australia, Brazil, Cambodia, Germany, Italy, Mexico, Venezuela). In a fourth class of countries (e.g., Malaysia, South Africa, Spain), it is perhaps too soon to issue a verdict on this question. The United States is difficult to classify in this typology because its ethnic distinctions are so multifarious that they are (according to one line of argument) less liable to form the basis for extreme political conflict.

[5] Because we lack good time-series indicators of ethnic conflict, it is not possible to test this question in a systematic fashion. Civil wars – though fairly easy to measure – have occurred largely in countries that are authoritarian or marginally democratic, offering little empirical leverage on our question.

[6] Brancati (2007).

[7] Cairns (1988: 159-60).

of historical development and historical accidents. They fight elections under different leaders, at different times, and on different issues before different electorates in separate jurisdictions endowed with distinctive constitutional responsibilities."[8] Similar observations have been made about India, Nigeria, Russia, and other federal polities.[9] Gunther and Mughan summarize a wide range of country studies: "in encouraging diversity, federalism tends to promote and ossify regionally distinctive cultural and political identities and traditions, as well as economic, social, and political concerns and priorities."[10] It would appear that federalism, when conjoined with an ethnically divided polity where ethnicities and territorial units coincide, is a recipe for disjointed federal/territorial politics.

Granted, the explicit purpose of federal unions is sometimes to grant official recognition to minority groups. However, granting recognition should not be confused with solving age-old conflicts. Indeed, official recognition of ethnic status may serve only to confirm and to reinforce latent ethnic hostilities. Autonomous regions, Svante Cornell argues, "may . . . isolate the minority and prevent its members from political or economic participation in the larger sphere of the state. Accordingly, it makes dialogue between groups within the society difficult, alienates component groups from one another, and leads to segregation."[11] In this respect, the effect of federalism is similar to the oft-noted effect of official ethnic recognition in other venues – for example, for purposes of classifying citizens in a census, assigning positions in the state bureaucracy, or appointing members to political bodies (e.g., "affirmative action").[12] The "boundary" problem inherent in all assertions of ethnicity[13] has an official stamp wherever ethnically homogeneous regions enjoy constitutional status. The granting of semi-sovereignty by the central state authority has the same political effect as the granting

[8] Ibid.

[9] On Canada, see Cairns (1988). On India, see Dikshit (1975) and Hardgrave (1994). On Nigeria, see Somide (2001: 23) and Suberu (2001). On Russia and the former Soviet republics, see Bunce (2004), Cornell (2002), Leff (1999), and Roeder (1991). On South Africa, see Horowitz (1991). More generally, see Kymlicka (1998), Nordlinger (1972), and Snyder (2000).

[10] Gunther and Mughan (1993: 296-7).

[11] Cornell (2002: 251).

[12] Galanter (1984).

[13] Barth (1969).

of (full) sovereignty by international institutions: it legalizes and legitimizes the quest for regional identity and full sovereignty. Adegboyega Somide notes that in Nigeria, the creation of ethnic states "has resulted in ethnic enclaves which ossify rather than dissolve allegiances," thus magnifying "ethnic separateness."[14] If the majority-controlled state is also occasionally oppressive to the minority in question (or if claims of abuse are credible to the minority in question), then its ethnicity-enhancing effects are doubled. "There is a fine line between legitimating difference and undermining commonality," note Valerie Bunce and Stephen Watts.[15]

We must also consider these institutional features at the elite level. Here, regional political systems established by a federal constitution offer secure berths for "ethnic" politicians. At the same time, they rarely offer a convenient staging ground for ethnic-minority politicians with higher ambitions. This is because getting to the top of an ethnically based territorial government usually demands an ethnic affiliation, precisely the sort of reputation that may preclude gaining power at the national level. Without such options, what is left to regional politicians is the pursuit of further autonomy, that is, independence. For the ambitious politician the prospect of being a head of state or a high-ranking member of a newly formed nation may be more attractive than remaining as a regional politician in a polity where one's group will never attain majority status. Insofar as elites have the power to shape political realities, the incentive structure of an ethnically divided federal polity is in this respect dangerously centrifugal.

Finally, federalism may set in motion a tit-for-tat game of ethnic defection in which groups threaten violence or secession in return for concessions. A federal arrangement establishes a framework for this centrifugal dynamic, one in which each side has an incentive to engage in brinksmanship. This may have disastrous consequences, since sentiments of ethnic hostility, once called into play, are difficult to dispel.[16] Thus, secession, an extreme form of ethnic and regional conflict, may be fostered rather than mediated by the existence of a federal structure. Cornell summarizes the matter this way: "The institution of

[14] Somide (2001: 23).
[15] Bunce and Watts (2005).
[16] Horowitz (1985: 624), Cornell (2002: 250).

autonomous regions is conducive to secessionism because institutionalizing and promoting the separate identity of a titular group increases that group's cohesion and willingness to act, and establishing political institutions increases the capacity of that group to act."[17]

In unitary polities, by contrast, all high-ranking positions are at the center, or are connected to the center, and extra-constitutional institutions such as political parties and interests tend to mirror this centralist orientation. If there is, in addition, a low threshold for representation (a matter we discuss later), ambitious politicians representing ethnic minorities will find it fairly easy to gain a foothold in the national legislature, and may even join the ruling coalition or play a pivotal role in the formation of a government. They are thus impelled to play to national themes and to preserve a national image. While they may continue to represent ethnic constituencies, they must resist centrifugal tendencies if they wish to occupy a position of prominence on the national stage. Institutional incentives thus compel them to forsake "ethnic" politics for "national" politics, or at least to keep the former within appropriate bounds.

[17] Cornell (2002: 252-3). McGarry and O'Leary (1993: 34-5) conclude that "federalism has a poor track-record as a conflict-regulating device in multi-ethnic states, even where it allows a degree of minority self-government. Democratic federations have broken down throughout Asia and Africa, with the possible exception of India, the survival of which is partly accounted for by the degree of central control possible in its quasi-federal system. Federal failures primarily occur because minorities continue to be outnumbered at the federal level of government. The resulting frustrations, combined with an already defined boundary and the significant institutional resources flowing from control of the their own province/state, provide considerable incentives to attempt secession, which in turn can invite harsh responses from the rest of the federation: the disintegration of the Nigerian and American federations were halted only through millions of deaths. As the ingenious federal engineering of the Nigerian second republic went down before a military coup the jury must remain out on the success or otherwise of democratic federalism in resolving Nigeria's ethnic dilemmas. India, the most successful post-colonial federation, faces secessionist movements in Kashmir and Punjab, and Canada is perennially threatened with the secession of Quebec.... Even the sham federations of the Soviet Union and Yugoslavia provided various ethnic movements with the resources to launch successful secessions during 1991-2.... Even relatively successful multi-ethnic federations appear to be in permanent constitutional crises. Not only do the division of powers need to be constantly renegotiated as a result of technological advances, economic transformations and judicial interventions, but to maintain stability supplemental consociational practices are often required at the federal and subcentral levels of government." See also Bunce (2004, 2005), Gunther and Mughan (1993: 296-7) and Snyder (2000: 40).

PARLIAMENTARISM

In a parliamentary system, elections are typically contests between political parties or coalitions of parties: rival teams that vie for power. Because parties are large organizations, with many leadership positions, it is fairly easy to incorporate diverse demographics within each prospective governing unit. Parties can easily accomplish the task of "descriptive" representation.[18]

In presidential systems, by contrast, the task of representing a diverse polity is more complicated, for the existence of a directly elected president establishes a winner-take-all political game at the apex of the polity.[19] This means that there is little scope for compromise and accommodation, particularly during the course of an election campaign where so much is at stake and there can only be one winner. It will be difficult for a presidential candidate, even if he is so inclined, to reach out to various ascriptive groups of which he is not personally a member. Despite strenuous efforts, a given politician cannot be both a Protestant and a Catholic, white and black, Notherner and Southerner. These diverse roles cannot be played (convincingly) by one person; they require a cast. But the constitutional role established by a presidential system is singular; hence the difficulty.

A winner-take-all electoral game does provide an incentive for candidates to occupy a position near the median, so as to attract as many voters as possible. This follows the Downsian model of two-party competition.[20] Since the presidential candidate is presumably freer of party encumbrances than a prime ministerial aspirant, we can expect him to enjoy somewhat greater latitude in this fence-straddling exercise. Where the shape of public opinion is single-peaked, a centrist dynamic may dominate. Yet severe political conflict is almost never encountered in situations where public opinion has a single peak. The problem of political conflict, insofar as it is a problem at all, concerns issues on which opinion is strongly divided (i.e., multipeaked) and invidious. There is no indication that the dynamics of Downsian

[18] Pitkin (1967).
[19] Lijphart (1999), Linz (1990, 1994), Linz and Stepan (1978), Stepan & Skach (1993).
[20] Downs (1957).

competition in a presidential election will successfully overcome the centrifugal nature of deep-seated ethnic animosities. Wherever cleavages are deep, that is, reinforced along several dimensions (rather than cross-cutting), we can expect that moves toward the center during a presidential election will be perceived by constituents as "rhetoric" or as a move to "co-opt" a group or an issue. Gestures count for little in an environment of heightened sensitivities. Wherever a majority ethic group exists, or can be formulated (from heretofore disparate identities), it will be in the interest of at least one candidate to champion the interests of the majority against the interests of the minority: Buddhists against Tamils (in Sri Lanka), whites against blacks (in the United States), and so forth. Ethnic conflict is at least as much a product of politicians representing the majority as of politicians representing minorities.

Between elections, the presidency also offers an awkward vehicle for compromise, since all important decisions taken within the executive branch are – de jure and usually de facto – the prerogative of one individual, the chief executive. Granted, the cabinet is often constructed with an eye toward inclusion. However, in a presidential system the cabinet is a subordinate body within a "hierarchical" executive; as such, it is unlikely to be of much service in the task of brokering agreements and mediating conflict. Everybody knows it is merely window dressing for the executive office of the president.

Legislatures, by contrast, are spheres in which compromise and accommodation are more easily played out. They are, to begin with, large. This might seem to be a trivial point, but it marks an important contrast between the presidency and the legislature. There are more people involved in critical roles in the latter, and hence a greater capacity to credibly represent dissident groups and deviant views. Second, all members of the legislature are, formally speaking, equals. Each has been elected from a district in the same manner as all the others. They are collegial bodies. Leadership exists, of course, and is usually quite strong. However, such leadership arises from the full assembly and is responsible to the assembly. Moreover, there is plenty of room in the leadership cadre for all sizeable constituencies (e.g., ethnic groups) who are likely to be accorded more than nominal importance. In short, it is quite easy to represent social cleavages politically in a parliamentary system (particularly if that system is proportional), and party leaders have every incentive to do so.[21] Thus, we anticipate that parliamentary systems will be more capable of mediating ethnic conflict than presidential systems, all other things being equal.

CLOSED-LIST PR

Scholars seem to have reached agreement on the point that PR systems are better at managing ethnic conflict than majoritarian systems.[22] Two basic features of PR make this outcome probable: the proportional distribution of seats and votes in a legislature, and the capacity to incorporate members from all relevant social groups on each party's list. PR systems thus allow for the representation of important social groups *across* parties and *within* parties. This dual or bilevel proportionality has direct and indirect effects in moderating social conflict.

Let us begin by looking at the interior life of political parties. Recall that a political party is a representational instrument, through which the views and interests of groups within society may be integrated into public policy – or not. The extent to which a party can effectively perform this role hinges, in part, on the electoral system within which it is situated. In an SMD system, the party's selection of candidates within each constituency is limited, by definition, to a single individual. Any party hoping to win that seat is well advised to choose a member of the dominant ethnic group in that district as its candidate. (Recall that we are concerned here with situations of severe ethnic conflict; under situations of moderate conflict, or no conflict, this stricture may not apply.) Thus, a simple deductive model of electoral competition

[21] Of course, presidential systems also have legislatures. But these assemblies are not as well equipped to integrate diverse constituencies. First, there are fewer positions to go around. With the cabinet chosen by the president, and party leadership a relatively informal affair, the "leadership" may consist of a handful of individuals, even in a legislature of hundreds. Second, the positions that are available lack definition (at least from the perspective of the general public) and public prominence. The "speaker," the party leaders, and the chairs of important committees may wield significant power, but they rarely catch the attention of the general public. Thus, groups already disposed to feel excluded by a polity are unlikely to be mollified by the leadership positions available to them in a presidential assembly. Regardless of whether a legislature in a presidential polity is "weak" or "strong," we doubt that it will have the same integrative effects as an assembly in a parliamentary system.

[22] Cohen (1997), Horowitz (1985), Lijphart (1968, 1977, 1984b, 1999), Saideman et al. (2002).

suggests that all relevant parties will select members of the same ethnic group as candidates within every electoral district in an SMD polity, leaving all other ethnic groups within each district effectively unrepresented. The dynamics in an MMD electoral system are quite different. The larger district size, coupled with each party's ability to name an entire list of candidates (corresponding to the number of seats in that district), means that it will be easy to include members of all sizeable ethnic groups on each party's list. A deductive model of electoral competition suggests that party-list nominations will be inclusive, while SMD nominations will be exclusive. Of course, larger ethnic groups may dominate the higher positions on each party's list; in this respect, PR systems may be exclusionary. Even so, it is much easier to grant a prominent place to a minority candidate when the list of candidates representing a party is long than when it consists of only one member. And popular parties can expect to elect several candidates from each multimember district. So, all in all, we anticipate a significant inclusionary effect operating *within* each party in a PR system.[23]

Now let us turn to the dynamics of interparty competition. Majoritarian electoral systems are often noted for establishing a confrontational, winner-take-all dynamic at the legislative level, one that is similar to that established by a separate-powers constitution at the presidential level. There is only one winner of a single-member seat,

[23] Dominguez (1998: 79) notes that in many Anglophone Caribbean nations, "the first-past-the-post electoral system and the small size of parliaments gravely weakened the capacity of the legislature to represent political minorities or to balance the executive. Elections produced large parliamentary majorities, denying even large minority parties adequate representation in parliament. Moreover, parliament was left with few means to check unbridled executive power. Almost one-third of the region's parliament members are also cabinet members. In effect, they are constitutionally debarred from independent and critical stances in relation to the executive because they are also in the executive." A more extreme example of plurality-assisted conflict is provided by Northern Ireland during the Stormont era (1920-71). O'Duffy (1993: 134) comments, "The fragmentation of the nationalist bloc was facilitated by the futility of constitutional representation of its minority interests.... During this time the unionist bloc was able to maintain hegemonic control over both local and provincial government through the (often abused) plurality system of representation. As a result of its inability to challenge unionist hegemony through constitutional politics, moderate nationalism never completely eclipsed the physical-force tradition within the nationalist bloc. This allowed the Irish Republican Army to retain a certain degree of legitimacy and cohesion despite military failures." See also Ward (1994: 110–12, 115, 117).

just as there is only one winner in a presidential contest; it is the same phenomenon writ small and multiplied many times. Here, conflicts are likely to be understood as zero-sum, with clear winners and losers. The stakes in such a contest are likely to be high, and the capacity for abuse by the winning party correspondingly great. Losers may fear that they will not survive to fight another day. Even if the party survives, leaders of the losing party(ies) may feel disgraced by their defeat. They may even refuse to admit defeat, for the simple reason that doing so would entail a loss of position within the party. In such circumstances, the opt-out clause is attractive – a unilateral withdrawal from government, a constitutional challenge, or, at the extreme, insurrection.

This head-to-head, us-against-them contest occurs in virtually every constituency, even if several parties are represented at the national level. Majoritarian electoral systems are conflictual not only because they have a tendency to create two-party (or two-coalition) competition at the national level but also because they have a tendency to create two-party or two-candidate competition at the local level. Indeed, it is rare to find three-cornered races at the constituency level. And even in those cases where three viable candidates face off, the local election still creates a winner-take-all dynamic.

This brings us to a second point. In majoritarian electoral systems, winning parties often take office with something less than an absolute majority of votes cast. If there is a significant "third party" effort, the winner is likely to have received a good deal less than an absolute majority. The wasted-vote phenomenon means that candidates and their supporters who end up with less than a plurality may feel that they are left empty-handed. Even if they have won a significant portion of their district's vote – or, at a national level, of the nationwide vote – they may have few or no seats in their possession at the end of the day. This is likely to engender resentment among losers, who see themselves as deprived of electoral representation corresponding to their level of support in the electorate. Elections quickly lose their legitimacy when votes cast bear only a distant relationship to seats won. The fairness of a majoritarian system is especially difficult to explain to minority groups whose representation in national affairs is thereby compromised. Aggrieved ethnic groups are often ready to impute the worst motives to their adversaries. Plots will be suspected. Counterplots may be hatched. Such situations may quickly spin out of control.

Majoritarian electoral systems also tend to accentuate the spatially demarcated (i.e., segregated) nature of a polity. In Britain, for example, a secular trend of regionalization in party support has occurred for the better part of a century. Mitchell and Seyd note that this has something to do with the changing demographics of the regions. Even so, "the properties of plurality rule exacerbate this regional cleavage, and often result in the parties concentrating their resources on a few marginal seats." The Westminster electoral system, they conclude, "builds in incentives for both [national] and regional parties to concentrate their support, rather than spread it across a large number of seats."[24] We should keep in mind that wherever ascriptive identities form the basis of sharp social conflict, the relevant groups are usually divided by region. A majoritarian system naturally accentuates this spatial decomposition of a geographically divided electorate, thus reinforcing the segregated – "territorial" – nature of existing social conflict and instituting political relationships between leaders and followers that are constructed on pride of place. Ethnicity and regionalism are a potent combination.

In this context, closed-list PR systems may be preferred precisely because they tend to nationalize political conflict. National ideologies, rather than territory, provide the leitmotif of electoral competition. It may not be immediately clear why this would be so, since most ethnic territories are large enough to encompass an entire multimember district. The fact that ties between district and ethnicity are less sharp in PR systems has to do with the dynamic of electoral conflict, where all votes count (so long as a party is able to surpass the threshold). This means that a vote for party X is just as useful in one district as in another. There are virtually no wasted votes. Quite a different dynamic obtains in a winner-take-all electoral environment. Here, the trick is to obtain more votes than one's opponents in as many districts as possible; minimal-winning electoral victories in constituencies across the country maximize a party's political power in the legislature. Since we are concerned here with the interaction between electoral systems and ethnic conflict, let us imagine an electorate in which ethnicity is a ready vehicle for electoral combat, that is, a latent identity that political

[24] Mitchell and Seyd (1999: 103).

elites might choose to emphasize if it suits their electoral purposes. A party with a latent ethnic majority in a district (i.e., where that party's "natural" constituency is a numerical majority) has an incentive to emphasize ethnic themes in order to stimulate turnout and party loyalty in that district. This would of course work against them in districts where they are in a minority, but within "their" (ethnic-majority) districts we can assume that they pursue an ethnic strategy. Similarly, their opponents have an incentive to pursue ethnic strategies of voter mobilization in districts where they claim a majority of the citizenry. Thus, it is reasonable to assume that ethnic strategies will be pursued in virtually all districts (the exception being those few districts where a single ethnic group does not predominate). Since these strategies are being pursued by the dominant party in each constituency, it is likely that this will be the dominant strategy nationally, even though party leaders – concerned with national-level results and perhaps with a broader view of politics – may resist. Politics is irredeemably local in most SMD polities.

At the same time, many, and perhaps most, districts are noncompetitive in majoritarian polities. Thus, it is natural to suppose that conflicts will be muted in these districts, though minority groups, effectively disenfranchised by the electoral system, may still harbor grievances, and opposition candidates will jump and shout. Most of the action, and most of the media attention, is likely to be focused on a few competitive districts, for upon these results control of the legislature often hinges. These districts are apt to be divided between the competing ethnic groups; they mirror the sharpest cleavage at the national level (whatever that may be). These are the "bleeding Kansas" districts. Again, the situation may be profitably contrasted with a closed-list PR system, where a vote is equally valuable regardless of its geographic location. As a rule, we expect conflict to heighten where stakes are large and results hinge on voting in ethnically divided districts. This is precisely the situation that majoritarian electoral rules establish wherever polities are ethnically divided.[25]

[25] Majoritarian electoral rules may have less deleterious effects in a polity that is divided among three or more groups. Here, the dynamic of party competition may encourage a cooperative, nonethnic style of politicking, particularly if no single group holds a majority in any electoral district. However, these are also the polities that we would expect, for a host of additional reasons (having nothing to do with the electoral system), to be less conflictual. Recent work on ethnic conflict highlights the fact

There is one important objection to everything we have said to this point. It might appear that the dynamics of PR competition would encourage a more "ethnic" style of campaigning in an ethnically divided polity, since it should be easy to mobilize a latent constituency nationally, even if that constituency is small and scattered throughout the country. One can imagine a veritable host of ethnically based parties within an ethnically diverse country like the United States – a Catholic party, a Protestant party, a Jewish party, an African-American party, and so forth.

Even so, we surmise that ethnic partisanship, should it occur, is less destructive in a PR system than in a majoritarian electoral system. In our view, it is not the representation of groups according to ethnicity that is harmful to governance but rather the failure of parties to effectively *mediate* conflict, peacefully and constitutionally. If they can accomplish the latter – and there is no reason to suppose otherwise – then we expect a happy outcome. Indeed, ethnic parties are a familiar feature of European polities, and they do not seem, on the whole, to have played an irresponsible role in political life. Arguably, direct participation in political affairs by organized religious and cultural groups has a moderating effect on ethnic identity over time. Ethnicity and politics *can* mix comfortably. Religions do not necessarily "religify" politics; more often, politics secularizes religion.[26] This pattern is observable in contemporary Turkey, as well as in most of Europe and Latin America over the past century.[27] Arguably, African polities, with ethnic cleavages that are at least as salient as those characterizing Europe in previous decades, would be better off if the principle of

that ethnicities become most problematic as they approach a "polarized" situation – two groups with roughly equal numbers of adherents and including most of the citizenry. The ideal situation, observe Elbadawi and Sambanis (2002: 263), "is for groups to be proportionately represented so that governments can only be formed by coalitions across ethnic groups. For such coalition politics a high degree of ethnic diversity is a great advantage. A society divided into, say, only two ethnic groups, one somewhat larger than the other, in which the political contest is between two groups, will find a development-oriented bargaining equilibrium more fragile than one in which each of many groups has its own party."

Thus, the "worst" demographic setting (from the perspective of ethnic conflict) is accentuated by two-party competition resulting from electoral systems organized around single-member districts.

[26] Wald (1987).

[27] Mecham (2004).

ethnic representation were more fully accepted and more openly practiced. As it is, ethnic mobilization occurs, but only sub rosa, a matter of shame for those who participate. Here, one imagines, is an effective tool to bind the members of a polity to its government. In order for political parties to be effective they must represent the lived reality – that is, the most fundamental social identity – of their constituents. If this identity is predominantly ethnic, then the party system ought to reflect that identity. Closed-list PR systems, particularly if combined with unitary and parliamentary governments, offer an effective way to channel such sentiments without undermining democratic deliberation and the provision of public goods.

In considering the effect of an electoral system on ethnic conflict we must also consider its effect in the formation of interparty coalitions, both formal and informal, and at the electoral and governing stages. As a rule, plurality electoral systems tend to discourage coalitional behavior. In the archetypal situation of two-party dominance, no coalition is conceivable (except in exceptional circumstances posed by a foreign war or natural disaster); the electoral world is divided into "us" and "them." In a plurality electoral system where more than two parties compete (usually in different regions) it is somewhat more common for parties to create tacit electoral alliances, which may amount to little more than nonaggression pacts (agreements not to compete in each other's bailiwicks). This is coalitional behavior of a very primitive sort, and it is not the sort that is likely to have positive repercussions for moderating ethnic conflict or for enhancing the quality of government more generally. Donald Horowitz notes that SMD systems encourage electoral coalitions among parties that are most *distant* from each other programmatically and ethnically. This is because parties with similar profiles tend to be competitive in the same districts, and therefore find it difficult to reach a mutually acceptable entente. Thus, in three-way competitions in Nigeria, Uganda, Benin, and Punjab,

> the natural lines of partnership run between those parties that will not oppose each other at the polls. Pre-electoral negotiations between parties in strong competition with each other are difficult. Even when coalitions are freshly formed after the elections, direct competitors have more difficulty reaching agreement than noncompetitors do – the more so when the competitors have both been striving for the privilege of exclusively representing a single ethnic group.... The most likely coalition partners – parties that stood the least

chance of competing for the same clientele – were also those with programs completely antithetical to each other.[28]

This leads to coalitions that are incoherent (and hence less legitimate from a public perspective), as well as unstable.

In a PR system, by contrast, coalitions are virtually unavoidable, and tend to incorporate parties with similar ideological and demographic profiles. They also tend to be formal in nature, perhaps to the point of issuing a common platform and/or postcoalition agreement. They tend, finally, to endure through an entire electoral period (from one election to the next) and perhaps over the course of many decades. As a result, they typically command greater legitimacy in the public eye. Coalitions are a generally recognized fact of life in PR systems. (Parliamentarism also facilitates coalitions, because the choice of government is a formal decision taken by the legislature and will necessitate cross-party agreements whenever a single party cannot muster a majority on its own. Formal coalitions are less common in presidential legislatures, and for this reason PR and parliamentarism exert complementary effects on coalitional behavior.)

Ethnic diversity need not pose a problem of governance if diverse interests and identities can be integrated into the political process, assuring each group a formal position in the polity roughly proportional to the group's numerical strength. The solution to ethnic conflict within a democratic framework is thus not the denial of ethnicity, but rather its recognition: specifically, the formation of ethnically based parties that can adequately represent these groups, assuring members that their interests are being protected and their identities respected. Each has a place at the table in a centripetal polity.[29]

PR electoral rules foster the overall representativeness of government by giving multiple parties important positions in parliament. Of course, not all parties will be represented in every coalition government; even the largest coalitions are not all-inclusive (except in extraordinary circumstances, such as wartime). However, out-parties are often included in policy making at other levels, in either a formal or an informal capacity. It is a hallmark of multiparty parliaments

[28] Horowitz (1985: 377-8).
[29] Collier (2001).

to have active legislatures, where committees play important roles, where parties are represented on committees in rough proportion to their membership in the legislature, and where cross-party mechanisms of communication and deliberation are robust. In this fashion, elites from all sizeable parties are encouraged to participate in meaningful ways in the governance process. Most important, so long as they do not occupy extreme positions on the political spectrum – and are therefore "coalition-worthy" – such parties can realistically expect to be included in the governing coalition at some point in the not-too-distant future. This creates a strong incentive for leaders of minority parties to support the political process even when their party is out of power.

The most important point is the most obvious: in situations of high ethnic sensitivity and mutual distrust, it is essential to prevent any single group from dominating, or appearing to dominate, positions of power. PR makes this much less likely to happen. It is of course logically possible for a majority group to gain power through PR institutions, and thereby to enact prejudicial legislation against a minority. Some might regard the post-apartheid polity in South Africa as an example of this. Over the past two decades, the African National Congress (ANC), representing most of the black electorate, has monopolized power – effectively excluding parties representing whites and mixed races. In this respect, the ANC has followed Westminster practice. (South Africa was a British colony, inheriting a first-past-the-post single-member-district electoral system, which operated until the transition from apartheid to majority rule in the 1990s.) Even so, and despite their apparent monopoly of power, it is questionable whether the ANC has seriously discriminated against these minority groups. More important, for our purposes, the electoral history of PR over the past century suggests that the ANC is very unlikely to retain its single-party majority for very long. With the notable exception of Japan, there are no democratic countries with extended periods of single-party majority government arising from PR electoral rules.[30]

[30] In Italy and Sweden, although one party was hegemonic throughout most of the postwar era, that party was usually forced to rule in coalition with other parties, or in a single-party minority government. Note that because minority governments exist only with the tacit support of other parties, they are perhaps better regarded as a

Our discussion has focused on the contrast between PR and majoritarian electoral systems, as exemplified by the plurality systems employed in the United States and the United Kingdom. Of course, electoral systems are nearly infinite in their variety. Under the circumstances, we cannot undertake a systematic review of each variant and its probable effect on conflict mediation. Nonetheless, the outlines of such a discussion are already evident: electoral systems should be successful in mediating social conflict to the extent that they embody the twin characteristics of closed-list-PR: proportionality within, and between, parties. The closer an electoral system lies to this ideal, we argue, the greater its capacity to mediate severe political conflicts.[31]

CONCLUSIONS

This chapter has focused on three constitutional-level institutions that may be effective in moderating extreme conflict, the paradigmatic example of which is provided by "ethnic" conflict.[32] There are, of course, many other ways of addressing this sort of political problem. We do not mean to suggest that centripetal institutions – unitarism, parliamentarism, and closed-list PR – are the only solution. We simply maintain that, in most circumstances, these institutions are at least as good as, or better than, their counterparts – federalism, separate powers, and majoritarian or preferential-vote electoral systems.

form of coalition government (Strom 1990). Pempel (1990) offers a brief discussion of one-party-dominant party systems in Western democracies.

31 Accordingly, majority ("double-ballot") and single-transferable-vote ("STV") electoral systems allow for a somewhat greater proportionality between votes and seats than would be obtainable in a pure plurality system. As a secondary effect, they encourage more coalition building among parties than would be expected under plurality rules, but not as much as in PR systems. Block vote systems (where all seats in an MMD are allocated to the party winning the most votes) create majoritarian conflict among parties but offer parties the opportunity to accommodate a variety of groups on their lists. Mixed electoral systems, of course, combine SMD/plurality seats with MMD/party-list seats (in either a "parallel" or a "compensatory" fashion). We presume that their effect on ethnic conflict will roughly parallel the share of seats that assume a PR format.

32 This does *not* presume that ethnicity has any real (i.e., Platonic or otherwise essentialist) value. It presumes, merely, that at some point in time certain ascriptive identies may take on great salience in the political sphere.

Of other political-institutional alternatives we have little to say, since they surpass the boundaries of our investigation.[33] We add only a brief cautionary note: if these alternative conflict-reduction measures have the consequence of weakening political parties, they are likely to impede the quality of governance in a polity, for reasons discussed in the previous chapter. And if so, the longer-term prognosis for ethnic reconciliation is not favorable.[34]

One might briefly consider the case of Lebanon, as explored by Horowitz. From the national pact of 1943 to the civil war that began in 1975–76, Horowitz explains,

> Lebanon had an electoral system that encouraged moderation, that practically required interethnic coalitions, and that prevented the crystallization of allegiances around the overarching affiliations of Muslim versus Christian. Four electoral provisions were conducive to these results: reserved offices, reserved seats, interethnic tickets, and interethnic voting. All the major offices were reserved. The President was to be a Maronite, the prime minister a Sunni, the speaker of the house a Shiite, the vice-speaker a Greek Orthodox, and so on. By the same token, the ethnic composition of the legislature was prescribed by law; that of the cabinet, by custom. Although there were variations over time, generally most constituencies were multimember and multiethnic. The ethnic identity of each seat was specified. There was a common electoral roll, so that each voter, regardless of ethnic identity, cast a ballot for each seat. Candidates formed competing interethnic lists, appealing to the entire electorate.[35]

Rarely, concludes Horowitz, "has there been a system that placed as high a premium on intraethnic competition and interethnic cooperation."[36]

In the event, these rather intricate solutions did not succeed in moderating interethnic hostilities. By the mid-1970s, Lebanon collapsed

[33] The "consociational" model is similar to centripetalism insofar as it features PR electoral systems, but different in its emphasis on federalism. Other features (e.g., reserved seats) are quite specific to particular situations of ethnic conflict and do not bear directly on our arguments. See Lijphart (1968, 1977) as well as commentary in Andeweg (2000), Bachtiger et al. (2002), Bogaards (2000), Bohn (1980), Daalder (1974), Halpern (1986), Horowitz (1985), Keman (1997), Lehmbruch (1993), Lustick (1979, 1997), Luther and Deschouwer (1999), McRae (1974), and Norris (2002).

[34] Brown (2000), Esman (1993), Zartman (1995).

[35] Horowitz (1985: 633).

[36] Ibid.

into a brutal civil war, ended only by Syria's intervention and subsequent occupation of the country. One might cite many reasons for this tragic failure. But foremost among these may have been the failure of Lebanese democracy to develop strong political parties, ones that could effectively govern the new state, with all its fractious parts. As it happened, the institutions set up to prevent domination by a single group succeeded in that objective. However, the cost was a polity that was stalemated across all dimensions. And this stalemate manifestly did not lead to the pacification of ethnic enmities. On the contrary, the weak Lebanese state formed the backdrop for the creation of ethnic militias that eventually eclipsed the state. For example, Horowitz points out, "the fixed proportions of the system meant that it was impossible to increase the number of seats held by any group or for a group to occupy an office or seat assigned to another group. All that was left was to squabble over who, among members of a given group, would occupy a seat or office and, in the process of doing so, to maximize support from sources outside the group."[37] This meant that political conflict was personalistic, rather than partisan, intraethnic rather than cross-ethnic. Strong parties were virtually prohibited; instead, factions bit at each other's heels. "The absence of parties created an organizational vacuum, which facilitated the emergence of armed private militias. These gangs, some of them attached to parliamentary politicians, had much greater freedom than they would have had if real party organizations had existed and seen them early on as rivals for political authority."[38]

The point here is that the problem of ethnic conflict is not just a problem of keeping diverse groups from each other's throats. One can easily incapacitate the state apparatus so that no single group can hope to monopolize power – the "veto points" approach (see Appendix B). But in the long run, such a solution is unlikely to maintain the peace for the simple reason that it prevents the establishment of a workable government. We put forward the working hypothesis that ethnic conflict is created and fostered as much by the weakness of states as by their strength. The problem, to paraphrase Huntington, is too little capacity, not too much.[39] State failure, often understood as a product

[37] Ibid., 633–4.

[38] Ibid., 635.

[39] Huntington (1968).

of ethnic conflict, is also a cause of ethnic conflict. Minority groups rightly perceive danger whenever a power vacuum exists, for who – in the absence of an effective state apparatus – will protect them? Anxieties rise when it appears that another group might gain control of the military.

Arguably, ethnic conflict is a rational response to conditions of high uncertainty, uncertainty that is closely linked to state failure. David Lake and Donald Rothchild comment:

> Collective fears of the future arise when states lose their ability to arbitrate between groups or provide credible guarantees of protection for groups. Under this condition . . . physical security becomes of paramount concern. When central authority declines, groups become fearful for their survival. They invest in and prepare for violence, and thereby make actual violence possible. State weakness, whether it arises incrementally out of competition between groups or from extremists actively seeking to destroy ethnic peace, is a necessary precondition for violent ethnic conflict to erupt.[40]

State weakness, the authors note, contributed to the rise of ethnic violence in Eastern Europe following the end of the USSR and in Liberia, Somalia, and other African states. This is easy to explain, since situations of high uncertainty create a first-mover advantage. Groups feel the need to strike first, before their enemies have a chance to mobilize. Successful conflict mediation thus involves assuring both parties that there is an authoritative seat of power, that this center of authority can enforce agreements, and that it will not be captured by either side.

The advantage of centripetal institutions is clear: they include diverse interests and identities while also bolstering state capacity. Centripetal polities channel and moderate conflict, which is institutionalized through the party system, the legislature, and other collegial bodies. Strongly held political interests and identities are thereby integrated into the political process. This does not mean that conflict is suppressed. Rather, such conflict is limited to ritualized display – for example, floor votes and election manifestos – sufficient to convince party militants that their party represents them without interfering

[40] Lake and Rothchild (1997: 99).

with interparty deal making.[41] Over time, a moderation of hostilities should become manifest at the grass roots.

The flip side of our argument is that fragmenting institutions may encourage, rather than diminish, sectional, sectoral, and sect-based cleavages. The veto-points architecture provides incentives for rival groups to defect, whereas the existence of a central political authority gives leaders of various groups a strong incentive to come together. This is particularly the case when the institutions of central authority are group-based (e.g., parties, committees, a legislature, a cabinet) rather than singular (e.g., a presidency), and where the electoral system gives full scope to minority interests and ideals, as proportional systems generally do.

[41] It is important to point out that the social integration we envision is not simply the integration of elites (representing each social group), as stipulated by the theory of consociationalism.

4

Policy Coordination

Government is often conceptualized as a solution to societal coordination problems.[1] Yet the institutions of governance may also suffer from coordination problems. There are many variations on this theme – joint-decision traps, shirking, underproviding of public goods, overgrazing, the tragedy of the commons, common-pool problems, collective action problems, free-rider problems, prisoner's dilemmas, transaction-cost dilemmas, and so forth.[2] These are different ways of pointing out a central problem: quite often, when individuals, groups, or institutions pursue their own agendas (even with the best of intentions), the result is not what members of society at large would prefer. Coordination problems thus involve a conflict between the part and the whole, between individual and collective rationality.

In this chapter, we are concerned specifically with policy coordination, that is, success in coordinating among a national government's constituent parts: between legislature and executive, between backbenchers and party leaders, among parties, among diverse agencies, between national and subnational governments, and among subnational governments. Successful coordination among these institutions can help resolve many of society's collective problems.

[1] Hardin (1999).

[2] Hardin (1982), Olson (1965), Ostrom (1990), Ostrom and Walker (1997), Scharpf (1988), Shleifer and Vishny (1993), Williamson (1996). A defining feature of a coordination problem is that preferences are assumed to be stable. This is quite different from other sorts of political problems, as discussed elsewhere in this book.

Centripetal theory suggests two solutions to this species of political problem. The first is Hobbesian: the internalization of externalities by centralizing jurisdictions and responsibilities. This has the effect of minimizing coordination problems because there are no independent (in the sense of sovereign) sources of power left to coordinate. They have all been incorporated. The resulting decision, taken at a centralized level or delegated to an accountable authority, is more likely to consider the total (net) costs and benefits of a particular policy because that is its formal purview. (The reader must bear in mind that this argument, like all others in this book, is contingent upon an important assumption: that the polity is democratic.)

The second solution concerns the process by which policies are framed and debated. In a centripetal system, we anticipate a *collegial* style of policy deliberation. Centripetal constitutions promote collegial bodies such as the cabinet, cabinet committees, the legislature, legislative committees, party caucuses, commissions, regulatory bodies, and other group decision-making bodies. They also encourage a cooperative style of decision making within and among these various bodies. Our use of the term "collegial" therefore conveys both the prominence of collegial bodies (minimally defined) in a polity and the degree of collegiality that these bodies exhibit.

In sum, we argue that centripetal polities resolve coordination problems through authority and through more subtle matters of process. Where authority is centralized and inclusive actors have strong incentives to cooperate, differences are more likely to be resolved in ways that are collectively beneficial. Deliberation, in the broad sense of the term, is more likely to occur.

UNITARISM

For a variety of reasons, federal constitutions tend to induce fragmented systems of public administration. This, in turn, may induce a variety of coordination problems. To begin with, the existence of independent governments at regional and national levels creates duplication of effort and a confusion of political roles. Although some constitutions seek to assign unique policy responsibilities to each level of government, in practice these distinctive areas of responsibility are often difficult to maintain – or, if successfully maintained, lead to bad policy outcomes, the product of a too-rigid separation.[3]

A classic example of policy implementation gone awry – due, in no small part, to the constitutional constraints of a federal constitution – is told by Jeffrey Pressman and Aaron Wildavsky, who regale us with the endless problems involved in building a single aircraft hangar and ship terminal in Oakland, California. The goals of a federal program, created in 1966, were to reduce unemployment, ease racial tensions in Oakland, and, of course, to build a hangar and ship terminal. Yet four years after the initial appropriation bill had passed through Congress, the terminal was only partially built, the plans for the hangar were not yet complete, and only a small number of jobs for minorities had been created. The glacial progress of the program, and accompanying cost overruns, were not the result of bureaucratic incompetence, the authors explain, but rather of intergovernmental complexity. These two small and specific tasks involved the cooperation of seven federal agencies (the Economic Development Administration [EDA] of the Department of Commerce, the Seattle Regional Office of the EDA, the Oakland Office of the EDA, the General Accounting Office, the Department of Health, Education and Welfare, the Department of Labor, and the U.S. Navy), three local agencies (the mayor of Oakland, the city council, and the port of Oakland), and four private groups (World Airways Company, Oakland business leaders, Oakland black leaders, and conservation and environmental groups). These fourteen governmental and private entities had to agree on at least seventy important decisions in order to implement a law initially passed in Washington.[4]

[3] Although education policy, in principle, is a state and local prerogative in the American constitutional system, the fact is that governments at all levels pursue education policies. The same might be said for other social welfare policies, for infrastructure policies (e.g., roads and public transportation) – indeed, for policy in virtually every area except defense, which for practical reasons remains a federal prerogative. The prevailing metaphor for American federalism is the marble cake. The reason for this is quite simple. People care about these issues, and insofar as legislators have the capacity to respond to these public demands, they are more or less obliged to do so. This is the not-so-secret spring behind federal "encroachment" on state powers, as well as state encroachment on federal powers.

[4] Pressman and Wildavsky (1973: 95–6, 102–7), summarized in Wilson (1992: 68). See also Bardach (1977).

More recently, Martin Dimitrov finds that the enforcement of intellectual property rights laws across a sample of thirty-one countries is more zealous (greater effort is expended) and more effective in unitary than in federal states. "Under-enforcement and shirking occur in federal states, while higher enforcement rates are characteristic of unitary states."[5] Yet another fairly simple administrative task is rendered problematic when national and subnational authorities share administrative duties.

A different sort of problem concerns *over*regulation, and varying regulatory burdens across multiple jurisdictions. With respect to financial markets in Canada, *The Economist* reports:

> For more than 20 years, Canada's bankers, lawyers and money managers have been trying to persuade politicians that 13 different securities regulators are 12 too many.... Because securities law falls under the provinces' jurisdiction, each of the ten provinces and three federally administered territories has its own rules, plus a regulator to enforce them. Companies wanting to sell securities to investors across the country require permission from all 13 jurisdictions.... the frustrations are especially acute in licensing investment advisers, mutual-fund managers and other market participants; and for private placements, where three of the biggest provinces, Ontario, Alberta and British Columbia, have recently adopted differing rules. Estimates put the cost of regulation in Canada at about the same as Britain – with its far bigger markets – and more than double the cost in Australia. Almost 3,800 people do the job in Canada, compared with under 2,800 in Britain and 2,200 in Australia – neither of which has a notably lean regulatory apparatus for securities. Regional jealousies are part of the problem. Alberta maintains that it needs special rules to grease the wheels of investment in its oil and gas industry. Ditto, mining and venture capital in British Columbia. The chances are less than slight of Quebec signing on to a pan-Canadian agency, so long as a separatist government remains in office. The provinces are also loath to sacrifice a tidy source of revenue.[6]

As a final example, one must consider the ubiquitous problem of coordinating fiscal and monetary policy at national and subnational levels. Note that in a federal polity money is raised and spent at both levels, and – more important – subnational governments enjoy considerable autonomy in these decisions. In these circumstances, an absence of formal coordination between national and subnational governments

[5] Dimitrov (2003: 2).

[6] *Economist* (2002: 69).

has the potential to wreak financial havoc.[7] Erik Wibbels argues that three common coordination problems affect fiscal and monetary policy in federal polities: "(1) provincial fiscal policy can starve central governments of revenue sources, encouraging fiscal imbalance at the federal level; (2) monetary policy can generate inflation if federal authorities cover subnational fiscal imbalances via seignorage; and (3) federal indebtedness can increase if national governments assume provincial debt to ensure the solvency of provincial governments."[8]

Insofar as persistent deficit spending is a valid measure of bad fiscal governance, the experience of federal states is not encouraging. To be sure, fiscal balance is a hallmark of state governments in the United States, where it is often prescribed in state constitutions. However, it has not been characteristic of state governments in Argentina, Brazil, and India, where "large aggregate deficits, ranging from 15 to over 30 percent of total revenue, have been quite persistent since the mid-1980s."[9]

[7] The question of "fiscal federalism" has received enormous attention from scholars over the past few decades. Although it is sometimes assumed that the theory of fiscal federalism is synonymous with constitutional federalism, very few authorities on the subject take this view of the matter. Fiscal federalism, its leading exponent explains, "lays out a general normative framework for the assignment of functions to different levels of government and the appropriate fiscal instruments for carrying out these functions" (Oates 1999: 1121; see also Oates 1972; Rodden et al. 2003; Ter-Minassian 1997; Weingast 1995). Indeed, fiscal federalism is a theory of fiscal management with particular attention to the vertical delegation of power, *not* a constitutional theory in the usual sense of that term. This is obvious enough when one considers the fact that theories of fiscal federalism do not tell us which constitutional institutions one should adopt. Indeed, many advocates of fiscal federalism are agnostic on the question of constitutional federalism. Barry Weingast (2000: 8), for example, argues that constitutional federalism is irrelevant to regime performance and of only diffuse importance to fiscal federalism.

[8] Wibbels (2000: 688–9).

[9] Rodden and Eskeland (2003). Under federal auspices, "local governments might have strong reasons to believe that bailouts will be forthcoming if their interests are well represented in the central legislature, or if decisions in the legislature are made through regional log-rolling. In several ... cases ..., fiscally irresponsible governments obtained bailouts through their influence in the national legislature, trading votes with other legislators, or threatening to veto unrelated policy proposals. Some problems of horizontal bargaining are exacerbated if a few provinces are dominant in size. In many countries, a two-chambered legislature gives each region representation proportional to population in the lower chamber, with small regions relatively over-represented in the upper chamber. In such systems, small states have disproportionate power and their votes may be shifted cheaply in political bargaining. In one particularly troubling scenario, the central government might appear to be little

The problem of subnational deficits can be overcome if the central government imposes "hard" budget constraints on state governments (the usual prescription emanating from advocates of fiscal federalism). However, one must ponder whether this constraint is likely to be enforced in the typical federal polity. Recall that the institutions of federalism empower regional actors, encourage them to define themselves as regionalists, and grant them positions in the very same national councils that decide upon revenues and expenditures. Arguably, the more fragmented a regime, constitutionally speaking, the less likely it is that the central authority will be able to refuse "urgent" requests from state governments. Thus, we surmise that the norm of hard budgets is unlikely to be sustained through difficult economic times within constitutionally divided polities. Constitutional federalism, ironically, may be inimical to the precepts of fiscal federalism.[10]

In sum, unitary constitutions seem more likely to resolve coordination problems than federal constitutions for the simple reason that all facets of the polity are formally incorporated into a single sovereign entity. Regional governments, to the extent that they enjoy an independent political existence, are forced to abide by whatever directives are issued from the center, and the center has an incentive (through accountability processes normal to democratic governance) to solve those problems. This does not mean, of course, that unitary systems necessarily solve complex coordination problems. But they are more likely to, for they have the constitutional tools and democratic incentives to do so.

more than a loose coalition of log-rolling regional interest groups. This danger is most pronounced in formally federal systems, which usually include direct representation and constitutional protections for the states. These features, along with others…, can make national government beholden to subnational governments rather than to citizens" (Rodden et al. 2003: 16). See also Blanchard and Shleifer (2000), Jones et al. (2000), Prud'homme (1995), Suberu (2001: chapter three), and Treisman (1999).

10 The Cardoso government in Brazil refinanced state budget deficits on a "one last time" basis, and then banned future bailouts in an apparently tough measure of fiscal responsibility. But is the tough-love pledge credible, given the formidable power of regional governments in Brazilian politics (Samuels 2003)? Later, in 2003, *The Economist* noted that "some powerful governors and mayors are now pressing Lula [the current president] to go back on this ban" (*Economist* 2003: 8). For further consideration of this issue, see Braun et al. (2002: 139).

CLOSED-LIST PR

The causal effect of electoral systems in solving (or exacerbating) coordination problems rests upon their role in structuring the party system. We have argued, in chapter two, that closed-list PR electoral systems are likely to foster stronger parties than would be anticipated in similar polities with SMD or preferential-vote rules. Recall that one of the functions of a strong party is to nationalize and broaden policy debates. Issues, insofar as they reach the national stage, are likely to address national constituencies, for the low barriers to entry of a PR system mean that parties have an incentive to collect votes in all regions of a country. That being the case, it seems likely that parties in a PR legislature will have a larger foundation of shared perspectives and shared constituencies than would be likely in a legislature elected according to SMD or preferential-vote rules. Insofar as strong parties are effective in aggregating interests, a closed-list PR electoral system should reduce coordination problems.

Strong parties also serve to enhance the power of party leaders. Leaders of strong parties are better able to bargain effectively with each other, reaching across partisan divides, since they enjoy considerable insulation from their constituents on most issues – in particular, from very small, parochial interests. Moreover, any agreements reached among the parties are likely to hold. Enforceability is likelier, and with it a measure of credible commitment. These features at the leadership level should also alleviate problems of policy coordination within the national government and across different levels of government.

We must also consider the *number* of parties that gain entrance into the legislature, and thus constitute players whose interests must be coordinated. It is true that in some circumstances (e.g., in polities that are small and relatively homogeneous, or where heterogeneous elements are widely dispersed) it is possible for two or three parties to monopolize power at the national level under majoritarian electoral rules. Such has generally been the case in Belize, Botswana, Jamaica, and the United States. In this setting, "Duverger's Law" appears to be at work. If these polities adopted PR, their party systems would probably expand. In this respect, policy making in these countries is simplified. However, in polities that are large, or where heterogeneous groups exist and are geographically concentrated – a set that includes most countries in the developing world – it is not clear that there is any regular association between party systems and average district size. This is because SMD systems allow parties to become entrenched in particular districts, a natural support base where groups are regionally concentrated.[11] Note also that the settings in which Duverger's Law appears to work (i.e., countries that are small and homogeneous, or where heterogeneous elements are widely dispersed) are also countries in which coordination problems are likely to be minimal.

But the issue of party system size, despite its high visibility, is in many respects a red herring. In our view, problems of coordination are more strongly affected by the kind of parties that exist in a polity than by the sheer number of parties in that polity. Thus, while the causal effect of SMD electoral rules may be, in certain instances, to manufacture majorities, we must also be conscious of the effect that these manufactured majorities have on the process of governance. If the majority party, so created, is cobbled together from diverse parts – if, that is, there is little internal coherence, either sociologically or ideologically – then that party may no longer serve as a unitary actor, for it has scarcely solved the aggregation problem. In this circumstance, coordination problems may arise *within* the majority party that are as severe, and perhaps in some ways more damaging to good public policy, than coordination problems *across* smaller but more coherent parties.

PARLIAMENTARISM

Parliamentarism helps resolve coordination problems by virtue of the fusion of executive and legislative functions in the same body: the cabinet, which Bagehot referred to imaginatively as a buckle. Parliamentary systems foster agreement because they have to: the executive is chosen by, and responsible to, the legislature. Under the circumstances, it is simply not possible for a serious and enduring division to spring up among the major actors in this play: the prime minister, the cabinet, and the backbenchers. In the event that such a rift appears, it must

[11] Gerring (2005).

be resolved immediately by (a) elections, (b) the formation of a new government, or (c) a renewed commitment on the part of participating parties to support the existing government.

In a presidential system, by contrast, two separate institutions with overlapping powers, different constituencies, (usually) different electoral cycles, and (usually) a different partisan and ideological composition vie for power. For the most part, they are not on collegial terms with one another. Indeed, one often finds political conflict, overt and covert. Leaders of the executive and legislative branches, on cordial terms with one another when appearing before cameras, may do everything possible to knife each other in the back when the klieg lights dim. In any case, these two bodies are constitutionally programmed to disagree. A separate-powers system is an "invitation to struggle."[12]

This conflict stems from the fact that the tasks of legislating and administering (executing) cannot be entirely separated from each other, as the pure theory of separate powers (a la Montesquieu and Madison) supposes. To endow a directly elected president with the power of veto is to grant a power that can and will be used for legislative purposes. Similarly, to endow a legislature with the power to pass bills and appropriate revenue is to involve that legislature in the task of administration. Thus, instead of two branches with separate powers, a presidential constitution creates two branches sharing powers[13] – or, as we would phrase it, vying for power. To our knowledge, this conflict is routine in every democratic polity with a nonparliamentary executive.[14]

[12] Crabb (1992). Of course, partisan conflict persists even in a parliamentary system. When we say that there is no strong or enduring disagreement between the executive and the legislature, we refer to the majority grouping in the legislature – a single party, a coalition of parties, or a tacit coalition of parties underpinning a minority government. Whether partisan debate is fierce and overt, or muted and covert, depends upon whether the electoral system is majoritarian or closed-list PR, a matter discussed earlier. Here we restrict ourselves to relations between the executive and the majority grouping in parliament.

[13] Neustadt (1980).

[14] On post-communist polities, see Taras (1997). On the United States, see Fisher (1985), Hardin (1989), King (1983), and Wilson and Schramm (1994). On Latin American polities, see Mainwaring and Shugart (1997). On semi-presidential polities, see Elgie (1999). On presidential systems generally, see Eaton (2000), Haggard and McCubbins (2001), Lijphart (1992), Samuels (2007), Shugart and Carey (1992), and von Mettenheim (1997).

These are the direct effects, and they are considerable. Even so, the indirect effects of a parliamentary system on policy making may be even more significant. Woodrow Wilson was perhaps the first to perceive the ways in which the constitutional properties of a regime intertwine with matters of public administration. "The study of administration," he wrote in 1887, "is closely connected with the study of the proper distribution of constitutional authority."[15] To be efficient, a system of public administration "must discover the simplest arrangements by which responsibility can be unmistakably fixed upon officials; the best way of dividing authority without hampering it, and responsibility without obscuring it."[16] "The more power is divided," Wilson thought, "the more irresponsible it becomes."[17] It follows that effective public administration is fostered by parliamentarism, not by presidentialism. Within the former, the polity is endowed with a single principal (the cabinet) and multiple agents holding distinct (nonoverlapping) mandates. Centralized political systems have clear lines of authority and hence establish greater accountability between elected and appointed officials.

The contrast between decentralist and centralist visions of public administration is often illustrated by comparing two archetypal polities representative of these two ideals, the United States and the United Kingdom. While having a shared history and political culture, these two polities have vastly different administrative structures, as Terry Moe and Michael Caldwell point out.

> The British scheme is a model of rationality.... The Prime Minister and her Cabinet rely upon two well integrated, professional, hugely powerful central bureaus to control the entire bureaucracy and see their agenda implemented. [By contrast,] the American scheme is not a scheme at all. It is a hodgepodge of presidential and bureaucratic units, overlapping in function and conflicting in perspective, that presidents have tried to weld together through strategies

[15] Wilson (1887/1978: 12).

[16] Ibid.

[17] Ibid., 31. See also Banfield (1975), Bardach (1977), Ford (1898/1967, 1904/1970), Goodnow (1900: 258), Jasper (1990), Kagan (2001), Mainwaring and Samuels (2004), Moe (1989, 1990a, 1990b), Moe and Caldwell (1994), Pressman and Wildavsky (1973), Ray (1987), Riggs (1994, 1997), Robertson (1989), Sanyal and Mukhija (2001), Schneider (1993), Steinberg (1996), Weber (1978), Weyland (1996), and White (1955).

of centralization and politicization. They have enhanced their capacity for control in the process. But with a system so ill designed, authority so limited, and opposition so formidable, their actual control is far less than they need to meet the responsibilities thrust upon them.[18]

From this perspective, the principal-agency problem is much more severe wherever fragmentation in the elective branches and in public service exists. Divided authority leads to mixed messages, overlapping jurisdictions, and rigid and detailed rules of procedure ("red tape"). Bureaucratic malfeasance is easily buried in the chaos or, if discovered, is disavowed ("blame avoidance"). Parallel institutions cannot hold other institutions accountable precisely because each institution is formally independent. In short, decentralized power structures introduce coordination problems among political units wherever the actors are (a) multiple, (b) organizationally independent, (c) instilled with different perspectives and different organizational missions, and (d) empowered with an effective policy veto.

Let us unpack some of these arguments.

Administrative fragmentation. Administrative fragmentation is fostered by the fact of separate powers. Separate-powers systems foster multiple agencies with competing (overlapping) jurisdictions. There are several reasons for this. First, where governmental authority is fragmented it is easier to create than to destroy. Agencies gather constituencies around them, and these constituencies install themselves in legislative committees and subcommittees. The power of these constituencies can be felt in key (swing) districts and even nationally wherever voters are willing to cast their ballots on the basis of a single issue. Thus, when faced with a new or somewhat altered policy imperative, legislators often resort to the creation of a new agency whose mission may be only slightly different from that of an existing agency. This also provides a mechanism for legislators to institutionalize their policy preferences, as discussed earlier, since this agency can be created "from scratch" and will not have to integrate the missions and perspectives of existing agencies. Finally, the specificity of all agency mandates makes reorganization difficult; each revision of bureaucratic

[18] Moe and Caldwell (1994: 190–1).

responsibility compels a revision of law. As a consequence, separate-powers constitutions are often accompanied by jerrybuilt bureaucratic structures. New initiatives build on old initiatives, with scant attention to administrative logic.

Civil service. Public administration depends upon a close and cooperative relationship between elected officials (principals) and their unelected agents, the bureaucracy. In a parliamentary system, we expect to find a collegial relationship between the executive and the agencies under his or her command. In a separate-powers system, by contrast, the executive is embodied in the person of the president. He, like the monarch, is the sole constitutional authority within the executive branch. His advisors, including cabinet members, are personal appointees and may be relieved of their duties at any time (though not without incurring political costs, as we shall observe). In such an environment, it is easy to see why presidential executives tend to embody either a "hierarchical" model or one in which there is little formal organization at all (an "individualistic" model). In either case, it is clear that the operation of the executive branch revolves around the person of the president. It responds to his wishes; it moves by his command, or his (implicit) desires. Indeed, the American president overshadows the cabinet to such an extent that it scarcely meets our minimal definition of a collegial body.[19] A body so constituted does not usually act in a collegial manner. Cabinets in presidential systems are generally sidelined from policy-making power. They serve as adjuncts to the chief executive and are often considerably less influential than the president's personal advisors, who are themselves even less independent of the president and even less inclined to state their views frankly.[20]

Salvatore Schiavo-Campo and Pachampet Sundaram, on the basis of an extensive survey of executive offices around the world, conclude that "central policy formulation and coordination mechanisms take a different form in parliamentary and presidential systems of government – more structured and 'collective' in the former, more flexible and

[19] Lincoln's oft-repeated (and probably apocryphal) joke is truer today than when it was ostensibly uttered. At one cabinet meeting held during the Civil War, he is supposed to have looked around the room at a solid phalanx of opposition and responded as follows: "I see seven nays and one aye. I guess the ayes have it."

[20] Hess (1976).

dependent on [the] leader's personality in the latter."[21] The cabinet, like all collegial bodies, exemplifies a give-and-take, a mutual discussion of interests and ideals, that cannot be reduced to a simple zero-sum notion of power. Debate, deliberation, and (ultimately) a formal consensus characterize cabinet operations in parliamentary systems. While the cabinet is sidelined from power in a presidential system, and hardly operates in a collegial manner even when it is allowed to meet, it is the linchpin of parliamentary government. This single body, situated at the apex of polity, is perhaps the most important embodiment of collegiality in a political setting.[22]

In a parliamentary system, the collegial principle of decision making extends down to the career civil service, whose members are integrated into the cabinet as its functioning staff. Having only one master, their loyalty is unchallenged, and mechanisms of accountability (should that loyalty be abrogated) are easy to implement. The wayward bureaucrat has poor prospects in a parliamentary administration. (What government would trust him or her with an important assignment?) Thus, parliamentarism serves to unite the executive, the cabinet, and the career bureaucracy in a relatively cohesive governing unit.

By contrast, in a presidential system, the executive, the cabinet, and the bureaucracy are often at loggerheads. Bureaucracies must respond to competing demands emanating from the legislature, important constituencies, statutory restrictions, and their own agencies (whose views on these matters are apt to be somewhat parochial). Consequently, the executive in a presidential system cannot afford to place trust in his subordinates, for in no sense do they belong to him. Of the American executive branch, Bert Rockman writes,

> The basic themes of American governmental institutions are distrust and disaggregation. Together, they fuel suspicion. Presidents often come to divide the world into 'us' and 'them.' 'They' typically cannot be relied upon. 'They' will be seen as torpid, bureaucratically self-interested, and often uncommitted or

[21] Schiavo-Campo and Sundaram (2001: 33–4). See also Blondel and Manning (2002), Evans and Manning (2002), and Manning et al. (1999).

[22] Blondel and Muller-Rommel (1993, 1997), Laver and Shepsle (1994), Mackintosh (1962), Manning et al. (1999), Rhodes and Dunleavy (1995), Rustow (1955). For an excellent discussion of centripetal and centrifugal forces at work within the cabinet, see Andeweg (1988).

skeptical of presidential initiatives. Above all, 'they' will be seen as an uncontrollable source of hemorrhaging to the press. Unmediated by any tradition of, or basis for, a cabinet team, distance defines 'us' and 'them.'[23]

This schematic portrayal might be applied to any presidential system governed under democratic rules. Arguably, it describes *no* parliamentary system.

Esprit de corps. Another consequence of constitutional separation is that the civil service itself is fragmented. Studies of bureaucracies in advanced industrial nations routinely note the extreme isolation and instability of top-level American bureaucrats. Hugh Heclo summarizes:

Much more important than the experience or inexperience of political appointees as individuals is their transience as a group. Cabinet secretaries may bring with them a cadre of personal acquaintances to fill some of their subordinate political positions, but in general public executives will be strangers with only a fleeting chance to learn how to work together.... One of the most persistent themes in comments from political executives of all recent administrations is the absence of teamwork characterizing the layers of appointees. This absence of unifying ties is foreordained, given the fractionalized, changing, and job-specific sets of forces that make up the selection process. But it is not only methods of selection that put mutually reinforcing loyalties at a premium. Rapid turnover intensifies all the other problems of political teamwork.[24]

By contrast, parliamentary systems tend to foster a more cohesive pattern of behavior among political executives. Top bureaucrats identify as members of a single class; relationships are long-standing, and civil service tasks and identities cross agencies and issue categories. Communication patterns are wide-ranging, particularly at elite levels, and teamwork is the expected mode of operation. This is the classic "mandarin" pattern characteristic of Botswana, Japan, Germany, Mauritius, the United Kingdom, and most long-standing parliamentary democracies.[25]

23 Rockman (1981: 916). See also Aberbach, Putnam, and Rockman (1981), Cronin (1975), Golden (2000), Heclo (1986: 104), Hess (1976), Moe (1991), Nathan (1983), and Rourke (1991).

24 Heclo (1977: 104).

25 On OECD cases, see Aberbach et al. (1981), Campbell (1983), Dogan (1975), Page and Wright (2000), and Suleiman (1984). On Botswana, see Acemoglu et al. (2003), Carroll and Carroll (1997), Charlton (1991), du Toit (1995), Good (1994), Holm

Discretion and micromanagement. Legislation in presidential systems produces highly specific laws with provisions for all conceivable contingencies, thus depriving bureaucrats (as well as executives) of policy-making discretion.[26] This pattern of legislating derives from the incentives produced by a system of policy making in which legislative authority is divided. Consider, first, that the executive and the legislature are likely to embody divergent policy goals. Consider, second, that the barriers to changing legislation (once approved) are high. As a consequence, it is in the interest of legislators to institutionalize their policy preferences in law: their preferences are different from the executive's, and legislators have the capacity to ensure that their legacy is not distorted by the executive, or by future executives.

This dynamic may be contrasted with a parliamentary system, where the legislature (i.e., a majority of legislators) shares the policy perspectives of the executive (this is definitionally true insofar as the executive is chosen by the legislature) and has no means to institutionalize its preferences over this, or future, executives. Because laws can be changed by a simple majority in a parliamentary system, and all executives (except in the rare case of minority governments) have this majority at their disposal, it is not possible to institutionalize a policy legacy by writing strict and specific statutes, for these would simply be changed or ignored by future governments. Thus, legislators in a parliamentary system have neither the incentive nor the means to institutionalize their preferences in micro-legislation.

Returning to our contrast between the UK and the United States, Moe and Caldwell extrapolate the following:

> The American separation of powers system . . . should tend to bury its regulatory agencies in excessive bureaucracy and deny them the discretion they need to do their jobs well. Regulation should be relatively formal, legalistic, adversarial – and ineffective. The British parliamentary system, by contrast, should

(1994, 2000), and Holm and Molutsi (1989). On Mauritius, see Brautigam (1997), Carroll and Carroll (1997), Carroll and Jaypaul (1993), and Grey-Johnson (1994). For further discussion of bureaucratic organization and behavior, see the following discussion.

[26] This section builds on Feigenbamm et al. (1993: 63), Goodnow (1900: 102–3), Jasanoff (1997), Kagan (1995), Kagan and Axelrad (1997), Kelman (1981, 1990), Moe (1990a, 1990b), Moe and Caldwell (1994), Noll and Rosenbluth (1995: 128), Vogel (1986), and Wilson (1989). Contrast Tsebelis (1995).

> produce agencies that are relatively free from burdensome bureaucracy, and granted far more discretion to exercise their professional judgment in accommodating the complex contingencies that arise over time. By comparison to the American, British regulation should tend to be more informal, cooperative – and effective.[27]

Where legislative sovereignty is divided, politicians within the legislature have the motivation, and ample authority, to institutionalize their preferences, which are likely to be different from the preferences of the chief executive. Likewise, the president has an incentive to institutionalize her policy preferences. Both will resort to war by statute, and the more specific such statutes are, the more binding they are likely to be (this is particularly important in the likely event of a court challenge). Once written into law, these preferences are difficult to change, since they have statutory sanction, and the threshold for changing statutes in a separate-powers system is often quite high. Thus, all actors in a presidential system have an incentive to micromanage.

We should note that statutes with highly specific provisions are not always bad for the quality of governance. Yet most work on public administration emphasizes the benefits of bureaucratic discretion and the ill consequences of "red tape."[28] First, it is difficult to anticipate all the eventualities that a new piece of legislation may face; for this reason alone, flexibility is desirable. Second, when bureaucrats are told what to do under every contingency, they are constrained to behave in punitive ways with respect to the groups that they are assigned to regulate. Punitive bureaucratic actions lead to adversarial behavior on the part of these constituencies, which fosters further distrust between government and the private sector (or civil society). Private actors are likely to resist, to delay, to shift the battle to the judiciary, or to lobby for statutory change, rather than comply with the law. Indeed, more law, and more specific law, does not necessarily lead to more law-abidingness. As a rule, the more harsh and punitive the regulation, the greater the incentives for individuals and businesses under its thumb to circumvent it, perhaps by corrupt means. Poorly crafted laws and bureaucratic red tape create a situation in which regulations must be

[27] Moe and Caldwell (1994: 183). See also Goodnow (1900: 102–3) and Steinmo (1993).

[28] For a contrasting argument, see Lowi (1969).

broken in order to accomplish essential tasks of public administration. This is a recipe for bribery, since private citizens have a material interest in breaking the law. Thus, the absence of discretion may be a positive harm, and it may also prevent government from doing good. Certain sorts of regulation are virtually precluded because they require extensive cooperation from private groups. One thinks, for example, of industrial policy, but many other examples might be cited.

The politicization of the bureaucracy. We have already pointed out that bureaucrats in a separate-powers system serve many masters – the president, the relevant committees of the legislature, the various party leaders, their own agency officials, and the wording of the statute itself (as enforced by the judiciary).[29] It is this fact that leads to an attenuation of accountability between elected and unelected officials and, at the same time, to the politicization of public administration. In the words of one classic study of the American polity: "Uncertain lines of authority encourage American bureaucrats to play political roles – to cut deals with congressmen who can protect their agencies from central executive control, to pursue the interests of clienteles who can help to protect their programs, and to act as advocates for interests inadequately represented through the ostensible channels of political representation."[30] Under the circumstances, it is difficult for bureaucrats to resist the blandishments and threats of special interests, for these interests are duly constituted principals according to the logic of a decentralized polity.

Having considered the matter from the perspective of the bureaucrat, let us examine this state of affairs from the perspective of the most important principal, the executive. Executives in parliamentary systems have no need to appoint partisan bureaucrats or personal favorites. Because lines of accountability are clear, civil servants must be responsive to cues emanating from the executive. The personal and professional success of the individual bureaucrat in a centralized system is directly tied to his or her success in implementing the executive's commands and assuring the success of the agency he or she has been

29 Golden (2000).

30 Aberbach, Putnam, and Rockman (1981: 99). See also Golden (2000), Goodnow (1900: 82), Heclo (1977), Hojnacki (1996), Kagan (1995: 92), Krause (1999), Peters (1997: 237), and Wilson (1885/1956: 191).

charged with (success understood in terms of the executive's chosen mission). If the current executive does not like the flavor of the law that bureaucrats are (faithfully) administering, he can simply change the law. There is no need to alter the law by devious means, that is, by stacking the bureaucracy with appointees who will interpret the law in ways favorable to the executive. Thus, executives in centralized polities rightly prioritize merit over partisanship or personal loyalty in the appointment and promotion of civil servants. (Even if the executive were to appoint personal or partisan favorites to civil service positions, he would gain very little by doing so. Indeed, these officials might be less capable of achieving policy successes than officials appointed on merit alone, simply by virtue of having less experience and training in the requisite policy area.)

By contrast, presidential executives must "politicize" and "personalize" the administration of government because they cannot trust bureaucrats, who are, by the constraints of a decentralized constitution, beholden to many masters. Heclo elaborates:

> In . . . a regime of government and opposition, a system of career officials reaching to the very apex of departmental organization can be generally accepted as being 'neutral' between the political parties precisely because it is thoroughly unneutral as between the party in opposition and the government of the day. Serving the party in power to the fullest of one's professional competence, and then doing the same for any successor government becomes an affirmation, not a denial, of political neutrality.[31]

In a separate-powers system, by contrast,

> the separation of legislative and executive institutions ensures that, except in rare instances when tightly disciplined party government bridges the two branches, there is no central point for decision-making. Responsibility is diffused. If senior officials are to be politically neutral, who in Washington is the government and who the opposition?[32]

Perhaps the strongest evidence on this point comes from Sri Lanka, where the constitution was altered in 1978 from parliamentarism to semi-presidentialism. John Healey reports that under the first system,

[31] Heclo (1986: 104).

[32] Ibid. See also Aberbach, Putnam, and Rockman (1981), Golden (2000), Hess (1976), Moe (1991), Nathan (1983), Rourke (1991).

the public administration was competent and remained neutral and adaptable. With the shift to presidential rule in 1978, the neutrality of the civil service was partially undermined and the roles of politicians and bureaucrats became blurred. Though there still remains a strong culture of neutrality in the Sri Lankan senior civil service, its independence has somewhat declined. There has been little interest in greater civil service openness or reform. In sum, in Sri Lanka the civil service has become weaker as a countervailing power to the political leadership. Off-budget procedures have emerged which paralleled and partly stemmed from centralisation of presidential power. Parliament has been formally and effectively by-passed.[33]

Sri Lanka thus illustrates in a single case the argument that cross-case contrasts (between parliamentary and presidential polities) have often pointed to: parliamentary systems foster more accountable, and more professional, bureaucracies.

CONCLUSIONS

We have argued that centripetal institutions provide better opportunities for policy coordination than would be anticipated from decentralist institutions within a democratic framework. Naturally, decentralists view the problem of coordination quite differently. In this concluding section, we briefly contrast the two theories.

Decentralists offer several possible solutions to coordination problems that may arise across the heterogeneous political entities of a nation-state. First, they propose that such difficulties may be overcome through constitutional rules that restrict the ability of agents to defect from the general interest solution. Examples include balanced-budget requirements and restrictions on borrowing ("hard budgets").[34] Coordination problems may also be minimized when the realm of local political authorities is made to conform to the ambit of a specific problem area, so as to minimize externalities (within that jurisdiction). A third way of overcoming coordination problems is to insulate agencies from political pressures, so that general interest solutions can be reached without undue particularistic pressure. A fourth sort of mechanism enhances the ability of communities to make appropriate

[33] Healey (1995: 250–1).
[34] Weingast (1995).

decisions, such as increasing the level of face-to-face interaction among participants.[35] A final solution relies on the creation of multiple lines of control – multiple principals to which each agent is accountable, thus instituting a system of "horizontal" accountability. As summarized by Vincent Ostrom, "Fragmentation of authority among diverse decision centers with multiple veto capabilities within any one jurisdiction and the development of multiple, overlapping jurisdictions of widely different scales are necessary conditions for maintaining a stable political order which can advance human welfare under rapidly changing conditions."[36] Thus, for a variety of reasons, it has been argued that coordination problems are best addressed within the context of a decentralized polity.[37]

While space limitations preclude a detailed response to these influential arguments, we note a few difficulties. The most important point is practical. The most ingenious solutions are also often the least likely to be adopted – or, if adopted, are unlikely to be sustained. Big problems with societywide repercussions – that is, *political* problems – are rarely solvable by legislative fiat. Indeed, the very existence of a coordination problem testifies to the political difficulty of attaining a solution. As a general rule, the more serious the coordination problem, the more difficult the prospective political solution.

Consider again the oft-proposed norm of hard budgets – the refusal of a central government to finance deficits created by subnational spending within a federal polity. We pointed out that while the establishment of a hard budget norm might solve coordination problems in monetary and fiscal policy, the real question is whether such a norm could ever be established in a federal polity where such coordination problems exist. Given that politicians in a federal system are likely to have strong regional loyalties, and given that it may be politically necessary for them to uphold the (short-term) interests of their regions, one can see why it might be difficult for them to resist constituency pressure to bail out a local government. Similarly, to the degree that regional politicians benefit from a pork-barrel system of appropriations, it is against their interest to pass legislation that would take

[35] Hackett et al. (1994).
[36] Ostrom (1973: 112).
[37] Ostrom and Walker (1997).

this instrument out of their control (e.g., by inaugurating hard budget constraints). This problem is typical of many proposals that purport to solve coordination problems in fragmented polities. They seem very clever until one considers the political reality at hand.

Indeed, coordination problems in decentralist polities, if they are solved at all, are usually solved not by clever institutional devices but rather by side payments and logrolling. Side payments are particularistic goods (e.g., pork, personal favors, or outright bribes) provided to a veto holder in exchange for his or her support for a policy measure. Exchanges, or logrolling, are quid pro quo agreements to exchange support for various items, neither of which would pass of its own accord. Both side payments and exchanges allow for the solution of coordination problems, and in this sense may be regarded as beneficial to the quality of governance. However, side payments are intrinsically particularistic. Although they may allow for a general interest measure to pass, the cost (considered as a cumulative sum of many such transactions) is usually substantial. Exchanges are slightly less problematic, since they do not presume a particularistic payment. However, we suspect that here too is a bias against the public interest, for agreement is obtained on the basis of negotiations that have little to do with the policy effects of a measure. X supports Y's bill only because Y agrees to support X's bill. It is a matter of sheer luck if the bills that ultimately gain passage by means of side payments and/or logrolling also serve the commonweal. In short, we believe in the commonsensical truth that public interest debates are more likely than private interest side payments or quid pro quo exchanges to lead to public interest laws. If this is so, then decentralism is a highly problematic form of government. By enshrining the power of minority veto holders, a decentralist system necessitates the frequent use of side payments and exchanges in order to solve coordination problems. They provide the necessary grease to keep the machinery of government running. They are, for good reason, commonly associated with corruption.

In conclusion, let us sum up the argument in the following way. Centripetal institutions allow for the flexible administration of public law, maintaining power at central levels where it seems essential, and delegating power to national and subnational agencies where useful to achieve public interest goals. We despair of various attempts, exemplified by contemporary work in political economy, to manage the problem of delegation through the logic of some general rule or set of rules. Instead, we feel that the task of administration is generally too complex to capture in a rule-book format. The primary business of government is to puzzle through these complexities in light of the variety of normative goals that every law embraces and the complex political situation that every attempt at implementation brings into play. One reason why centripetalism may offer better administrative performance is that it grants government the liberty to engineer administrative details in a manner suitable to the contingencies of the policy and polity at hand, and to adapt to new circumstances, new ideas, and new evidence as the case may warrant. Flexibility requires authority, and a centripetal polity provides sufficient insulation for political elites so that they can "puzzle," as well as "power."[38]

[38] Heclo (1974).

PART TWO

EMPIRICS

We have now explored the theory of centripetalism at some length. We have argued that centripetal institutions are likely to foster party government (chapter two), to mediate and moderate extreme political conflict (chapter three), and to lead to better policy coordination across the multifarious institutions of the nation-state (chapter four). On this basis, we have reason to suspect that unitary, parliamentary, and closed-list PR institutions may lead to a higher quality of governance than democratic regimes governed by semi-sovereign regions, elected presidents, and majoritarian or preferential-vote electoral systems, all other things being equal.

The highly schematic nature of our theoretical discussion in the previous chapters is obvious. There is much more that could be said, and should be said, about these complex subjects. We are constrained by reason of space to a brief treatment of a very extensive subject. Fortunately, many of the topics treated fleetingly in the foregoing pages have been pursued at greater length by other scholars, as suggested by the copious footnotes to this text. Future work, we trust, will undertake others. We regard the present initiative as a summary and application of what we already know (or think we know), and what we still need to know about the role of democratic institutions in securing good governance.

In the second section of the book, we subject our main theoretical claims to empirical testing. In light of the elusive nature of the stipulated causal mechanisms, we focus our empirical strategy on the three constitutional-level institutions and their (hypothesized) distal effects. Chapter five addresses problems of definition and measurement connected with the three key institutions (unitarism, parliamentarism, and closed-list PR) and their combined causal impact (incorporated into a single summary variable). Chapter six lays out a set of policies and policy outcomes intended to test the quality of governance in a polity, and then explores how strongly centripetal institutions are associated with these outcomes in a series of cross-country regressions. Chapter seven assesses the empirical robustness of these findings and speculates upon their practical implications.

5

Hypotheses

The key to good government, we have argued, is to be found in institutions that successfully combine authority and inclusion within a democratic setting. Institutions must reach out to all interests, ideas, and identities (at least insofar as they are relevant to the issue at hand). And they must provide an effective mechanism for reaching agreement and implementing that agreement. This is the process of gathering together that culminates, over time, in good government

What sort of institutions are these, exactly? In chapter one, we suggested a number of possibilities in a preliminary sort of way (see Table 1.1). Among these options, we stipulate that three are so fundamental, and so far-reaching, that they deserve the appellation "constitutional." They are *unitarism*, *parliamentarism*, and *closed-list PR*. In this chapter, we elaborate a strategy for measuring these factors so that we might test their impact on the quality of governance.

However, our primary theoretical interest concerns not the independent effects of unitarism, parliamentarism, and closed-list PR but rather their combined effects on good governance. Thus, we place greatest emphasis on a variable that aggregates these factors in a single indicator, dubbed *Centripetalism*. Our central hypothesis is that, on balance, centripetal polities produce better governance than decentralist polities. (We follow the convention of capitalizing these terms only when they are employed as variables, so as to distinguish general concepts from empirical indicators that are specific to this project.)

UNITARISM

Unitary governments should promote better governance outcomes than federal governments, all else being equal. We conceptualize the former along two dimensions: (a) the *degree of separation* (independence) between national and territorial units, and – if any separation exists at all – (b) the *relative power* of the two players (the more power the center possesses relative to the periphery, the more unitary the system).

Of the many institutional factors that determine variation along these dimensions, two predominate: *federalism* and *bicameralism*. We therefore operationalize Unitarism as an additive variable with two components: nonfederalism and nonbicameralism.

Federalism is an institutionalized division or sharing of responsibilities between a national authority and semiautonomous regional units. Since this sharing of responsibilities takes a variety of forms and is not always formally prescribed (or is ambiguous in formal-constitutional terms), we utilize three coding categories for our *nonfederalism* variable: 0 = federal (elective regional governments plus constitutional recognition of subnational authority); 1 = semifederal (where there are elective governments at the regional level but in which constitutional sovereignty is reserved to the national government); and 2 = nonfederal (where regional governments, if they exist, are granted minimal policy-making power).[1]

In order to gauge the strength of unitarism we must also examine the status of territorial units within the national government. To the extent that territorial units receive special representation in the national legislature (different from what would be allocated by counting every ballot equally), we consider this a violation of the principle of unitarism. In practice, wherever this special consideration obtains it is found in the second ("upper") chamber. Thus, the second feature of unitarism concerns bicameralism, the sharing of policy-making power between two chambers at the national level. Bicameralism can also be

[1] Principal sources employed in coding: Alvarez et al. (1999), Derbyshire and Derbyshire (1996), Elazar (1991), Hicken and Kasuya (2001), McHenry (1997), Watts (1997), *The Database of Political Institutions* (Beck et al. 2000), *The Political Reference Almanac* (see polisci.com). For a more general discussion of the theory and intellectual history of federalism, see the discussion in chapter one and Beer (1993), Davis (1978), Forrest (1988), Mogi (1931).

defined across two dimensions: (a) the relative power of the two bodies (symmetrical if they are roughly equal in power, asymmetrical if the lower house dominates) and (b) the composition of the two bodies (congruent if the partisan distribution is roughly the same, incongruent if different).[2] Since, like federalism, bicameralism is often a matter of degree, we code *nonbicameralism* according to the predicted degree of asymmetry and incongruence: 0 = strong bicameral (the upper house has some effective veto power; the two houses are incongruent); 1 = weak bicameral (the upper house has some effective veto power, though not necessarily a formal veto; the two houses are congruent); 2 = unicameral (no upper house or a weak upper house).[3]

We construct the variable *Unitarism* by averaging the scores of each country together on these two components: nonfederalism and nonbicameralism. The combining of these two dimensions is justified by the fact that they are empirically linked (constitutional federalism is a necessary condition for strong bicameralism) and conceptually related (the purpose of a strong second chamber is usually to protect the powers and prerogatives of subnational units).[4] In a fully unitary state, territorial units (if any) have no constitutional standing, no independently elected territorial legislature, and minimal policy-making authority.

Before continuing, we should signal an important terminological ambiguity in the text. Sometimes, we employ "federalism" in the narrow sense, as just described. But, we also require a term to refer to the opposite of unitarism. Thus, we have often employed "federalism" in the previous discussion in this broader sense – as "nonunitary."

[2] Sometimes the degree of congruence is measured directly; more frequently, it is inferred by the electoral systems, electoral districts, electoral timing, and term lengths that apply to the two chambers.

[3] Principal sources employed in coding: Hicken and Kasuya (2001), Patterson and Mughan (1999), Tsebelis and Money (1997), *The Political Reference Almanac* (polisci.com).

[4] It is important to clarify that unitary government, as we use the term here, is quite different from administrative or fiscal centralization. The latter refers to a particular arrangement of powers and responsibilities between national and subnational units, involving issues such as whether revenue generation is decentralized, whether there are hard budgetary constraints on subnational units, whether there are clear lines of authority separating national and subnational responsibilities, whether local institutions are democratically run, and whether effective evaluative procedures are available (Bird and Vaillancourt 1998: 12–15; Burki et al. 1999; Fisman and Gatti 2002; Huther and Shah 1998; Oates 1972; Ter-Minassian 1997; Weingast 1995). Unitary governments may (and often do) institute policies suggested by the literature on fiscal federalism, as discussed in chapter four.

A further ambiguity concerns the implied counterfactual of our causal hypothesis. The unitarism thesis admits of several, quite different, counterfactuals, all of which we embrace (with several caveats). To say that unitarism is better than federalism (nonunitarism) is to say that: (a) a state that is currently federal would be better off as a unitary state; (b) a state that is currently unitary would be worse off as a federal state; (c) a state that is currently federal would be better off dividing into separate and independent (unitary) states; and (d) independent unitary states would be worse off if they joined together in a federal union.

There are two important caveats. First, in considering these alternatives, any change of status (unification or division) must be achieved peacefully. We agree, for example, that a federal system may be preferable to a unitary system if the latter is imposed by force (a dominant group at the center repressing resistant minorities at the periphery). Clearly, unitarism is not better in all circumstances.[5] If the transition process is coercive, all bets are off.[6]

Second, we propose that unitarism is preferable to federalism *in the long run*. Indeed, federalism may provide a useful structure for constitutional transition, either to a single consolidated state or to several independent (unitary) states. But it is not an optimal resting point. Thus, we would argue that the European Union, a currently evolving federal structure, may be preferable to a European continent of fully sovereign nation-states, but only if it transitions eventually into a unitary European state. In short, the achievement of good government rests (in part) on the peaceful achievement of a unitary structure in the long run. (Our measures of unitarism and centripetalism aim to capture precisely these long-run effects.)

PARLIAMENTARISM

Our second hypothesis is that parliamentary systems produce better governance than presidential systems. By *parliamentarism* we mean a

[5] See Lawson and Thacker (2003) on the case of Iraq.

[6] This is the same caveat that most proponents of federalism adopt. Thus, Wheare (1963: 35) argues that federalism is a workable arrangement only where it is freely chosen. Indeed, it is the implicit caveat attached to our other hypotheses, parliamentarism and closed-list PR. We propose that parliamentary systems are better than presidential systems *when freely chosen*.

system of government in which the executive (the prime minister and cabinet: collectively, "the government") is chosen by, and responsible to, an elective body (the legislature), thus creating a single locus of sovereignty at the national level.[7] *Presidentialism*, its contrary, is understood as a system where policy-making power is divided between two separately elected bodies, the legislature and the president. The president's selection is usually by direct popular election, though it may be filtered through an electoral college (as in the United States), and the rules pertaining to victory (i.e., by relative or absolute majority) vary from country to country. His or her tenure cannot be foreshortened by parliament except in cases of gross malfeasance.

In practice, between these two polar types we find many admixtures, known generically as "semi-presidential" systems. Thus, we conceptualize the parliamentary/presidential distinction as a continuum with two dimensions: (a) the *degree of separation* (independence) between president and parliament (unity = parliamentary; separation = presidential), and, if there is any separation at all, (b) the *relative power* of the two players (the more power the president possesses, the more presidential is the resulting system). We capture this complex reality with a three-part coding scheme: 0 = presidential; 1 = semi-presidential; 2 = parliamentary.[8]

Some notes on coding are in order. If a directly elected president exists but has no effective policy-making power, as in Iceland and Ireland, we consider the regime to be parliamentary. If a president is chosen by the legislature but enjoys a fixed term of office (cannot be removed by the legislature except in cases of gross malfeasance) and significant policy-making powers, as is generally the case in Bolivia, we consider the regime to be semi-presidential. If a president is chosen by popular election, enjoys significant policy-making power, but must

7 The precise terms used to refer to these institutions vary somewhat from country to country. Sometimes the prime minister is a "chancellor" or even a "president." The important point is that he or she is chosen by, and responsible to, the legislature.

8 Principal sources employed in coding: Alvarez et al. (1999), Delury (1999), Derbyshire and Derbyshire (1996), Diamond (1999), Golder (2005), Hicken and Kasuya (2001), *International Year Book and Statesmen's Who's Who* (2001), Jones (1995), Nohlen et al. (1999, 2002), *The Database of Political Institutions* (Beck et al. 2000), *The Political Reference Almanac* (polisci.com). For discussion of semi-presidentialism, see Elgie (1997, 1999), Nousiainen (1988, 2001), Shugart and Carey (1992), and Skach (2006). For a general discussion of separate powers, see chapter one and discussions in Gwyn (1965) and Vile (1967/1998).

share power with a prime minister chosen by the legislature, then we also code the system as semi-presidential. This is the most common form of semi-presidentialism, as currently found in France, Lithuania, Poland, Russia, and the Ukraine.

CLOSED-LIST PR

Our third hypothesis argues that closed-list PR electoral systems lead to better governance than majoritarian and other nonproportional systems. Empirically, three features of an electoral system bear critically on electoral system design: (a) district magnitude (M), (b) seat allocation rules (majoritarian or proportional), and (c) candidate selection rules. The centripetal ideal type is defined by M > 1, proportional seat allocation rules, and party-controlled candidate selection. This is the familiar *closed-list PR* electoral system.

Let us begin with the issue of district magnitude (M). Proportional representation refers generically to an electoral system in which there is a more or less proportional relationship between voting preferences and the allocation of seats in a legislature. To be sure, any representational system has some lower limit below which preferences cannot be translated into seats. Even if there are no statutory thresholds, a de facto limit is provided by the number of seats in a legislature and by the size of the district. Thus, if a legislature has 200 members and is chosen in a single nationwide district (M = 200), then the effective threshold is roughly 1/200th of the effective electorate, even under the most proportional rules of seat allocation.

We do not expect to find a perfectly linear relationship between proportionality and good governance. There is no reason to suppose, for example, that Israel and Denmark (two of the most proportional systems in the world) should experience better governance than Sweden or Spain (countries with moderately proportional electoral systems) by virtue of having more proportional seat-to-vote ratios. Thus, we approach the question of proportionality through a simple three-part coding system that recognizes important categorical differences among majoritarian systems, mixed-member majoritarian (MMM) systems (combining single-member and multimember districts in parallel [noncompensatory] lists, as in Russia and Mexico), and proportional electoral systems (M > 2 [binomial electoral systems are not considered to be proportional]). Mixed-member proportional (MMP) electoral systems, where extra seats are designed to rectify nonproportional outcomes achieved by single-member district contests (e.g., Bolivia, Germany, New Zealand, Venezuela), are classified as closed-list PR, since the principle of proportionality is preserved for the system as a whole.[9]

Majoritarian refers here to all single-member-district electoral systems, whether they employ first-past-the-post (plurality) rules, as in the well-known Westminster system, or majority (double-ballot) rules, as in France and many former French colonies. (Block vote systems are majoritarian at the interparty level, but not at the intraparty level, as will be discussed later.)

Usually, a higher district magnitude offers greater choice among parties to the elector. Indeed, district magnitude is the single most important factor in determining how many *effective* interparty choices (choices that might culminate in electing a representative to parliament) voters will have at their disposal as they enter the voting booth.

The question of intraparty choice is somewhat more complicated. Usually, where district magnitude is equal to one, constituency members will be able to determine the nomination of candidates (perhaps with some vetting from central party headquarters) and hence exercise a degree of intraparty choice. Of course, voters in the *general* electorate will be prohibited from exercising any choice in this matter, under most circumstances. Where district magnitude is greater than one ($M > 1$), it is common for candidate selection to be decided by party leaders (at either the regional or national level), with less input from local party members. Thus, all things being equal, district magnitude is inversely correlated with intraparty choice.

There are, of course, other features of an electoral system that may affect the degree to which the general electorate intervenes in intraparty choices (candidate selection). They include (a) mandatory write-in ballots (e.g., the Philippines); (b) multiple lists constructed by factions of the same party (e.g., Colombia, Uruguay); (c) the single-transferable vote (STV); (d) the alternate vote (AV); (e) the single nontransferable

9 M refers to the average (mean) district magnitude in a legislature. On MMM and MMP systems, see Shugart and Wattenberg (2001).

vote (SNTV); and (f) "open-list" systems of PR where only preferential votes determine the order of candidates on a party's list (as in pre-reform Italy) or where preferential voting is mandatory.[10] Wherever electoral systems employ one of these preferential voting options, which we refer to as *strong preferential voting* (to distinguish them from the more usual, and less consequential, forms of preferential voting), we code such countries as 0 on our three-part coding scale. This recoding affects only a handful of countries during some portion of the 1960–2000 period: Australia, Brazil, Chile, Colombia, Estonia, Finland, Greece, Ireland, Italy, Japan, Jordan, Luxembourg, Malta, Nauru, Papua New Guinea, Peru, the Philippines, Poland, Sri Lanka, Switzerland, Taiwan, Uruguay, and Vanuatu. (It should also be noted that some of the countries just listed are, by virtue of missing data or authoritarian rule, already excluded from our statistical analyses.)[11]

Another important deviation from pure PR or pure majoritarianism consists of a relatively rare electoral system known as the *block vote*, employed in Bermuda, Djibouti, Ecuador, Jordan, Kuwait, Laos, Lebanon, the Maldives, Mali, Mauritius, Mongolia, the Philippines, Senegal, Singapore, Thailand, Tunisia, and the U.S. Virgin Islands at various points during the 1960–2000 period.[12] Here $M > 1$ but seats are allocated on a winner-take-all basis, so that the party winning a plurality within a district captures all seats in a district. Electors cast either as many votes as there are seats available (and may be allowed to cross lists) or a single vote for a party (in effect, a party-list vote).[13] Note that in order to qualify as a block vote system in our typology the electoral system must be based on party lists (even if voters are allowed to exercise a preferential vote); if ballots list only individual candidates (without party affiliation), then it is classified

[10] In the latter case, we assume that in order for intraparty preference voting to upstage party leaders in the selection of candidates there must be no default candidate ranking on the ballot that voters might fall back on as a voting cue (lists are "unranked").

[11] For work on intraparty preference voting and its variants (e.g., STV, SNTV), see Bowler and Grofman (2000), Carey and Shugart (1995), Grofman et al. (1999), Karvonen (2004), and Katz (1986).

[12] We exclude Fiji from this list because its legislative seats are chosen from separate ethnic lists (Lal and Larmour 1997).

[13] Sometimes the single-vote system is called a "party block vote" to distinguish it from the more common block vote system in which voters have as many votes as there are seats.

as a strong-preferential voting system. The block vote system is even more majoritarian than the single-member-district system insofar as it adopts the winner-take-all electoral principle in multimember districts. However, political parties, rather than individual candidates, compete against each other. This makes it easy for party leaders to include members of key minority groups on their lists. Usually, this system is considerably more inclusive than an electoral system based on single-member districts because parties have incentives to present diverse lists, including all significant minority social groups within a constituency, and because the electoral dynamic itself is apt to be somewhat less confrontational.[14] It also seems to uphold the strength and cohesion of party leadership, since candidate selection is still, for all practical purposes, a party monopoly (even where open-list voting is possible). Thus, we code block vote systems 1 on our three-part scale.

A final deviation from pure PR consists of polities where a majority of seats in the legislature (we refer, as always, to the lower or dominant chamber, if the legislature is bicameral) are reserved for a particular social or ethnic group *if* such seat reservations ("communal rolls") involve a significant departure from the one-person/one-vote principle (i.e., if they entail significant malapportionment between the designated groups). Such cases (e.g., Fiji) are coded as 0 on our three-point scale. We do not introduce other forms of malapportionment into our coding schema, as these deviations generally have less severe consequences.

In summary, we approach all electoral systems according to their deviation from the principles articulated at the outset: high district magnitude (M), proportional seat allocation rules, and closed candidate selection rules. Thus, we code the Closed-list PR variable as follows: 0 = majoritarian or preferential-vote; 1 = mixed-member majority (MMM) or block vote; and 2 = closed-list PR.[15]

[14] On the Mauritius experience, see Mathur (1997a, 1997b). On Mali, see Vengroff (1994).

[15] Countries are excluded from this classification if a majority of seats in the lower, or more powerful, house are appointed or are elected through a system of reserved seats, as in Fiji and Hong Kong. Note that where coding principles conflict, the lower coding prevails. Thus, although the Philippines employs an MMP electoral system, it also employs mandatory write-in ballots, a provision that classifies the electoral system as strong preferential vote. Hence, the Philippines is coded as 0, rather than 1, in the current period. Principal sources employed for coding: Golder (2005), Hicken and

HISTORICAL CODING

The most complex issue of coding involves the temporal dimension of our primary variables: Unitarism, Parliamentarism, and Closed-list PR. We suppose that it takes time for constitution-level institutions to exert an appreciable effect on governance outcomes. A country switching from a presidential to a parliamentary system (or establishing a parliamentary system in a newly democratic or independent setting) should not expect to see immediate, dramatic changes in the quality of governance. Instead, these effects are likely to register over time as new institutional rules begin to structure the actions and expectations of political actors.[16] Thus, we expect institutions to have modest short-term effects and more substantial, wide-ranging long-term effects. In order to capture the temporal element of institutional design, we construct *stock* measures of Unitarism, Parliamentarism, and Closed-list PR, summed from 1900 up to the observation year, with a 1 percent annual depreciation rate.

A country's score on each of these variables counts toward its stock so long as the country was minimally democratic in that year. (Recall that these variables have no meaning, or a very different meaning, in authoritarian contexts.) We employ a relatively low threshold of democracy because we wish to include as many plausible cases as possible in our analysis and because we feel that the logic of centripetalism should be operative so long as there is a modicum of multiparty competition. Thus, we include a country-year in our analysis if it obtains a score greater than zero – on a scale that ranges from −10 to 10 – on the Polity2 measure of democracy.[17] Our intent here is not to

Kasuya (2001), Massicote and Blais (1999), Nohlen et al. (1999, 2002), Reynolds and Reilly (1997), Shvetsova (1999), the EPIC Project (http://www.epicproject.org), the Interparliamentary Union web site (http://www.ipu.org), *The Database of Political Institutions* (Beck et al. 2000), *The Political Reference Almanac* (polisci.com). For general discussions of the theory and history of proportional representation, see chapter one and Carstairs (1980), Farrell (2001), Hart (1992), and Noiret (1990).

[16] Gerring et al. (2005).

[17] Marshall and Jaggers (2002). Because the Polity2 democracy score does not contain data for several countries (mostly micro-states), we impute missing values using the following alternative measures of democracy: the Freedom House Political Rights

define democracy per se, but rather to establish the empirical boundaries of the study. To the extent that our definition is too lenient, we expect that it biases the results against our hypotheses, for we anticipate that centripetal institutions will be less effective in less democratic settings.

Since our primary theoretical interest is in the combined effect of Unitarism, Parliamentarism, and Closed-list PR, we add together these three historical, depreciated stock variables to create an aggregate variable, *Centripetalism*, that forms the centerpiece of the empirical analysis to follow. Our central research hypothesis is that centripetal polities – those with unitary, parliamentary, and closed-list PR institutions – enjoy better governance than their decentralist counterparts.

Table 5.1 provides a complete list of all countries meeting our minimal definition of democracy in the year 2000, a total of 124 cases, ranked by their historical Centripetalism scores (as just described), along with their contemporary (raw) scores on all four variables.[18] We hypothesize that countries at the top of this list have better political institutions and should therefore experience better governance outcomes, ceteris paribus. The following chapter tests this argument empirically. Henceforth, the terms Unitarism, Parliamentarism, Closed-list PR, and Centripetalism – if capitalized – will refer to the historical sum, or stock, of these variables, stretching from 1900 to the observation year, with an annual depreciation rate of 1 percent.[19] Descriptive statistics for these four variables are included in the appendix to chapter six.

indicator (Gastil, various years), Bollen's (1993) Liberal Democracy variable, Vanhanen's (1990) Competition measure, and Banks's (1994) Legislative Effectiveness and Party Legitimacy variables.

[18] Note that a recently democratized polity, even if fully centripetal in its current institutions, would not be high on this list because of the historically weighted and summed measures used to generate this variable.

[19] The value for a country receives a weight of 1 in the observation year and is depreciated by one percent each year moving back in time. These values are then summed to create the stock variables.

TABLE 5.1. *Centripetalism in democratic polities, 2000*

		Contemporary				Stock
Rank	Country	Unit	Parl	PR	Cent	Cent
1	Denmark	2	2	2	6	356.02
2	Sweden	2	2	2	6	353.75
3	Iceland	2	2	2	6	339.46
4	Norway	1.5	2	2	5.5	335.38
5	Belgium	0.5	2	2	4.5	321.23
6	The Netherlands	1.5	2	2	5.5	302.05
7	Austria	1.5	2	2	5.5	270.87
8	New Zealand	2	2	2	6	264.85
9	Costa Rica	2	0	2	4	255.05
10	UK	2	2	0	4	252.73
11	Luxembourg	2	2	0	4	246.07
12	Israel	2	2	2	6	244.87
13	Germany	0	2	2	4	233.19
14	Finland	2	2	0	4	227.05
15	Japan	1.5	2	1	4.5	224.02
16	Ireland	2	2	0	4	220.99
17	Turkey	2	2	2	6	199.96
18	Canada	1	2	0	3	191.29
19	South Africa	0.5	2	2	4.5	189.98
20	Greece	2	2	0	4	189.17
21	Spain	1	2	2	5	187.44
22	France	1.5	1	0	2.5	177.16
23	Portugal	2	2	2	6	171.16
24	Mauritius	2	2	1	5	141.13
25	Italy	1	2	1	4	140.56
26	Sri Lanka	1.5	1	0	2.5	137.98
27	Liechtenstein	2	2	2	6	137.97
27	San Marino	2	2	2	6	137.97
28	Australia	0	2	0	2	126.79
29	Malta	2	2	0	4	124.22
30	Cyprus (Greek)	2	0	2	4	121.02
31	Jamaica	1.5	2	0	3.5	120.52
32	Botswana	2	2	0	4	118.62
33	Bolivia	0.5	1	2	3.5	114.77
34	Trin. & Tobago	1.5	2	0	3.5	113.49
35	Guatemala	2	0	2	4	112.85
36	Slovak Rep.	2	2	2	6	109.70
37	Czech Rep.	1.5	2	2	5.5	105.84
38	W. Samoa	1.5	2	0	3.5	105.16
39	Barbados	1.5	2	0	3.5	103.79
40	Honduras	2	0	2	4	101.96
41	Nauru	2	2	0	4	98.11
42	Estonia	2	2	2	6	97.39

TABLE 5.1 *(continued)*

		Contemporary				Stock
Rank	**Country**	**Unit**	**Parl**	**PR**	**Cent**	**Cent**
43	Ecuador	1.5	0	0	1.5	97.27
44	Thailand	1.5	2	1	4.5	95.73
45	Malaysia	0.5	2	0	2.5	89.35
46	Fiji	1.5	2	0	3.5	89.00
47	Guyana	2	0	2	4	88.69
48	Bahamas	1.5	2	0	3.5	85.85
49	India	0	2	0	2	83.77
50	Dominica	2	2	0	4	82.55
50	Tuvalu	2	2	0	4	82.55
51	PNG	1.5	2	0	3.5	80.48
52	South Korea	2	1	1	4	80.02
53	St. Lucia	2	2	0	4	79.35
53	St. Vin. & G.	2	2	0	4	79.35
54	Suriname	2	1	2	5	79.18
55	Uruguay	2	0	0	2	78.78
56	Venezuela	1	0	2	3	72.17
57	El Salvador	2	0	2	4	69.53
58	Grenada	1.5	2	0	3.5	67.12
59	Vanuatu	1.5	2	0	3.5	66.60
60	Ethiopia	0	2	0	2	66.48
61	Switzerland	0	1	0	1	63.76
62	Belize	1.5	2	0	3.5	63.73
63	Solomon Is.	1	2	0	3	61.92
64	Bulgaria	2	2	2	6	61.89
65	Panama	2	0	1	3	60.46
66	St. Kitts & N.	1	2	0	3	59.51
67	Slovenia	2	2	2	6	57.37
68	Chile	1	0	0	1	55.09
69	Antigua & Barb.	1	2	0	3	54.63
70	Latvia	2	2	2	6	54.60
71	Poland	1.5	1	2	4.5	52.98
72	Hungary	2	2	1	5	52.33
72	Namibia	2	1	2	5	52.33
73	Argentina	0.5	0	2	2.5	49.38
74	Moldova	2	1	2	5	47.81
74	Sao Tome & P.	2	1	2	5	47.81
75	Albania	2	2	1	5	47.53
76	Kiribati	1.5	1	0	2.5	47.14
77	Lithuania	2	1	1	4	45.52
78	Romania	1.5	1	2	4.5	45.29
79	Dominican Rep.	1	0	1	2	43.96
80	Cape Verde	2	1	2	5	43.24
81	Cambodia	1	2	2	5	42.99

(*continued*)

TABLE 5.1 *(continued)*

		Contemporary				Stock
Rank	Country	Unit	Parl	PR	Cent	Cent
82	Nicaragua	2	0	2	4	41.86
83	Paraguay	1.5	0	2	3.5	41.37
84	Macedonia	2	2	1	5	41.22
85	Colombia	0.5	0	0	0.5	40.67
86	Andorra	2	2	1	5	38.63
87	Bangladesh	2	2	0	4	38.25
87	Benin	2	0	2	4	38.25
88	Nepal	1.5	2	0	3.5	36.63
89	Mali	2	1	1	4	34.59
89	Marshall Islands	2	2	0	4	34.59
90	Madagascar	2	0	0	2	32.31
91	Ukraine	2	1	1	4	31.66
92	Mongolia	2	1	0	3	31.41
93	Armenia	2	1	1	4	30.52
94	Philippines	0.5	0	0	0.5	29.40
95	Georgia	2	0	1	3	28.69
96	Monaco	2	2	0	4	27.17
97	Mozambique	2	0	2	4	26.23
98	Lesotho	2	2	0	4	25.12
99	Niger	2	0	2	4	24.78
100	Guinea-Bissau	2	0	2	4	23.25
101	CAR	2	1	0	3	23.18
102	Indonesia	2	1	2	5	21.75
103	Taiwan	1.5	1	0	2.5	21.62
104	Zambia	2	0	0	2	19.12
105	Russia	0	1	1	2	17.30
106	Seychelles	2	0	0	2	15.45
107	Malawi	2	0	0	2	13.59
108	Palau	2	0	0	2	11.70
109	Ghana	2	0	0	2	9.80
110	Micronesia	1	0	0	1	9.56
111	Nigeria	0	0	0	0	8.23
112	Iran	2	0	0	2	7.88
113	Croatia	1.5	1	1	3.5	6.97
114	Mexico	0	0	1	1	6.79
115	Senegal	2	0	1	3	3.00
116	Brazil	0	0	0	0	0.00
116	United States	0	0	0	0	0.00

Unit = unitarism; Parl = parliamentarism; PR= closed-list proportional electoral system; Cent = Centripetalism; Stock Cent = sum of depreciated (1%) Unit, Parl, and PR stocks. N = 124.

6

Cross-National Tests

Having introduced our theoretical hypotheses and independent variables, we turn now to questions of research design. We begin with a brief discussion of how one might go about measuring that ineffable state of grace known as "good governance" and proceed to a discussion of methods and a description of variables used in the analysis. The chapter concludes with a presentation of the empirical results.

MEASURING GOOD GOVERNANCE

In order to provide an empirical test of the causal effects of centripetal institutions on good governance we must arrive at a set of indicators that accurately measures the quality of governance in a country. Some might argue that this is an impossible quest. Perhaps these matters simply cannot be measured. Doubts notwithstanding, most observers are fairly comfortable making qualitative judgments about extreme cases of misgovernance such as is found today in the Democratic Republic of Congo (formerly Zaire) or in Somalia (the classic "failed state"). We have no trouble at all concluding that the quality of governance is worse in these countries than it is, say, in northern Europe. The fact that we can make such judgments at all is testament to the existence of a set of norms that we apply to governments – all governments. What are these norms? What are the components of good/bad governance? What is it that we expect governments to do, and how might these outcomes be measured, and hence more systematically compared?

A good outcome measure of governance, for present purposes, must balance four criteria. It must have a fairly clear normative import; it must be related (plausibly) to basic-level political institutions; it must be cross-nationally and temporally valid; and it must provide adequate data coverage. We discuss these features briefly, before introducing the specific measures that we will employ.

First, we understand good governance as any governmental process, policy, or policy outcome that furthers the public interest. Appendix A presents an extended discussion of this concept. For present purposes, we assume that it is possible to identify policies that have either predominantly favorable, or predominantly unfavorable, effects on citizens living within a political community, considered over the long run. Such policies (or processes or policy outcomes) can be regarded as measures of good/bad governance.[1]

Second, we seek to identify governance measures that might plausibly be connected to constitutional-level institutions. If a measure of governance is determined almost entirely by societal factors or international pressures and has little to do with the shape of domestic politics, it provides a poor test of our hypotheses about the role of political institutions.

Third, chosen indicators must measure what they purport to measure and must do so across diverse cultural and institutional settings. This is usually referred to as a problem of *concept validity*. Otherwise, cross-national empirical tests have little meaning.

Finally, the chosen measures must provide sufficient data coverage to allow for global comparisons through time. A measure restricted to a single region, or a single period of time, will not provide sufficient empirical leverage on the questions of interest.

Unfortunately, no single empirical measure fully achieves all four desiderata. Generally, policy outcomes are clearer in normative import

[1] Of course, there is often a degree of uncertainty about such judgments. Not everyone agrees that trade openness is a valid measure of good governance. However, the disagreements over this issue among economists center largely upon whether there is a robust positive association between measures of trade openness and outcomes like growth and human development that are generally approved. The skeptics claim that the association is weak and perhaps nonexistent. But few economists today claim that trade openness leads to *worse* economic outcomes. Thus, it seems fair to conclude, as a general rule, that policies advancing trade have a beneficial – or, at worst, indifferent – effect on the public interest. Thus, we regard policies as useful measures of good/bad governance so long as their error range is one-tailed.

but harder to connect (causally) to constitutional institutions. We all agree that economic prosperity is desirable, but to what extent can a country's economic performance be plausibly attributed to its constitutional structure? Processes and policies generally exhibit the opposite traits; they are plausibly linked to political institutions but more ambiguous in their substantive effects. While it is fairly easy to demonstrate that constitutional factors affect a country's aggregate revenue stream (considered as a share of GDP), it is somewhat harder to establish that higher revenue streams are indicative of good governance.

In our view, the only way to overcome these problematic features, inherent in all measures of governance, is to adopt a basket of indicators that range across diverse issue areas and include both policies and policy outcomes. Our confidence in the empirical results rises as the number of independent tests increases, so long as the causal patterns remain reasonably consistent.

Applying these four criteria, we identify eleven dependent variables, grouped into three broad categories: *political development*, *economic development*, and *human development*. Following is a brief description of each indicator. (The chapter appendix provides descriptive statistics and source information.)

Political Development

The concept of political development is closely related to the notion of state capacity, that is, the power, strength, ability, capability, efficiency, or effectiveness of a state. More specifically, political development refers to the capacity of a state to maintain control over its claimed territory (its monopoly on the use of organized violence), to resist societal pressures (its "autonomy"), and to transform society (its "developmental" capacity).[2] We measure this wide-ranging concept using four indicators: tax revenue, telephone mainlines, participation, and democratic volatility.[3]

[2] For other definitions of state capacity and related concepts, similar for the most part to our own, see Huber (1995: 167) and Skocpol (1985: 15–17).

[3] As discussed in chapter one, a critical component of centripetalism is that it is both authoritative and inclusive. Though all of our political development variables capture both of these aspects to one degree or another, the third (participation) addresses the inclusion aspect most directly.

Tax Revenue. Tax revenue is perhaps the most common measure of political development.[4] We must assume, of course, that a government's extractive capacity is a reasonably good indication of its capacity, and inclination, to perform public interest tasks. This is not a universally shared assumption. According to the "grabbing hand" view of government, state actors are interested primarily in maximizing their own prerogatives – in particular, their rents.[5] However, our own empirical analyses (not shown), where we employ revenue as an independent variable, belie this skeptical view. Whatever the motivations of state actors, government revenue is strongly correlated with other good governance outcomes.[6] On empirical grounds alone, then, a good case can be made for revenue as an indicator of state capacity. The variable employed here measures aggregate tax revenues (compulsory, unrequited, nonrepayable receipts for public purposes collected by the central government, including interest collected on tax arrears and penalties collected on nonpayment or late payments of taxes), considered as a percentage of GDP.[7] The statistic is net of refunds and other corrective transactions.

Telephone Mainlines. A country with well-developed and well-maintained physical infrastructure, including transportation and communications networks, should be well placed to grow and to enhance the quality of life.[8] For our purposes, it is important to identify a measure of infrastructural development that (a) has the same utility in every country (i.e., it is not more useful in Ghana than in Switzerland), (b) is as easy or difficult to construct and maintain everywhere (thus imposing similar costs on all governments), and (c) is sensitive to government policy (i.e., it is a public sector activity or is closely regulated by the government).

Telephone service seems an ideal candidate on all three scores. Its utility is universal. (Indeed, some economists regard it as an excellent

[4] See, for example, Cheibub (1998) and Lieberman (2002).

[5] Buchanan and Tullock (1962), Friedman (1962/1982), Hayek (1944), Levy (1988), Shleifer and Vishny (1998).

[6] Analysis by authors (available on request).

[7] World Bank (2003a).

[8] Knack and Keefer (1995).

predictor of long-run economic growth.)[9] It offers similar construction and maintenance challenges across countries, and the remaining differences – such as the level of development or size of a country – can easily be measured and controlled for in the analysis.[10] Finally, telephone service is typically either publicly provided or subject to extensive regulation. Thus, its effectiveness and reach is largely a product of governmental activity or inactivity. For all these reasons, telephone service seems a useful indicator of the capacity of governments around the world to foster infrastructural development. Whether "telecom" is efficient or inefficient should be captured by the number of people who enjoy the service of a telephone, all else being equal.[11] Our measure counts telephone mainlines (telephone lines connecting a customer's equipment to the public switched telephone network) per 1,000 people.[12]

Participation. The quality of democracy and political development rests in part on the participation of citizens in political life. As pointed out in chapter one, centripetal institutions should be both authoritative and inclusive. Among the many ways to measure participation, voter turnout provides a consistent metric for spatial and temporal comparisons. Using Vanhanen's data, we measure political participation as the percentage of the adult population voting in national elections.[13] Because voting is compulsory in some countries, we control for such laws using dummy variables for three categories of obligatory voting regulations: those with applied sanctions, those with sanctions that are not applied, and those with no sanctions.[14]

[9] See Canning and Fay (1993), Easterly and Levine (1997).

[10] By contrast, roads, rivers, and airports are variable in nature, importance, and ease of construction; these means of communication and transportation depend a great deal on the landscape and may function differently in different places. For country A, road service may be essential; for country B, it may be dispensable, owing to abundant navigable rivers and/or seaports.

[11] The rising use of cellular technology to replace landline telephone service would seem to make this variable less useful as an effective measure of infrastructure. However, our analysis spans the years 1964 to 2000, a period during which landlines were clearly dominant.

[12] World Bank (2003a).

[13] Vanhanen (1990, 2000).

[14] Countries with applied sanctions include Australia, Belgium, Cyprus, Fiji, Luxembourg, Nauru, Singapore, and Uruguay. Countries with nonapplied sanctions include

Democratic Volatility. While we control for a country's history of democracy (see the following discussion), and while our sample is limited to minimally democratic country-years, there remains room for significant variation in the quality and stability of democracy. Political instability can be unsettling not just in political terms, but also in economic and social arenas. Instability and unpredictability can undermine policy cohesion, shorten political leaders' time horizons, deter foreign and domestic investment, and trigger capital flight. We calculate democratic volatility as the moving five-year sum of the standard deviation of a country's Polity2 score.[15] Higher scores indicate higher regime volatility.

Economic Development

Economic development refers primarily to those government policies that are thought to have important, and fairly direct, ramifications for economic growth and prosperity. This assumes, of course, that pro-growth policies, and growth itself, have generally positive effects on human welfare. This is a fair assumption, we think, with the following explanatory caveats.

First, and most important, it is important to keep in mind that GDP per capita, and GDP-enhancing policies, are by no means the only – or even the primary – measures of good governance. In this study, income forms only one of many indicators, and is complemented by direct measures of human development performance (to be discussed). Taken in conjunction with these other factors, economic prosperity is an indispensable component of good governance. Any government that cannot sustain respectable growth rates is probably not doing its job well.

Second, we assume that whatever negative externalities might arise from growth – for example, environmental destruction or income inequality – are counterbalanced by positive effects.[16] Note that even

Argentina, Brazil, Chile, Ecuador, Egypt, Greece, Italy, Liechtenstein, Paraguay, Peru, and Turkey. Those with no sanctions include Bolivia, Costa Rica, the Dominican Republic, Guatemala, Honduras, Mexico, and Thailand (Bilodeau and Blais 2005: 16).

[15] Marshall and Jaggers (2002).

[16] Of course, growth need not cause environmental destruction, if "sustainable development" is a viable long-range goal (World Bank 2003b).

if the welfare generated by economic growth is unevenly distributed, growth is still preferable to economic stagnation or decline. Over the long term, we can expect that the benefits of GDP growth will extend to a country's poorest inhabitants. "Pro-poor" patterns of economic development are always preferable to inegalitarian ones. However, since we lack good measurements of annual fluctuations in economic inequality within the developing world, we must examine per capita income as an independent outcome (leaving aside the question of its distribution).[17] Similarly, we assume that pro-growth *policies* do not detract from social welfare along other dimensions. Although we do not investigate these matters here, in a companion study we have examined the relationship between pro-growth economic policies and human development. In that study, we found that many orthodox ("neoliberal") economic policies– including some of the indicators examined here – foster improved human development, independent of their putative growth-inducing effects.[18]

Our analysis encompasses policy- and outcome-based measures of economic development. Policy indicators include two measures of trade openness (import duties and trade openness). Policy outcomes include per capita income and growth volatility.

Trade. In trade policy, we follow Smithian orthodoxy. All other things being equal, we expect that a more open trade policy – that is, fewer barriers to the entry and exit of goods and services – will benefit a country in the long run. We shall not rehearse the familiar arguments, pro and con.[19] But we do wish to call attention to one oft-neglected point. Advocates of restrictive trade policies often posit an omniscient and nonpolitical (above the fray) policy maker, one who can pick winners and losers and impose costs on interest groups as economic logic dictates. The Japanese MITI model and the examples of Korea and Taiwan loom large. There is, of course, continual debate about the

[17] We have analyzed inequality (Gini coefficient) with very strong confirmatory findings for all of our variables of interest, but we do not report the results here because of concerns about the quality of the data.

[18] Gerring and Thacker (2006).

[19] Reviews of the "free trade" perspective can be found in Bhagwati (1998), Edwards (1989), Frankel and Romer (1999), Krueger (1997), Sachs and Warner (1995), and Srinivasan and Bhagwati (1999). For more critical views, see Rodriguez and Rodrik (2001), and Rodrik (1997, 1999).

role of trade protection in the outstanding economic growth performance of these three economies over the postwar decades. But what bears emphasis is how little the economic policy bureaucracies of the developing world resemble MITI, and how few leaders have the vision and the authority of Park Chung-hee. Thus, these examples, intriguing as they may be, are likely to remain exceptions to the rule. Most countries, and in particular most developing countries, would likely be better off individually with a blanket free trade policy rather than as selective protectionists. (It is even easier to argue that they would be better off collectively. But this observation takes us beyond the realm of the current study, which assumes a country-centered perspective on economic and human development.)

Relative openness can be measured in a variety of ways. Our first measure counts the value of import duties collected by the central government as a share of total imports.[20] Import duties are all levies collected on goods at the point of entry into the country, including levies for revenue purposes or import protection, whether on a specific or an ad valorem basis, as long as they are restricted to imported products.

Another approach to the question of trade policy focuses on the policy result: total imports and exports as a share of GDP (logarithm).[21] This indicator captures the overall inward or outward orientation of an economy and reflects, in part, the effect of trade policies on actual patterns of trade. Following the logic just discussed, we assume that higher levels of trade promote higher standards of living, ceteris paribus.

Per Capita Income. Per capita income, or GDP per capita, is a measure of societal income, or the real value (in constant 1995 dollars) of total production within an economy during the course of a year as a ratio of the total population (logarithm).[22] We choose to measure economic performance as a level, rather than an annual-change (i.e., growth), variable because our interest is in the level of prosperity attained in a given country, rather than its short-run rate of change. This is also in

[20] World Bank (2003a).

[21] Ibid. Some examine imports only, rather than imports and exports. Because we emphasize the import side with the previous variable, we focus here on the overall trade orientation of an economy. In any event, these two statistics are highly correlated, and the regression results are much the same.

[22] Ibid. Small amounts of missing data are imputed using Penn World Tables 6.1 (Heston, Summers, and Aten 2002).

keeping with our approach to other governance outcomes; for example, we measure the level of trade from year to year, not the change in trade from year to year. Note, however, that because we include the level of per capita income in 1960 in the estimation, we are controlling for base year conditions. Thus, what we are really measuring here are long-term improvements over time, from 1960 to the observation year. Given a certain level of economic development (i.e., controlling for initial conditions that we may not be capturing otherwise), what kinds of institutions promote better economic performance over the long run?

Growth Volatility. Apart from the level of economic prosperity and long-run growth, the degree of economic stability in a country may be a useful indicator of good governance. Long-term rates of growth and annual income levels may not reveal relevant patterns in the annual perturbations that affect the quality of economic governance and development in a country. In order to capture this phenomenon empirically, we use a strategy similar to that used in our measure of democratic volatility: a moving five-year sum of the standard deviation of the real rate of growth per capita.[23]

Human Development

Human development, our third and final governance area, refers generally to "the improvement of the human condition so that people live longer, healthier and fuller lives."[24] Logically, this is the final outcome of interest to any study of governance. (We are not interested in political or economic development per se; our interest in these matters is stimulated by the assumption that they have positive ramifications for the quality of human life.) We divide this subject into two general areas: health (infant mortality, public health expenditure) and education (total schooling).[25]

[23] Calculated using data from World Bank (2003a).

[24] Ranis and Stewart (2000: 49). See also Ravallion (1997), Sagar and Najam (1998), and Srinivasan (1994).

[25] To reduce sample bias, we interpolate missing data for variables measuring infant mortality and total schooling. Because these variables are all heavily trended, we do not anticipate that interpolation introduces new systematic biases in the data.

Infant Mortality. The infant mortality rate (IMR) is defined as the number of children who perish during the first year of life, per 1,000 live births.[26] This statistic is widely available, generally reliable, and characterized by high variance, thus providing maximum leverage for empirical analysis. From a normative perspective, it also enjoys priority over other mortality indicators, since the loss of an infant's life represents the loss of nearly a whole life, while mortality experienced later in the life cycle represents the loss of a portion of a life. Finally, infant mortality rates are affected by many government policies and are thus an important outcome-based measure of good governance.[27]

Health Expenditure. Health expenditure refers to the public expenditure of government funds for health-related purposes, considered as a percentage of GDP.[28] This includes "recurrent and capital spending from government (central and local) budgets, external borrowings and grants (including donations from international agencies and nongovernmental organizations), and social (or compulsory) health insurance funds."[29] While many governments suffer from the leaky bucket problem, where expenditures do not always translate effectively and efficiently into improved health outcomes,[30] this policy measure helps capture the input side of public health.

[26] Logarithm, World Bank (2003a).

[27] Child mortality, another option for measuring the status of the least advantaged, is less widely available than IMR. In any case, it correlates almost perfectly with infant mortality (R = 0.98), so we can anticipate virtually identical results in an analysis of under-five mortality rate and IMR. For discussion of IMR relative to other indicators of human development, see Adetunji (1995), Bos, Vu, and Stephens (1992), Gerring, Thacker, and Alfaro (2006), Hill (1991), Hill et al. (1999), and United Nations (1991, 1999).

[28] World Bank (2003a).

[29] World Bank (2002).

[30] Among works focused on the developing world, several studies find that social policies account for variation in human development (Anand and Ravallion 1993; Bidani and Ravallion 1997; Caldwell 1986; Cremieux et al. 1999; Dreze and Sen 1989; Ghai 2000; Halstead et al. 1985; McGuire forthcoming; Meerman 1979; Mehrotra and Jolly 1997; Muhuri 1995; Ranis et al. 2000; Selowsky 1979; Vallin and Lopez 1985; van de Walle and Nead 1995; Wennemo 1993). But the majority does not. Existing studies indicate, in the words of one recent review, that "cross-national differences in public spending on health account for essentially *none* of the differences in health status" (Filmer and Pritchett 1999: 1310; see also Barlow and Vissandjee 1999; Filmer et al. 2000; Kim and Moody 1992; McKeown 1967; Moon 1991; Musgrove 1996; Poikolainen and Eskola 1988; Pritchett and Summers 1996; and Rogers and Wofford 1989).

Total Schooling. Education policies and outcomes are difficult to measure reliably, and a wide variety of indicators might be used to capture human development in the area of education. Among these (none of which boasts particularly good data and coverage), we choose to focus here on total schooling, defined as "the average number of years of schooling achieved by the average person in each country."[31]

ESTIMATION TECHNIQUES

Our empirical analyses employ a time-series – cross-section (TSCS) format.[32] Although often preferable to simple cross-sections, we should note that this sort of data is subject to simultaneous spatial and temporal difficulties. Regrettably, we are unable to employ unit-based fixed effects to address spatial issues (such as unobserved heterogeneity) because our causal variables do not vary sufficiently from year to year. Their movement through time is sluggish.[33] We do, however, employ a set of regional "fixed effects" to remove much of the sample heterogeneity and a wide variety of other control variables, including a geographically weighted version of the dependent variable, to help remedy spatial problems. With regard to temporal issues, we employ a statistical correction for first-order serial correlation and a time-trend variable to control for possible spurious correlations between heavily trended independent and dependent variables. In addition, we lag most independent variables one period behind the dependent variable as a guard against endogeneity.

Control Variables

Model specification issues are inevitably critical in statistical studies of observational data. A lack of appropriate controls can call results into

31 Barro and Lee (2000).

32 We employ Newey-West standard errors, which assume a heteroskedastic error distribution and are a TSCS equivalent of Huber/White/sandwich, or "robust," standard errors (Newey and West 1987). While Newey-West is a common approach in economics, it is less frequently used in political science. We employ it here because it achieves the goals discussed earlier and is somewhat less computationally expensive than the alternatives. In any event, results are quite similar in other formats (e.g., with a Prais-Winsten feasible generalized least squares approach with panel corrected standard errors and an AR1 correction for autocorrelation).

33 Wilson and Butler (2003). See also Beck (2001: 285), Beck and Katz (2001: 492–93), and Wooldridge (2002: 286).

question. Conversely, including excessive, theoretically ambiguous, and/or empirically weak controls can make the analysis unwieldy and often inconsistent. In order to avoid problems of under- and overspecification we mine the literature on various topics captured by our dependent variables, identifying eight broad categories and fourteen specific controls to employ throughout the empirical analysis: geography (latitude, distance from the nearest financial center), economics (GDP per capita), region (Africa, Asia, Latin America/Caribbean, Western Europe), legal origin (English), socialism, demography (population), mineral wealth (oil, diamonds), ethnic fractionalization, and democratic stock. Where appropriate, we add or substitute a small number of additional controls (to be specified). Evidently, each dependent variable may call forth a somewhat different model specification. The chapter appendix lists the sources for each of these variables, along with descriptive statistics.

Expectations for our control variables are relatively straightforward. GDP per capita (logarithm) should be associated with better governance outcomes. Dummy variables for Africa and Latin America are expected to have a negative impact on governance, while expectations for Asia are mixed (e.g., lower tax revenues, but higher levels of schooling). The Western Europe dummy variable should show a positive relationship with good governance; it should also help control for any spurious correlation between Europe's centripetal governments and our governance indicators. We anticipate that a significant period of socialist rule has negative effects on political and economic development and positive effects on human development. Having an English legal origin (by virtue of being a former English colony) is assumed to produce better governance outcomes. To the extent that countries farther from the equator have better governance, latitude (absolute value, scaled to 0–1, logarithm) should correlate with better outcomes. Ethnic fractionalization is usually expected to hamper government performance. To the extent that having a large population (total population, logarithm) makes certain tasks of government more difficult, population might be expected to diminish the quality of governance. Distance (in thousands of kilometers) from the nearest financial center (Tokyo, New York, or London) is intended to capture the negative impact of geographic distance from the "cores" of the international economy. Oil production levels (millions of barrels per day per capita) and diamond production levels (rescaled to billions of metric carats per year per capita) capture the "resource curse," controlling for level of development.[34] Yet these resources may also contribute to government revenue; as such, expectations are somewhat mixed.

A country's regime history is likely to influence the quality of governance.[35] Thus, we include a variable that captures the cumulative democratic history of each country over the course of the twentieth century, measured in the same manner as our explanatory variables, as an historical stock from 1900 to the observation year, depreciated at the rate of 1 percent annually. We anticipate that a longer history of democratic rule should improve a country's governance. Including this variable should also help disentangle the effects of centripetal institutions from democracy itself; controlling for a country's democratic history, we examine the effects of its history of centripetal institutions.

We employ additional variables in selective regressions, as appropriate. Protestant (as a percentage of total population) is included in some analyses of political development. Muslims (as a percentage of total population) is included in the analysis of human development outcomes. Prior research has suggested that a Protestant heritage may improve state capacity,[36] while having a large Muslim population may impede human development.

In order to address additional spatial issues we include a control variable that measures the average value of the dependent variable across all countries, weighted by the inverse of the geographic distance (in kilometers) of each country from the country in question. (In the case of GDP per capita, the average value of the dependent variable is weighted by each country's share of trade with the

[34] Some indicators measure the export value of these last two items as a percentage of all exports or of GDP. We believe that this confuses two issues: the extent of natural resources in a country and the degree of its economic development or export orientation, which is implicit in the denominator. Since it is the first, not the second, that we wish to measure, it seems preferable to employ a "raw" per capita measure of natural resources.

[35] Gerring et al. (2005).

[36] Gerring and Thacker (2004).

observed country, rather than by the inverse of the geographic distance between the countries. Results are virtually identical using either control variable.) The assumption is that countries lying close to one another may display similar values for extraneous reasons (culture, geography, diffusion, and so forth). Thus, we anticipate a positive sign for this variable. The inclusion of this variable in all regressions should help minimize possible spatial autocorrelation in the sample.

We also employ a time trend variable to control for any spurious temporal correlation between any pair of similarly trended dependent and independent variables. This variable should be signed in whatever direction a given dependent variable is trended over time (e.g., negative for infant mortality and positive for GDP per capita).

Because no standard benchmark model exists for any of these outcomes, we report two initial tests for each dependent variable. The first is a full model, including all the variables just discussed. The second is a reduced-form model that sequentially deletes variables that do not pass the threshold of statistical significance ($p < 0.10$ in two-tailed tests) in the expected direction. Additionally, we conducted a series of sensitivity tests (not reported), adding and removing additional control variables in order to gauge their effect on Centripetalism. The addition and/or removal of these controls has little effect on our results, suggesting that the results presented here are robust to a wide variety of alternative specifications.

In order to minimize possible endogeneity between left- and right-side variables, we measure two control variables in the first year of our dataset (1960), rather than on an annual basis. This applies to GDP per capita and population, two variables that arguably could be affected by governance outcomes (our eleven dependent variables) in the contemporary period. In addition to being more consistent with the historical nature of our argument, using a base year for GDP per capita helps achieve two statistical goals. First, it addresses the problem of endogeneity between GDP per capita and our dependent variables. Several of our outcome variables could arguably affect GDP per capita levels. While the use of a lag does not remove all possible endogeneity from the model, in the absence of viable instruments a long lag such as the one used here offers at least some protection.[37] Second, by controlling for the starting point of each country, we control for a host of historical, cultural, and geographic factors that may not be represented in the model.

Where we are less concerned about endogeneity issues we allow indicators to vary from year to year, but lag them by one year (except in the case of the geography-weighted dependent variable, which is contemporaneous). We treat other controls, such as region, legal origin, fractionalization, distance from the nearest financial center, and Protestantism, as constant through time.

Since the theory of centripetalism applies only within a democratic framework, we limit all regression analyses to country-years that are minimally democratic (Polity2 > 0), as discussed in chapter five. Resulting samples vary in size from 80 to 141 countries, and from 11 to 53 observation years. Most analyses begin in the 1950s or 1960s and end in or around 2000.

RESULTS

We regress each of eleven outcomes representing good governance against Centripetalism and its component parts, along with relevant controls. Recall that each of the constitutional variables is intended to measure a country's institutional *stock* along that dimension, as discussed in chapter five. These stock measurements extend back to 1900, with an annual depreciation rate of 1 percent. We test each of these four variables separately because of high levels of multi-collinearity (see chapter appendix).

Tables 6.1 to 6.11 contain the results for these analyses. For each dependent variable, we present five separate models. Column one presents the fully specified model with Centripetalism, our summary measure, as the independent variable of interest. This is the principal model upon which we base our substantive conclusions and interpretations. Column two presents a reduced-form model that eliminates

[37] The alternative to the use of a base year is the employment of instrumental variables in place of per capita income, but there are no viable instruments that can feasibly be used in this particular case. We anticipate that any remaining endogeneity – likely quite minimal – biases the results against our hypotheses, by "soaking up" some of the variation that might otherwise be attributed to our variables of interest.

any control variables that do not obtain a 0.10 level of statistical significance in the expected direction. Columns three through five present full-model results for the three subcomponents of Centripetalism: Unitarism, Parliamentarism, and Closed-list PR.

The overall fit of these models is quite good, with F values all significant at better than the 0.0001 level. (In other words, there is a minuscule chance that all the variables used in these models are collectively not significant.) The R^2 values range from 0.21 to 0.90, with most falling in the 0.50 to 0.80 range.[38] For the most part, control variables behave as expected.[39] Among the more consistent performers we find GDP per capita (1960), socialism, population (1960), and democracy stock. Not surprisingly, wealthy, small, long-term democracies tend to be better governed, while socialism's effects cut both ways, depending on the outcome under consideration. Some of the regional variables, along with distance from the nearest financial center, ethnic fractionalization, and latitude, show mixed patterns, significant in some estimations but not in others. English legal origin, Protestant (where included), and oil and diamond production perform less well. This suggests that once one controls for a country's institutional history, its cultural and legal traditions and the "resource curse" do not exert substantial independent effects across this range of governance outcomes.

Table 6.12 summarizes the findings from Tables 6.1 to 6.11 for our key variables of interest. Results appear quite strong for Centripetalism, the composite variable. Even the most skeptical may be convinced that institutions crafted on the centripetal model are unlikely to depress the overall quality of governance in a country. The point may seem trivial, but from a practical perspective it is important to recall the first (apocryphal) stricture of the Hippocratic oath: do no harm.[40] There is, so far as we can tell, little reason to suspect that a constitutional

[38] The R^2 values are harvested from the first "phase" of Newey-West regressions, before the error correction process.

[39] Because they are intended to correct for possible spatial and temporal problems in the data rather than to test any substantive hypothesis, we do not analyze the results for our geography/trade-weighted or time trend control variables.

[40] This stricture is not actually found in the Hippocratic oath, though the idea may owe its origins to Hippocrates (http://www.geocities.com/everwild7/noharm.html, http://en.wikipedia.org/wiki/Hippocratic_Oath).

change to unitarism, parliamentarism, or closed-list PR would have negative effects on the quality of governance in a country.[41] Only in the case of total schooling is Centripetalism associated with poor governance, and it shows no apparent relationship to growth volatility. On the positive side, Centripetalism is associated with higher tax revenues, more telephone mainlines, higher levels of political participation, more democratic stability, lower import duties, more trade, higher average incomes, fewer infant deaths, and larger public health expenditures.

The preponderance of the evidence thus rests in favor of centripetal institutions, rather than decentralized ones. Institutions that pull toward the center, maximizing the twin goals of authority and inclusion in a democratic setting, are on the whole associated with higher levels of political, economic, and human development.

To be sure, there is considerable variation in results across the three component institutions, as demonstrated in Table 6.12. Parliamentarism shows a particularly strong relationship with good governance, while results for Unitarism are somewhat less consistent. Closed-list PR shows a mixed pattern, though it is, on balance, associated with good governance. Of the three components of centripetalism, electoral system rules appear to have the least impact on governance.

In the following chapter, we address some of the methodological issues involved in assessing the strength of this evidence. While far from conclusive, we argue that the regression tests reviewed in this chapter are more than merely suggestive.

[41] The one important caveat to this conclusion is that institutional changes must be achieved in a peaceful and relatively consensual manner. This is a plausible – and widely shared – assumption. It is much less likely that an institutional innovation will achieve desirable results if it is imposed from the top against strenuous objections at the grassroots level. Note that the question of regime type is quite different. Here, the initial imposition of a democratic order is sometimes necessary, and warranted, and need not guarantee the failure of that regime. Sometimes dictators must be deposed by violence. But when the topic of concern turns to what sort of political institutions a democracy should adopt, it seems reasonable to presume that whatever changes might be adopted will have the support of (at the very least) a majority, and will not arouse virulent opposition. We do not wish to sanction undemocratic changes towards unitarism, parliamentarism, or closed-list PR.

TABLE 6.1. *Tax revenue*

	1	2	3	4	5
Centripetalism	0.028***	0.0221***			
	(0.004)	(0.003)			
Unitarism			0.057***		
			(0.007)		
Parliamentarism				0.046***	
				(0.008)	
PR					0.024***
					(0.007)
Geography-weighted DV	5.005***	5.7340***	5.453***	5.043***	5.253***
	(0.752)	(0.725)	(0.797)	(0.772)	(0.783)
GDP per capita (ln), 1960	1.466***	0.9335***	1.671***	1.219***	1.503***
	(0.290)	(0.204)	(0.290)	(0.304)	(0.292)
Africa	1.744*		1.547*	1.552	1.714*
	(0.952)		(0.939)	(0.968)	(0.942)
Western Europe	7.894***	6.5524***	8.184***	8.098***	8.792***
	(0.755)	(0.745)	(0.747)	(0.733)	(0.696)
Asia	−3.824***		−3.469***	−3.936***	−3.051***
	(0.594)		(0.579)	(0.643)	(0.565)
Latin America/ Caribbean	−0.510		−1.014*	−0.043	−0.845
	(0.562)		(0.563)	(0.573)	(0.574)
Socialism	9.342***	7.7413***	9.236***	9.239***	9.403***
	(1.071)	(0.892)	(1.089)	(1.066)	(1.060)
English legal origin	5.438***	3.8290***	5.391***	4.043***	5.051***
	(0.536)	(0.376)	(0.562)	(0.492)	(0.586)
Latitude (ln)	−0.623*		−0.678**	−0.635*	−0.187
	(0.331)		(0.333)	(0.336)	(0.317)
Ethnic fractionalization	−5.656***	−3.6300***	−5.250***	−6.319***	−5.976***
	(0.965)	(0.856)	(0.976)	(1.036)	(1.040)
Population (ln), 1960	−0.610***	−0.8663***	−0.584***	−0.755***	−0.687***
	(0.091)	(0.092)	(0.090)	(0.086)	(0.095)
Protestant	−0.044***		−0.039***	−0.041***	−0.041***
	(0.007)		(0.008)	(0.008)	(0.008)
Distance financial center	0.304***		0.339***	0.273***	0.377***
	(0.096)		(0.086)	(0.103)	(0.100)
Oil production per capita	3.235		7.241***	4.078*	3.101
	(2.410)		(2.549)	(2.350)	(2.516)
Diamond production per capita	−0.130		−0.099	−0.146	−0.160
	(0.155)		(0.151)	(0.156)	(0.154)
Demo stock	−0.001		−0.001	0.001	0.003***
	(0.001)		(0.001)	(0.001)	(0.001)
Trend	0.054**	0.0532**	0.058***	0.060***	0.064***
	(0.022)	(0.023)	(0.022)	(0.022)	(0.023)

TABLE 6.1 *(continued)*

	1	2	3	4	5
Constant	6.392*	15.453***	5.0378	11.252***	8.261**
	(3.405)	(2.453)	(3.483)	(3.301)	(3.416)
Observations	*1,643*	*1,643*	*1,643*	*1,643*	*1,643*
Countries	*105*	*105*	*105*	*105*	*105*
Sample period	*1969–2000*	*1969–2000*	*1969–2000*	*1969–2000*	*1969–2000*
R–square	*0.643*	*0.606*	*0.629*	*0.627*	*0.620*
Prob >F	*0.000*	*0.000*	*0.000*	*0.000*	*0.000*

Dependent variable: aggregate tax revenues, as a percentage of GDP (World Bank 2003a). Estimator includes a correction for first-order autocorrelation. Sample is limited to country-years that are minimally democratic (Polity2 > 0). Newey-West standard errors in parentheses. *p < 10%; **p < 5%; ***p < 1%.

TABLE 6.2. *Telephone mainlines*

	1	2	3	4	5
Centripetalism	0.001**	−0.00004			
	(0.0003)	(0.0003)			
Unitarism			0.001		
			(0.001)		
Parliamentarism				0.005***	
				(0.001)	
PR					−0.001**
					(0.001)
Geography-weighted DV	−0.208***		−0.219***	−0.156***	−0.230***
	(0.058)		(0.059)	(0.058)	(0.059)
GDP per capita (ln), 1960	0.754***	0.7622***	0.757***	0.732***	0.755***
	(0.079)	(0.061)	(0.079)	(0.078)	(0.078)
Africa	−0.789***	−0.7589***	−0.802***	−0.762***	−0.817***
	(0.143)	(0.100)	(0.144)	(0.140)	(0.143)
Western Europe	−0.482***		−0.460***	−0.558***	−0.441***
	(0.077)		(0.077)	(0.076)	(0.076)
Asia	−0.390***		−0.382***	−0.453***	−0.385***
	(0.139)		(0.139)	(0.139)	(0.139)
Latin America/ Caribbean	0.121		0.110	0.196**	0.109
	(0.077)		(0.076)	(0.077)	(0.076)
Socialism	0.306**	0.3952***	0.306**	0.284*	0.302**
	(0.146)	(0.137)	(0.146)	(0.146)	(0.146)
English legal origin	0.025		0.011	−0.040	−0.030
	(0.069)		(0.070)	(0.065)	(0.070)
Latitude (ln)	0.330***	0.2705***	0.336***	0.295***	0.340***
	(0.054)	(0.049)	(0.055)	(0.053)	(0.054)
Ethnic fractionalization	−0.126		−0.118	−0.180	−0.123
	(0.117)		(0.118)	(0.115)	(0.119)
Population (ln), 1960	−0.062***	−0.0989***	−0.063***	−0.063***	−0.066***
	(0.012)	(0.011)	(0.013)	(0.012)	(0.012)
Protestant	−0.002*		−0.001	−0.002**	−0.001
	(0.001)		(0.001)	(0.001)	(0.001)
Distance financial center	−0.075***	−0.049***	−0.074***	−0.080***	−0.074***
	(0.011)	(0.011)	(0.011)	(0.011)	(0.011)
Oil production per capita	−0.430***	−0.4761**	−0.347**	−0.507***	−0.265*
	(0.143)	(0.163)	(0.142)	(0.134)	(0.146)
Diamond production per capita	0.066***		0.066***	0.064***	0.067***
	(0.015)		(0.015)	(0.015)	(0.015)

TABLE 6.2 *(continued)*

	1	2	3	4	5
Demo stock	0.001***	0.0005***	0.001***	0.0003	0.001***
	(0.0002)	(0.0002)	(0.0002)	(0.0002)	(0.0002)
Trend	0.050***	0.0514***	0.051***	0.049***	0.051***
	(0.002)	(0.002)	(0.002)	(0.002)	(0.002)
Constant	−3.884***	−3.7921***	−3.881***	−3.654***	−3.796***
	(0.770)	(0.630)	(0.784)	(0.752)	(0.765)
Observations	2,131	2,173	2,131	2,131	2,131
Countries	126	128	126	126	126
Sample period	1964–2000	1964–2000	1964–2000	1964–2000	1964–2000
R-square	0.796	0.781	0.795	0.800	0.796
Prob > F	0.000	0.000	0.000	0.000	0.000

Dependent variable: telephone mainlines per 1,000 people, natural log (World Bank 2003a). Estimator includes a correction for first-order autocorrelation. Sample is limited to country-years that are minimally democratic (Polity2 > 0). Newey-West standard errors in parentheses. *p < 10%; **p < 5%; ***p < 1%.

TABLE 6.3. *Participation*

	1	2	3	4	5
Centripetalism	0.051***	0.046***			
	(0.006)	(0.004)			
Unitarism			0.083***		
			(0.015)		
Parliamentarism				0.054***	
				(0.016)	
PR					0.076***
					(0.009)
Geography-weighted DV	−0.926		−0.697	−0.807	−0.929
	(0.679)		(0.711)	(0.716)	(0.687)
GDP per capita (ln), 1960	1.786***	2.398***	2.105***	1.739***	2.030***
	(0.495)	(0.404)	(0.510)	(0.500)	(0.495)
Africa	−0.301		−0.296	−0.240	−0.025
	(1.814)		(1.791)	(1.813)	(1.814)
Western Europe	0.830		1.766	2.225*	2.310**
	(1.239)		(1.259)	(1.242)	(1.167)
Asia	−2.041*	−2.131**	−1.113	−1.549	−0.506
	(1.240)	(0.961)	(1.250)	(1.345)	(1.203)
Latin America/ Caribbean	−1.435	−2.060**	−2.142**	−1.254	−1.915*
	(1.109)	(0.853)	(1.073)	(1.138)	(1.100)
Socialism	6.474***	6.788***	6.467***	7.376***	7.039***
	(2.165)	(1.428)	(2.218)	(2.216)	(2.170)
English legal origin	−1.514*		−1.796*	−3.203***	−1.320
	(0.919)		(0.927)	(0.824)	(0.933)
Latitude (ln)	1.381***	1.091**	1.472***	1.583***	2.181***
	(0.484)	(0.487)	(0.497)	(0.491)	(0.488)
Ethnic fractionalization	−18.740***	−19.235***	−18.353***	−19.360***	−18.876***
	(1.506)	(1.568)	(1.564)	(1.698)	(1.669)
Population (ln), 1960	−0.217		−0.224	−0.475**	−0.320*
	(0.203)		(0.212)	(0.192)	(0.194)
Protestant	−0.011		−0.001	−0.008	−0.011
	(0.011)		(0.012)	(0.012)	(0.011)
Distance financial center	−0.499***	−0.460***	−0.465***	−0.457**	−0.407**
	(0.184)	(0.177)	(0.180)	(0.189)	(0.193)
Oil production per capita	14.808**		20.709***	17.497**	13.268*
	(7.130)		(7.144)	(6.993)	(7.352)
Diamond production per capita	−1.276***	−1.182***	−1.233***	−1.303***	−1.281***
	(0.166)	(0.147)	(0.165)	(0.168)	(0.163)
Demo stock	0.0001		0.003	0.007***	0.008***
	(0.003)		(0.003)	(0.002)	(0.002)
Trend	0.277***	0.260***	0.293***	0.285***	0.302***
	(0.031)	(0.029)	(0.032)	(0.032)	(0.031)

TABLE 6.3 *(continued)*

	1	2	3	4	5
Applied turnout sanctions	7.175***	7.707***	7.779***	6.282***	7.102***
	(1.248)	(1.076)	(1.386)	(1.372)	(1.318)
Nonapplied sanctions	3.597***	4.880***	3.817***	4.580***	4.554***
	(1.388)	(1.077)	(1.334)	(1.298)	(1.359)
No turnout sanctions	−9.039***		−8.367***	−6.110***	−8.928***
	(1.167)		(1.169)	(1.124)	(1.123)
Constant	13.413**	4.644	10.262	18.961***	13.750**
	(6.722)	(4.540)	(6.952)	(6.422)	(6.589)
Observations	2,310	2,316	2,310	2,310	2,310
Countries	121	122	121	121	121
Sample period	1960–97	1960–97	1960–97	1960–97	1960–97
R-square	0.580	0.560	0.569	0.561	0.572
Prob > F	0.000	0.000	0.000	0.000	0.000

Dependent variable: voter turnout as a percentage of the adult population voting in elections (Vanhanen 2000). Estimator includes a correction for first-order autocorrelation. Sample is limited to country-years that are minimally democratic (Polity2 > 0). Newey-West standard errors in parentheses. *p < 10%; **p < 5%; ***p < 1%.

TABLE 6.4. *Democratic volatility*

	1	2	3	4	5
Centripetalism	−0.001*	−0.0013***			
	(0.001)	(0.0004)			
Unitarism			−0.001		
			(0.001)		
Parliamentarism				−0.003*	
				(0.001)	
PR					−0.001
					(0.001)
Geography-weighted DV	2.881***	3.3890***	2.915***	2.884***	2.913***
	(0.924)	(0.899)	(0.924)	(0.919)	(0.925)
GDP per capita (ln), 1960	−0.064		−0.068	−0.051	−0.068
	(0.054)		(0.054)	(0.055)	(0.054)
Africa	0.409*	0.5461***	0.418*	0.412*	0.413*
	(0.216)	(0.149)	(0.218)	(0.216)	(0.218)
Western Europe	−0.195		−0.227*	−0.179	−0.226*
	(0.124)		(0.124)	(0.130)	(0.121)
Asia	0.048		0.030	0.077	0.024
	(0.172)		(0.171)	(0.180)	(0.170)
Latin America/ Caribbean	−0.160		−0.148	−0.190	−0.150
	(0.132)		(0.132)	(0.131)	(0.132)
Socialism	−0.489*		−0.495*	−0.483*	−0.496*
	(0.277)		(0.278)	(0.277)	(0.278)
English legal origin	−0.329***	−0.1608**	−0.307***	−0.275***	−0.321***
	(0.104)	(0.068)	(0.102)	(0.100)	(0.108)
Latitude (ln)	0.184**		0.177**	0.195**	0.170**
	(0.081)		(0.081)	(0.083)	(0.080)
Ethnic fractionalization	0.373*		0.372*	0.395*	0.379*
	(0.216)		(0.219)	(0.215)	(0.215)
Population (ln), 1960	0.014		0.017	0.017	0.017
	(0.021)		(0.021)	(0.020)	(0.021)
Protestant	0.004***		0.004***	0.004***	0.004***
	(0.001)		(0.001)	(0.001)	(0.001)
Distance financial center	0.001		−0.001	0.003	−0.001
	(0.022)		(0.022)	(0.023)	(0.022)
Oil production per capita	−0.499		−0.577	−0.492	−0.492
	(0.425)		(0.416)	(0.416)	(0.426)
Diamond production per capita	−0.073***		−0.074***	−0.072***	−0.073***
	(0.021)		(0.021)	(0.020)	(0.021)

TABLE 6.4 *(continued)*

	1	2	3	4	5
Demo stock	−0.003***	−0.0022***	−0.003***	−0.003***	−0.003***
	(0.0003)	(0.0002)	(0.0003)	(0.0003)	(0.0003)
Trend	−0.001		−0.002	−0.001	−0.002
	(0.003)		(0.003)	(0.003)	(0.003)
Constant	1.840***	1.0814***	1.816***	1.646***	1.802***
	(0.638)	(0.074)	(0.652)	(0.634)	(0.637)
Observations	2,595	3,333	2,595	2,595	2,595
Countries	125	141	125	125	125
Sample period	1960–2000	1950–2002	1960–2000	1960–2000	1960–2000
R-square	0.225	0.205	0.224	0.225	0.224
Prob > F	0.000	0.000	0.000	0.000	0.000

Dependent variable: five-year moving sum of the standard deviation of Polity2 (calculated from Marshall and Jaggers 2002). Estimator includes a correction for first-order autocorrelation. Sample is limited to country-years that are minimally democratic (Polity2 > 0). Newey-West standard errors in parentheses. *p < 10%; **p < 5%; ***p < 1%.

TABLE 6.5. *Import duties*

	1	2	3	4	5
Centripetalism	−0.0233*** (0.004)	−0.0080** (0.004)			
Unitarism			−0.0647*** (0.008)		
Parliamentarism				−0.0490*** (0.008)	
PR					−0.0015 (0.006)
Geography-weighted DV	−2.8968 (1.826)		−3.4654* (1.837)	−3.3100* (1.879)	−3.6063* (1.905)
GDP per capita (ln), 1960	−2.9247*** (0.545)	−2.3431*** (0.353)	−3.1951*** (0.532)	−2.7198*** (0.571)	−2.9829*** (0.565)
Africa	3.0063* (1.591)	3.1928** (1.489)	3.3672** (1.622)	3.3749** (1.625)	3.3723** (1.679)
Western Europe	−1.9713*** (0.735)	−1.7617*** (0.670)	−2.1973*** (0.671)	−2.0357*** (0.698)	−3.1584*** (0.661)
Asia	2.2439** (1.089)	1.9210* (1.119)	1.9792* (1.050)	2.3765** (1.102)	1.5731 (1.111)
Latin America/ Caribbean	0.3195 (0.865)	1.6095** (0.650)	0.8461 (0.868)	−0.2072 (0.894)	0.5864 (0.881)
Socialism	−5.5794*** (1.142)		−5.7786*** (1.131)	−5.4455*** (1.163)	−5.7437*** (1.162)
English legal origin	−0.682 (0.546)		−0.8298 (0.540)	0.6365 (0.556)	0.1395 (0.593)
Latitude (ln)	0.5366 (0.570)		0.6389 (0.577)	0.5935 (0.567)	0.13 (0.588)
Ethnic fractionalization	−1.4309 (1.188)		−2.4235* (1.262)	−1.2449 (1.200)	−1.4434 (1.258)
Population (ln), 1960	−0.7416*** (0.191)		−0.7503*** (0.178)	−0.5879*** (0.192)	−0.5894*** (0.204)
Distance financial center	0.3512*** (0.108)	0.5458*** (0.099)	0.3203*** (0.107)	0.3894*** (0.111)	0.2675** (0.110)
Oil production per capita	0.9443 (1.516)		−3.0936** (1.445)	0.6673 (1.428)	−0.7239 (1.546)
Diamond production per capita	−0.2332 (0.177)		−0.267 (0.183)	−0.2275 (0.177)	−0.2042 (0.178)
Demo stock	0.0055*** (0.002)		0.0063*** (0.002)	0.0042** (0.002)	0.0006 (0.002)
Trend	−0.1080*** (0.032)	−0.1647*** (0.031)	−0.1078*** (0.031)	−0.1118*** (0.032)	−0.1258*** (0.032)
Constant	55.228*** (4.604)	39.9012*** (4.576)	58.272*** (4.689)	50.980*** (4.720)	53.075*** (4.685)

TABLE 6.5 *(continued)*

	1	2	3	4	5
Observations	1,411	1,436	1,411	1,411	1,411
Countries	97	98	97	97	97
Sample period	1969–99	1969–99	1969–99	1969–99	1969–99
R-square	0.508	0.454	0.523	0.503	0.487
Prob > F	0.000	0.000	0.000	0.000	0.000

Dependent variable: import duties, as a percentage of imports (World Bank 2003a). Estimator includes a correction for first-order autocorrelation. Sample is limited to country-years that are minimally democratic (Polity2 > 0). Newey-West standard errors in parentheses. *p < 10%; **p <; 5%; ***p < 1%.

TABLE 6.6. *Trade*

	1	2	3	4	5
Centripetalism	0.0007***	−0.0001			
	(0.0002)	(0.0002)			
Unitarism			0.0012***		
			(0.0003)		
Parliamentarism				0.0015***	
				(0.0004)	
PR					0.0005*
					(0.0003)
Geography-weighted DV	−0.1000	0.3096***	−0.0916	−0.1142	−0.1007
	(0.079)	(0.094)	(0.078)	(0.079)	(0.078)
GDP per capita (ln), 1960	−0.0322**		−0.0271*	−0.0392***	−0.0296**
	(0.014)		(0.015)	(0.015)	(0.015)
Africa	−0.1585***		−0.1612***	−0.1637***	−0.1586***
	(0.047)		(0.047)	(0.048)	(0.047)
Western Europe	0.4460***	0.2846***	0.4608***	0.4450***	0.4706***
	(0.038)	(0.038)	(0.037)	(0.037)	(0.037)
Asia	0.0945**	0.1732***	0.1032**	0.0799*	0.1124**
	(0.046)	(0.045)	(0.046)	(0.047)	(0.046)
Latin America/ Caribbean	−0.2003***	−0.1620***	−0.2100***	−0.1884***	−0.2053***
	(0.035)	(0.026)	(0.035)	(0.035)	(0.035)
Socialism	0.4597***		0.4639***	0.4579***	0.4657***
	(0.057)		(0.057)	(0.058)	(0.057)
English legal origin	0.1596***	0.0852***	0.1574***	0.1251***	0.1511***
	(0.027)	(0.023)	(0.026)	(0.026)	(0.028)
Latitude (ln)	−0.0682***		−0.0668***	−0.0718***	−0.0584***
	(0.019)		(0.019)	(0.020)	(0.019)
Ethnic fractionalization	0.3836***		0.3908***	0.3708***	0.3780***
	(0.046)		(0.047)	(0.046)	(0.047)
Population (ln), 1960	−0.2446***	−0.2270***	−0.2450***	−0.2472***	−0.2465***
	(0.006)	(0.007)	(0.006)	(0.006)	(0.007)
Distance financial center	−0.0236***	−0.0280***	−0.0229***	−0.0247***	−0.0224***
	(0.005)	(0.005)	(0.005)	(0.005)	(0.005)
Oil production per capita	0.0532		0.1354	0.0607	0.0615
	(0.124)		(0.120)	(0.117)	(0.125)
Diamond production per capita	0.0145**		0.0147**	0.0142**	0.0145**
	(0.006)		(0.006)	(0.006)	(0.006)
Demo stock	−0.0001		−0.0001	−0.0001	0.00002
	(0.0001)		(0.0001)	(0.0001)	(0.0001)

TABLE 6.6 *(continued)*

	1	2	3	4	5
Trend	0.0097***	0.0110***	0.0100***	0.0096***	0.0101***
	(0.001)	(0.001)	(0.001)	(0.001)	(0.001)
Constant	6.9492***	6.6413***	6.9047***	7.0703***	6.9705***
	(0.202)	(0.132)	(0.205)	(0.200)	(0.202)
Observations	2,522	2,601	2,522	2,522	2,522
Countries	126	132	126	126	126
Sample period	1960–2000	1960–2000	1960–2000	1960–2000	1960–2000
R-square	0.708	0.636	0.707	0.708	0.706
Prob > F	0.000	0.000	0.000	0.000	0.000

Dependent variable: exports and imports as a percentage of GDP, natural log (World Bank 2003a). Estimator includes a correction for first-order autocorrelation. Sample is limited to country-years that are minimally democratic (Polity2 > 0). Newey-West standard errors in parentheses. *p < 10%; **p < 5%; ***p < 1%.

TABLE 6.7. *GDP per capita*

	1	2	3	4	5
Centripetalism	0.0004***	0.0004**			
	(0.0002)	(0.0002)			
Unitarism			0.0001		
			(0.0004)		
Parliamentarism				0.0035***	
				(0.001)	
PR					−0.0007**
					(0.0003)
Trade-weighted DV	0.0335**	0.0438***	0.0333**	0.0271*	0.0319**
	(0.015)	(0.015)	(0.015)	(0.014)	(0.015)
GDP per capita (ln), 1960	0.7978***	0.7732***	0.7993***	0.7778***	0.7985***
	(0.070)	(0.051)	(0.071)	(0.071)	(0.070)
Africa	−0.1644*		−0.1674*	−0.1660*	−0.1710*
	(0.095)		(0.096)	(0.093)	(0.095)
Western Europe	−0.0778*		−0.0602	−0.1347***	−0.0532
	(0.044)		(0.046)	(0.041)	(0.045)
Asia	0.1365		0.1452	0.0799	0.1435
	(0.092)		(0.092)	(0.095)	(0.093)
Latin America/ Caribbean	0.0501		0.047	0.0912**	0.0482
	(0.047)		(0.046)	(0.046)	(0.046)
Socialism	−0.4382***	−0.3966***	−0.4344***	−0.4616***	−0.4348***
	(0.106)	(0.110)	(0.106)	(0.103)	(0.105)
English legal origin	−0.009		−0.0218	−0.0498	−0.0381
	(0.039)		(0.041)	(0.039)	(0.040)
Latitude (ln)	0.2151***	0.1981***	0.2204***	0.1901***	0.2198***
	(0.045)	(0.040)	(0.046)	(0.042)	(0.045)
Ethnic fractionalization	−0.3077***	−0.4115***	−0.3098***	−0.3305***	−0.3119***
	(0.072)	(0.068)	(0.072)	(0.071)	(0.072)
Population (ln), 1960	−0.0220***	−0.0173**	−0.0236***	−0.0237***	−0.0250***
	(0.008)	(0.007)	(0.008)	(0.007)	(0.008)
Distance financial center	−0.0520***	−0.0472***	−0.0513***	−0.0565***	−0.0514***
	(0.006)	(0.008)	(0.006)	(0.006)	(0.006)
Oil production per capita	0.3814**		0.4132***	0.3213**	0.4591***
	(0.150)		(0.143)	(0.137)	(0.148)
Diamond production per capita	0.1336***		0.1337***	0.1326***	0.1337***
	(0.008)		(0.008)	(0.008)	(0.008)
Demo stock	0.0005***	0.0006***	0.0006***	0.0003*	0.0006***
	(0.0002)	(0.0001)	(0.0002)	(0.0002)	(0.0002)

TABLE 6.7 *(continued)*

	1	2	3	4	5
Trend	0.0150***	0.0152***	0.0153***	0.0140***	0.0154***
	(0.001)	(0.001)	(0.001)	(0.001)	(0.001)
Constant	1.4004**	1.4116***	1.4240**	1.6556***	1.4683**
	(0.633)	(0.477)	(0.646)	(0.640)	(0.635)
Observations	2,523	2,523	2,523	2,523	2,523
Countries	124	124	124	124	124
Sample period	1960–99	1960–99	1960–99	1960–99	1960–99
R-square	0.896	0.886	0.895	0.898	0.896
Prob > F	0.000	0.000	0.000	0.000	0.000

Dependent variable: GDP per capita, in constant 1995 dollars, natural log (World Bank 2003a). Estimator includes a correction for first-order autocorrelation. Sample is limited to country-years that are minimally democratic (Polity2 > 0). Newey-West standard errors in parentheses. *p < 10%; **p < 5%; ***p < 1%.

TABLE 6.8. *Growth volatility*

	1	2	3	4	5
Centripetalism	−0.0009	−0.0013			
	(0.001)	(0.001)			
Unitarism			−0.0003		
			(0.002)		
Parliamentarism				−0.0048**	
				(0.002)	
PR					0.0001
					(0.002)
Geography-weighted DV	2.1740***	2.7969***	2.1835***	2.1601***	2.1856***
	(0.558)	(0.583)	(0.559)	(0.559)	(0.558)
GDP per capita (ln), 1960	0.1442		0.141	0.1718	0.1418
	(0.179)		(0.180)	(0.186)	(0.179)
Africa	−0.2655		−0.2575	−0.2659	−0.2562
	(0.329)		(0.329)	(0.330)	(0.330)
Western Europe	−0.5971***	−1.1354***	−0.6320***	−0.5354***	−0.6369***
	(0.182)	(0.109)	(0.183)	(0.178)	(0.181)
Asia	−0.8598***	−1.1534***	−0.8758***	−0.7918***	−0.8773***
	(0.294)	(0.151)	(0.293)	(0.306)	(0.294)
Latin America/ Caribbean	−0.3424		−0.3333	−0.3983	−0.3345
	(0.246)		(0.246)	(0.248)	(0.245)
Socialism	2.5821***	2.3101***	2.5740***	2.5984***	2.5729***
	(0.490)	(0.458)	(0.490)	(0.488)	(0.489)
English legal origin	0.4307***		0.4535***	0.4996***	0.4604***
	(0.163)		(0.163)	(0.169)	(0.174)
Latitude (ln)	−0.2364		−0.2461	−0.2102	−0.2482
	(0.181)		(0.183)	(0.181)	(0.181)
Ethnic fractionalization	−0.069		−0.0663	−0.0356	−0.0626
	(0.347)		(0.348)	(0.345)	(0.347)
Population (ln), 1960	−0.1862***		−0.1830***	−0.1843***	−0.1822***
	(0.034)		(0.034)	(0.033)	(0.033)
Distance financial center	0.0294		0.028	0.0351	0.0278
	(0.027)		(0.027)	(0.027)	(0.027)
Oil production per capita	−0.1044		−0.1786	−0.0439	−0.173
	(0.522)		(0.508)	(0.503)	(0.536)
Diamond production per capita	−0.0469		−0.0471	−0.0456	−0.0471
	(0.043)		(0.043)	(0.043)	(0.043)
Demo stock	−0.0023***	−0.0015***	−0.0025***	−0.0022***	−0.0025***
	(0.001)	(0.0003)	(0.001)	(0.001)	(0.001)
Trend	−0.0243***	−0.0259***	−0.0249***	−0.0231***	−0.0249***
	(0.004)	(0.004)	(0.004)	(0.005)	(0.004)
Constant	6.6277***	5.5002***	6.5851***	6.3291***	6.5562***
	(1.818)	(0.308)	(1.849)	(1.847)	(1.826)
Observations	*2,610*	*2,903*	*2,610*	*2,610*	*2,610*

TABLE 6.8 *(continued)*

	1	2	3	4	5
Countries	125	132	125	125	125
Sample period	1960–2000	1954–2000	1960–2000	1960–2000	1960–2000
R-square	0.258	0.227	0.257	0.259	0.257
Prob > F	0.000	0.000	0.000	0.000	0.000

Dependent variable: five-year moving sum of the s.d. of real per capita GDP growth (calculated from World Bank 2003a). Estimator includes a correction for first-order autocorrelation. Sample is limited to country-years that are minimally democratic (Polity2 > 0). Newey-West standard errors in parentheses. *p < 10%; **p < 5%; ***p < 1%.

TABLE 6.9. *Infant mortality*

	1	2	3	4	5
Centripetalism	−0.0005***	−0.0006***			
	(0.0002)	(0.0002)			
Unitarism			−0.0008**		
			(0.0004)		
Parliamentarism				−0.0022***	
				(0.001)	
PR					0.0003
					(0.0003)
Geography-weighted DV	0.1415		0.1518	0.1333	0.1431
	(0.108)		(0.109)	(0.109)	(0.109)
GDP per capita (ln), 1960	−0.3009***	−0.2880***	−0.3041***	−0.2899***	−0.3027***
	(0.037)	(0.025)	(0.037)	(0.037)	(0.037)
Africa	0.3544***	0.3790***	0.3579***	0.3532***	0.3591***
	(0.068)	(0.052)	(0.069)	(0.068)	(0.068)
Western Europe	0.0544		0.0428	0.0799**	0.0292
	(0.040)		(0.040)	(0.039)	(0.040)
Asia	−0.127		−0.1306	−0.0989	−0.1365
	(0.084)		(0.084)	(0.085)	(0.084)
Latin America/ Caribbean	0.2245***	0.2132***	0.2326***	0.1969***	0.2258***
	(0.050)	(0.036)	(0.050)	(0.050)	(0.050)
Socialism	−0.3528***	−0.4336***	−0.3556***	−0.3463***	−0.3597***
	(0.079)	(0.077)	(0.080)	(0.079)	(0.080)
English legal origin	0.0018		0.0028	0.0349	0.0235
	(0.030)		(0.030)	(0.029)	(0.030)
Latitude (ln)	−0.0507		−0.0514	−0.0386	−0.0565
	(0.035)		(0.035)	(0.034)	(0.035)
Ethnic fractionalization	0.5206***	0.5378***	0.5151***	0.5384***	0.5265***
	(0.059)	(0.052)	(0.060)	(0.058)	(0.059)
Population (ln), 1960	0.0312***	0.0157**	0.0314***	0.0326***	0.0337***
	(0.008)	(0.007)	(0.008)	(0.008)	(0.008)
Muslim	0.0050***	0.0047***	0.0050***	0.0050***	0.0050***
	(0.001)	(0.001)	(0.001)	(0.001)	(0.001)
Distance financial center	0.0432***	0.0391***	0.0428***	0.0456***	0.0424***
	(0.005)	(0.005)	(0.005)	(0.005)	(0.005)
Oil production per capita	−0.3137***		−0.3720***	−0.2882***	−0.3685***
	(0.112)		(0.107)	(0.103)	(0.109)
Diamond production per capita	0.0022		0.002	0.0027	0.002
	(0.010)		(0.010)	(0.010)	(0.010)
Demo stock	−0.0008***	−0.0009***	−0.0008***	−0.0007***	−0.0009***
	(0.0001)	(0.0001)	(0.0001)	(0.0001)	(0.0001)

TABLE 6.9 *(continued)*

	1	2	3	4	5
Trend	−0.0312***	−0.0308***	−0.0314***	−0.0307***	−0.0316***
	(0.001)	(0.001)	(0.001)	(0.001)	(0.001)
Constant	7.2781***	7.5228***	7.3054***	7.1504***	7.2405***
	(0.378)	(0.235)	(0.386)	(0.372)	(0.377)
Observations	2,634	2,683	2,634	2,634	2,634
Countries	126	129	126	126	126
Sample period	1960–2000	1960–2000	1960–2000	1960–2000	1960–2000
R-square	0.814	0.805	0.814	0.816	0.814
Prob > F	0.000	0.000	0.000	0.000	0.000

Dependent variable: number of infant deaths between ages zero and one, natural log (World Bank 2003a). Estimator includes a correction for first-order autocorrelation. Sample is limited to country-years that are minimally democratic (Polity2 > 0). Newey-West standard errors in parentheses. *p < 10%; **p < 5%; ***p < 1%.

TABLE 6.10. *Health expenditure*

	1	2	3	4	5
Centripetalism	0.0031***	0.0024***			
	(0.001)	(0.001)			
Unitarism			0.0024		
			(0.002)		
Parliamentarism				0.0033*	
				(0.002)	
PR					0.0058***
					(0.002)
Geography-weighted DV	2.8961***	2.7859***	2.8659***	2.7972***	2.7990***
	(0.478)	(0.498)	(0.489)	(0.484)	(0.477)
GDP per capita (ln), 1960	0.6201***	0.6766***	0.6296***	0.6114***	0.6209***
	(0.081)	(0.071)	(0.082)	(0.081)	(0.081)
Africa	0.0875		0.0265	0.0199	0.0571
	(0.222)		(0.224)	(0.220)	(0.225)
Western Europe	0.2024		0.3259	0.2845	0.286
	(0.203)		(0.202)	(0.204)	(0.197)
Asia	−0.8660***	−0.8539***	−0.8436***	−0.8852***	−0.8293***
	(0.214)	(0.175)	(0.217)	(0.217)	(0.218)
Latin America/ Caribbean	−0.3285**	−0.4623***	−0.3711**	−0.3316*	−0.3772**
	(0.166)	(0.130)	(0.168)	(0.171)	(0.166)
Socialism	0.9846***	0.7772***	0.9892***	0.9725***	1.0272***
	(0.233)	(0.212)	(0.232)	(0.236)	(0.231)
English legal origin	−0.0046		−0.0559	−0.1276	0.0415
	(0.133)		(0.135)	(0.132)	(0.138)
Latitude (ln)	−0.1558		−0.1308	−0.1418	−0.1157
	(0.104)		(0.104)	(0.104)	(0.104)
Ethnic fractionalization	−0.9271***	−0.8401***	−0.8962***	−0.9367***	−0.9399***
	(0.245)	(0.219)	(0.250)	(0.245)	(0.247)
Population (ln), 1960	−0.0338	−0.0824***	−0.0407	−0.0449	−0.0416
	(0.028)	(0.028)	(0.029)	(0.028)	(0.028)
Distance financial center	−0.0297		−0.0287	−0.0302	−0.0262
	(0.024)		(0.025)	(0.025)	(0.025)
Oil production per capita	−0.5204		−0.1795	−0.315	−0.7757*
	(0.422)		(0.415)	(0.427)	(0.443)
Diamond production per capita	−0.0248		−0.0204	−0.0218	−0.024
	(0.027)		(0.026)	(0.026)	(0.028)
Demo stock	0.0009**	0.0008**	0.0013***	0.0012***	0.0013***
	(0.0004)	(0.0003)	(0.0004)	(0.0004)	(0.0003)

TABLE 6.10 *(continued)*

	1	2	3	4	5
Trend	0.023	0.0273*	0.0259*	0.0260*	0.0245*
	(0.015)	(0.015)	(0.015)	(0.015)	(0.015)
Constant	−3.0173*	−2.8140*	−3.0601*	−2.8447*	−2.8579*
	(1.625)	(1.500)	(1.648)	(1.638)	(1.608)
Observations	*1,104*	*1,117*	*1,104*	*1,104*	*1,104*
Countries	*122*	*124*	*122*	*122*	*122*
Sample period	*1989–99*	*1989–99*	*1989–99*	*1989–99*	*1989–99*
R-square	*0.63*	*0.603*	*0.625*	*0.625*	*0.631*
Prob > F	*0.000*	*0.000*	*0.000*	*0.000*	*0.000*

Dependent variable: public health expenditures as a percentage of GDP (World Bank 2003a). Estimator includes a correction for first-order autocorrelation. Sample is limited to country-years that are minimally democratic (Polity2 > 0). Newey-West standard errors in parentheses. *p < 10%; **p < 5%; ***p < 1%.

TABLE 6.11. *Schooling*

	1	2	3	4	5
Centripetalism	−0.0025***	−0.0054***			
	(0.001)	(0.001)			
Unitarism			−0.0029**		
			(0.001)		
Parliamentarism				−0.0066***	
				(0.001)	
PR					−0.0019*
					(0.001)
Geography-weighted DV	1.1379		0.5835	0.5572	0.7241
	(1.202)		(1.226)	(1.215)	(1.265)
GDP per capita (ln), 1960	1.4280***	1.2795***	1.4087***	1.4889***	1.4133***
	(0.058)	(0.058)	(0.059)	(0.059)	(0.059)
Africa	−1.9718***	−0.8433***	−1.9420***	−1.9064***	−1.9765***
	(0.164)	(0.122)	(0.168)	(0.164)	(0.171)
Western Europe	−1.0711***		−1.0993***	−0.9955***	−1.1190***
	(0.129)		(0.133)	(0.130)	(0.132)
Asia	1.0365***	1.6990***	0.9463***	1.0898***	0.9263***
	(0.218)	(0.164)	(0.215)	(0.220)	(0.214)
Latin America/ Caribbean	−0.9475***		−0.9025***	−1.0136***	−0.9328***
	(0.164)		(0.168)	(0.166)	(0.166)
Socialism	3.1972***	3.7379***	3.2622***	3.2677***	3.2692***
	(0.238)	(0.203)	(0.235)	(0.228)	(0.236)
English legal origin	0.1563		0.2023**	0.3071***	0.1846*
	(0.100)		(0.095)	(0.095)	(0.103)
Latitude (ln)	0.3236***	0.2877***	0.3055***	0.3296***	0.2838***
	(0.084)	(0.064)	(0.083)	(0.085)	(0.081)
Ethnic fractionalization	0.8410***		0.8118***	0.8901***	0.8932***
	(0.200)		(0.203)	(0.201)	(0.195)
Population (ln), 1960	−0.1438***	−0.2093***	−0.1253***	−0.1139***	−0.1257***
	(0.028)	(0.028)	(0.029)	(0.027)	(0.028)
Muslim	−0.0183***	−0.0150***	−0.0182***	−0.0182***	−0.0181***
	(0.001)	(0.002)	(0.001)	(0.001)	(0.001)
Distance financial center	0.1118***		0.1061***	0.1194***	0.1056***
	(0.018)		(0.018)	(0.018)	(0.019)
Oil production per capita	1.8902**		1.6757**	1.9623**	1.8851**
	(0.800)		(0.792)	(0.789)	(0.799)
Diamond production per capita	0.0879***		0.0896***	0.0949***	0.0917***
	(0.022)		(0.023)	(0.022)	(0.022)
Demo stock	0.0023***	0.0035***	0.0021***	0.0022***	0.0019***
	(0.0002)	(0.0003)	(0.0002)	(0.0002)	(0.0002)

TABLE 6.11 *(continued)*

	1	2	3	4	5
Trend	0.0700***	0.0736***	0.0696***	0.0719***	0.0690***
	(0.004)	(0.003)	(0.004)	(0.004)	(0.004)
Constant	−8.2501***	−6.1220***	−8.4027***	−9.3632***	−8.4869***
	(0.666)	(0.677)	(0.695)	(0.662)	(0.688)
Observations	*1,896*	*1,935*	*1,896*	*1,896*	*1,896*
Countries	*80*	*81*	*80*	*80*	*80*
Sample period	*1960–98*	*1960–98*	*1960–98*	*1960–98*	*1960–98*
R-square	*0.838*	*0.798*	*0.837*	*0.839*	*0.836*
Prob > F	*0.000*	*0.000*	*0.000*	*0.000*	*0.000*

Dependent variable: total average years of schooling (Barro and Lee 2000). Estimator includes a correction for first-order autocorrelation. Sample is limited to country-years that are minimally democratic (Polity2 > 0). Newey-West standard errors in parentheses. *p < 10%; **p < 5%; ***p < 1%.

TABLE 6.12. *Summary of empirical tests*

	Independent Variables			
Dependent Variables	**Cent**	**Unit**	**Parl**	**Closed-list PR**
Political Development				
Tax revenue	++	++	++	++
Telephone mainlines	++		++	– –
Participation	++	++	++	++
Democratic volatility	+		+	
Economic Development				
Import duties	++	++	++	
Trade/GDP	++	++	++	+
GDP per capita	++		++	– –
Growth volatility			++	
Human Development				
Infant mortality	++	++	++	
Public health expenditures	++		+	++
Total schooling	– –	– –	– –	–
Summary				
Good governance (+ or ++)	*9/11*	*5/11*	*10/11*	*4/11*
Bad governance (– or – –)	*1/11*	*1/11*	*1/11*	*3/11*

Summary of Centripetalism results based on full models from Tables 6.1–6.11. ++ and + indicate statistical significance at the 0.05 and 0.10 levels, respectively, in the expected direction. – – and – indicate statistical significance at the 0.05 and 0.10 levels, respectively, in the unexpected direction. Empty cell indicates that there is no statistically significant relationship.

APPENDIX: DESCRIPTIVE STATISTICS

Independent Variables

Moments and Distribution

	Unitarism			Parliamentarism			Closed-list PR			Centripetalism		
	Score	Observations		Score	Observations		Score	Observations		Score	Observations	
	0–25	1,489	(45%)	0–25	1,618	(49%)	0–25	2,493	(75%)	0–71	1,698	(51%)
	25–51	773	(23%)	25–51	508	(15%)	25–51	247	(7%)	71–143	677	(20%)
	51–77	532	(16%)	51–77	418	(13%)	51–77	214	(6%)	143–215	535	(16%)
	77–103	336	(10%)	77–103	462	(14%)	77–103	234	(7%)	215–287	299	(9%)
	103–129	203	(6%)	103–129	327	(10%)	103–129	145	(4%)	287–361	124	(4%)
	All	3,333	(100%)	All	3,333	(100%)	All	3,333	(100%)	All	3,333	(100%)
Mean	39.2			40.5			20.2			99.9		
Min.	0			0			0			0		
Max.	128.97			128.97			128.97			128.97		
S.D.	33.4			39.1			33.5			85.3		

Includes only country-years surpassing a minimal threshold of democracy (Polity2 score > 0). N = 3333. Period: 1950–2002. Percentages rounded to nearest integer.

Correlation Matrix

	Unitarism	Parliamentarism	Closed-list PR
Parliamentarism	0.68***		
Closed-list PR	0.47***	0.26***	
Centripetalism	0.89***	0.83***	0.70***

Control Variables

Variable	Source	Obs.	Mean	S.D.	Min.	Max.
GDP per capita (ln), 1960	World Bank (2003a)	2,886	7.622	1.354	−0.034	10.175
Africa	Authors' coding	3,333	0.110	0.313	0.000	1.000
Western Europe	Authors' coding	3,333	0.246	0.431	0.000	1.000
Asia	Authors' coding	3,333	0.115	0.319	0.000	1.000
Latin America/Caribbean	Authors' coding	3,333	0.243	0.429	0.000	1.000
Muslim	CIA (n.d.)	3,333	8.184	21.509	0.000	99.800
Applied turnout sanctions	Bilodeau and Blais (2005)	3,333	0.068	0.251	0.000	1.000
Nonapplied sanctions	Bilodeau and Blais (2005)	3,333	0.105	0.307	0.000	1.000
No turnout sanctions	Bilodeau and Blais (2005)	3,333	0.056	0.230	0.000	1.000
Socialism	LaPorta et al. (1999)	3,333	0.082	0.274	0.000	1.000
English legal origin	LaPorta et al. (1999)	3,333	0.401	0.490	0.000	1.000
Latitude (ln)	LaPorta et al. (1999)	3,329	−1.355	0.845	−4.500	−0.341
Ethnic fractionalization	Alesina et al. (2003)	2,668	0.356	0.237	0.000	0.879
Population (ln), 1960	World Bank (2003a)	2,866	15.104	2.051	9.616	19.891
Protestant	CIA (n.d.), Johnstone (1993)	3,333	21.108	30.550	0	98
Distance financial center	Authors' calculations	3,288	3.538	2.660	0.000	9.677
Oil production per capita	Humphreys (2005)	2,794	0.014	0.056	0.000	0.742
Diamond production per capita	Humphreys (2005)	2,794	0.131	1.080	0.000	15.575
Demo stock	Marshall and Jaggers (2002)	3,333	146.165	252.937	−429.154	637.628
Trend	Authors' calculations	3,333	82.166	15.046	50.000	102.000

Dependent Variables

Variable	Source	Obs.	Mean	S.D.	Min.	Max.
Tax revenue	World Bank (2003a)	1,643	22.507	8.524	1.640	50.573
Telephone mainlines (ln)	World Bank (2003a)	2,173	4.484	1.577	−0.916	6.659
Participation	Vanhanen (2000)	2,316	39.516	15.563	0.000	70.200
Democratic volatility	Marshall and Jaggers (2002)	3,333	0.752	1.695	0.000	8.955
Import duties	World Bank (2003a)	1,436	8.726	8.552	0.000	60.059
Trade (ln)	World Bank (2003a)	2,601	4.171	0.606	2.078	5.672
GDP per capita (ln)	World Bank (2003a)	2,523	8.190	1.451	4.627	10.937
Growth volatility	World Bank (2003a)	2,903	3.250	2.722	0.252	30.275
IMR (ln)	World Bank (2003a)	2,683	3.214	0.945	0.875	5.381
Health expenditure	World Bank (2003a)	1,117	3.867	1.933	0.180	13.410
Total schooling	World Bank (2003a)	1,896	6.292	2.636	0.520	12.049

7

Assessing the Evidence

In chapter six, we presented evidence of a causal relationship between centripetal institutions – as embodied in Unitarism, Parliamentarism, and Closed-List PR and in a combined variable, Centripetalism – and good governance. In this chapter, we critically assess the plausibility of these apparent relationships and reconsider our choice of methods.

In doing so, we are fully cognizant of potential problems and limitations. We have already mentioned the generic difficulties that affect any study focused on basic-level constitutional institutions and distal governance outcomes. There is little change in these institutions through time, so the leverage for causal analysis comes mostly from spatial variation. Yet, across-unit heterogeneity is extreme, requiring the inclusion of myriad control variables, which can never fully compensate for the nonexperimental characteristics of the research design.

These sorts of difficulties prompt some methodologists to forswear use of cross-national regression techniques,[1] a conclusion we find a bit extreme. The relevant question, in our view, is not whether a given method stands above some imagined bar of acceptable truth-probability, but rather whether it offers the best possible empirical test of the question at issue. We think that our approach to these questions satisfies the practical test of human knowledge. Ours is emphatically a pragmatic, not an absolute, epistemology.[2]

[1] Freedman (1991), Kittel (2006).

[2] Dewey (1938), Gerring (2001: epilogue).

PROBLEMS OF ROBUSTNESS, BRIEFLY CONSIDERED

We begin with the problem of nonrandomized treatment. It is conceivable that centripetal institutions are more likely to be adopted where prospects for good governance are already propitious, in which case our key variables may be proxying for other, unmeasured factors. In order to gauge the robustness of our findings in the face of this identification problem, we employed a series of instruments for Centripetalism in two-stage least squares estimations.[3] Results from these instrumental-variable estimations are at least as strong as the findings presented here – and in some cases stronger – thus providing some assurance that the effects reported here are not simply the product of nonequivalent treatment and control groups. Yet we do not have a great deal of confidence in the two-stage models. All of the possible instruments available to us violate at least one of the assumptions of instrumental-variable analysis: either they are poorly correlated with Centripetalism, or they are correlated with the error term (i.e., they are probable causes in their own right of good/bad governance in the contemporary period).[4] Thus, we do not regard this technique as an appropriate one for the present analysis, and do not report the results here.

In any case, we think it unlikely that the choice of constitutional institutions reflects a country's future prospects for good or bad governance. To be sure, whether a country becomes unitary or federal, parliamentary or presidential, closed-list PR or majoritarian depends in part on a country's colonial heritage, its size and heterogeneity, and on patterns of government that obtain in a regional or historical context. However, these exogenous influences are relatively easy to model and appear as controls in our regression tests. Other factors influencing constitutional choice are more or less stochastic and do not seem to accord with a country's proclivity to good or bad governance. In some

[3] Chosen instruments for Centripetalism include democracy stock (logged), latitude, ethnic fractionalization, religious fractionalization (Alesina et al. 2003), Western Europe (dummy), state history, social conflict (a compilation of measures from Marshall 1999), instability (a compilation of measures from Banks 1994), and population size (1960, logged).

[4] For a general discussion of IV analysis, see Reiss (2003). For a discussion focused specifically on the problem of finding good instruments for political institutions, see Acemoglu (2005).

instances, for example, federal institutions have been chosen because of their anticipated success in resolving conflict among heterogeneous groups (e.g., Canada, India, Switzerland, and the United States). In other instances, unitarism has been viewed as the cure for precisely the same set of conflicts. This is the approach taken by all currently unitary states, whose populations were once – and in many cases remain – fractious and diverse (e.g., France, the United Kingdom). In short, it all depends. It is not the case, therefore, that federalism is chosen only in instances of high conflict or great heterogeneity.

One must also consider the fact that constitution makers generally have notoriously short time horizons. They are usually interested in installing a system that will benefit them personally, their parties, or their constituencies. In this respect, the type of constitution a country arrives at is the product of a highly contingent political battle, with little or no bearing on a country's long-term governance potential.

Finally, one must reckon with the dubious assumptions made by each contending group (or by voters, if the agreement is ratified by the populace). Presidential systems, for example, are commonly viewed as installing "strong" government; however, most political scientists believe that parliamentarism fosters energy and efficiency in the executive. Thus, even where calculations by constitution makers extend to the long-term quality of governance in a polity, they are of dubious significance in achieving that result. Precisely because framers do not know which constitutional factors lead to good governance, whatever wisdom and far-sightedness they may possess is of little practical import.

For all these reasons, we think it fair to regard a country's choices among constitutional institutions as a largely stochastic phenomenon with respect to the outcomes of interest in this study: long-term patterns of good or bad governance.

Now, let us consider the specific formats used to evaluate the cross-national evidence. The regression models adopted here represent our best guess as to the proper specification of highly complex causal relationships.[5] In identifying appropriate controls, we canvassed a wide

[5] Approaches such as this one evolve over time. The present analysis draws in part on Gerring, Thacker, and Moreno (2005), but has some differences. The present empirical tests incorporate a slightly modified set of control variables, a somewhat

range of exogenous factors that might be associated with better or worse governance. (A list of these additional controls is available from the authors.) Variables were retained if they were empirically robust or if a strong theoretical argument could be made for their inclusion in the benchmark equation. We offered two tests of the primary hypothesis, one representing a "full" set of controls and the other a more limited ("reduced-form") set of controls. In most cases, the coefficients and standard errors for our variables of theoretical interest remain stable across these two models, offering further assurance that results are not an artifact of arbitrary specification choices. We conducted further tests on a wide range of other possible control variables (not reported here) to assess their impact on our core results and found no others the inclusion or exclusion of which consistently altered our results.

We have not attempted to test causal mechanisms directly. This is an important task, but not one that is easily undertaken. The most important obstacle is empirical. Most of the presumed causal pathways from constitutional-level institutions to governance are difficult to measure and, as such, resistant to cross-national analysis. For example, while we believe that the cohesiveness of political parties matters a great deal to the quality of governance, and that party strength arises in large part from the shape of constitutional institutions, we are at a loss to measure party strength through time and across a large sample of countries. (This does not mean that the concept of party strength is unmeasurable; it simply means that political scientists have not yet solved this formidable conceptual and empirical challenge. John Carey's work on party voting in democratic legislatures is exemplary, but as yet incomplete.)[6]

Another complication arises from the irregular nature of each set of causal mechanisms. In most cases, there are likely to be myriad pathways leading from centripetal institutions to good governance, and great unpredictability among them. Sometimes causal path A may be determinative; at other times causal path B may be so. Under the circumstances, it would be difficult for a single empirical model to

different collection of dependent variables, and a different method for calculating R^2 values. They also add results for the component parts of the Centripetalism variable (Unitarism, Parliamentarism, and Closed-list PR). Even so, overall results are substantively the same.

[6] Carey (2002).

capture all of these capillaries, even if all the intermediate variables could be precisely and accurately measured. Thus, one is constrained to examine exogenous causes and distal outcomes, without a clear sense of how, *precisely*, X might lead to Y. For these reasons, the question of causal mechanisms is addressed in a frankly speculative fashion (see chapters two, three, and four).

Now let us consider the outcomes at issue in these empirical analyses. The reader will note that various measures of good/bad governance are by no means entirely independent of each other. The eleven chosen dependent variables have important interactions. Political development is dependent upon economic and human development, and vice versa. Each might be regarded, to a certain extent, as a causal mechanism as well as an outcome. We have not attempted to model these interrelationships. Except for the inclusion of a control for baseline GDP per capita, we treat each outcome as discrete. Although the appeal of a "complete" model is tantalizing, we are skeptical about whether such a model could ever be utilized with any degree of confidence, particularly in a time-series format. A poor general model (of anything) is worse than no model at all, for all results become contingent upon every assumption in the model. Thus, after considering the options, we opt for a relatively simple model with fewer moving parts, that is, fewer assumptions.

Additional concerns arise regarding the manner in which we compute our centripetal variables. Recall the historical nature of the theory. We do not expect institutions to exert their effects overnight. It takes time for them to alter or shape perceptions, incentives, interests, and behavior. At the same time, we do not expect the institutional makeup of a country fifty years ago to exert as much influence as its more recent status. This situation calls for an historical perspective, but not one that treats time in a linear fashion. Thus, we constructed our additive variables by adopting a (relatively low) rate of depreciation to discount more distant years (see chapter five). As a diagnostic, we also tested several alternative methods for measuring the historical stock of these political institutions, including a 5 percent depreciation rate and a variety of other historical weighting schemes. None of these alternative stock measurements showed appreciably different results, so long as the depreciation rate was relatively low. By contrast, when governance outcomes are regressed against *contemporary* Centripetalism scores (no historical stock), empirical results are somewhat weaker, though still broadly consistent with those presented here. Such a finding is consistent with the historical nature of our theory.

Centripetalism is understood in this study as a simple aggregate index, with each of its three components weighted equally. Of course, there are many alternative ways to compile such an index. We experimented with various multiplicative terms in order to test the possibility that Unitarism, Parliamentarism, and Closed-list PR might affect each other's relative performance. We found no significant interaction effects of this nature, so the assumption of additivity seems justified.[7]

In the tests shown here, we adopt a minimal threshold of democracy (Polity2 > 0), under the assumption that the work of centripetal institutions will be accomplished whenever a semblance of multiparty competition is present. We also conducted tests that impose a higher threshold of democracy (Polity2 > 5). (This applies both to the construction of the stock centripetalism variables and to the sample of observations upon which governance outcomes are tested.) This somewhat smaller sample of "high-quality" democracies reveals broadly similar relationships between centripetal institutions and governance outcomes. Some results are slightly stronger, others slightly weaker. In any case, no systematic differences appear. There is no reason to suppose, therefore, that results are driven by our choice of a low democracy threshold.

While this investigation has interrogated numerous governance outcomes, it certainly does not purport to be comprehensive. Indeed, no study of this nature could possibly be exhaustive, for the field of possible indicators of good and bad governance is essentially limitless. Any outcome that may be understood as having a positive or negative effect on the public interest, is plausibly related to basic-level constitutional structures, and provides reliable data coverage across a sample of countries could be enlisted as a dependent variable. We have focused only on outcomes in three policy areas – political development, economic development, and human development – and on variables that measure a selective set of dimensions across these vast areas. Thus, although our data analysis includes many of the most

[7] We also conducted tests that exclude nonbicameralism from the Unitarism component of Centripetalism (so that Unitarism = nonfederalism) and obtained substantively similar results.

commonly employed indicators of governance, we cannot preclude the possibility that additional measures might provide a slightly different picture of centripetalism's causal effect. Further research is warranted, and no doubt will be forthcoming.

WHY NOT A "CASE STUDY" APPROACH?

Before concluding this chapter it may be helpful to contrast the chosen style of analysis – the cross-country regression – with another approach that has often been applied to this genre of question. Traditionally, scholars interested in the effects of constitutions have focused on a single country or a small set of similar countries, examining the relationship between particular constitutional features and governance outcomes over some period of time. This is the *case study* approach to governance.[8] While we lean heavily on this style of evidence in part one of the book (focusing on the vexing question of causal mechanisms), we believe that the case study method has limited potential for testing causal relations between structural institutions and distal outcomes. Understanding these limitations may help to bolster our methodological choice of a cross-country regression model, despite the shortcomings associated with this method.

Note that democratic polities rarely undergo changes in their basic constitutional features. Unitary countries tend to remain unitary and federal countries federal. The same applies to the separation of powers and electoral systems. These features are fairly constant over many decades, and sometimes over centuries. Where change does occur, it tends to be subtle and incremental. Thus, France evolved from a parliamentary to a semi-presidential system from the Fourth Republic to the Fifth. Other countries have also made subtle alterations in their electoral systems, but few have transitioned from majoritarian to closed-list PR, or vice versa. In sum, there is minimal variation through time in the institutions of theoretical interest among the world's democracies. Equally problematic is the fact that the small temporal variation that does occur is usually accompanied by additional changes that might also affect the quality of governance in a country. This means that covariational patterns discovered between constitutional changes and changes in the quality of governance in a given country are difficult to

[8] For example, Weaver and Rockman (1993).

interpret. There are no "natural experiments" in constitutional design that might help us to judge the governance effects of constitutional-level institutions.

Consequently, the most useful variation in democratic constitutional institutions is spatial rather than temporal. Of course, this spatial variation would be amenable to small-N cross-case analysis if countries with very similar cultural, socioeconomic, and historical features adopted different political institutions. Unfortunately, the empirical pattern does not conform to the "most-similar" template. Countries with similar cultures and historical experiences tend also to have similar institutions. The parliamentary system is common in Europe, for example, while presidential systems are the norm in the Americas. These empirical collinearities are problematic for any analysis, but they pose particular difficulties for the case study method.[9]

Moreover, since our principal causal hypothesis concerns the *combined* effects of all three constitutional institutions, judging these effects in a case study format would require situations (a) where a country changes from centripetal to decentralist or vice versa, or (b) where centripetal and decentralist polities stand side by side (i.e., they are similar in all respects except that one is centripetal and the other decentralist). These sorts of cases simply do not exist.

A final problem is perhaps most significant, methodologically speaking. We anticipate that constitutions have diffuse, probabilistic effects across a wide range of governance outcomes but do not have overwhelming or deterministic effects upon any single outcome. This sort of causal relationship is virtually impossible to examine in a case study format, where relationships must typically be (a) strong and (b) highly consistent in order to be detected.[10]

It is said that some theories attempt to explain 10 percent of the variance across 100 cases, while others attempt to explain 100 percent of the variance across 10 cases. We argue that the relationship between political institutions and governance more closely approximates a situation of the former sort. Constitutional institutions exert a small

[9] Gerring (2004, 2007). A "most-different" systems research design is also problematic, for reasons explored in Gerring (2007). Even if it were potentially useful, it offers little help here. Countries that differ greatly in their cultural and historical backgrounds typically have very different institutional arrangements as well.

[10] Gerring (2004, 2007), Sekhon (2004).

influence across a very wide range of policy outcomes. Their effects are broad and diffuse. This means that an analysis focusing on a small number of cases or a small number of outcomes will underestimate the cumulative causal effects of these institutions.

For these reasons, we believe that cross-national regression analysis offers a more useful test of our hypotheses than the more traditional method of case study analysis. A global approach to governance expands the scope of evidence, maximizes variance on relevant explanatory and outcome variables, and mitigates problems of case selection. By no means do we wish to suggest that cross-country regressions are unproblematic. Many preferable research designs may be imagined. Indeed, global regressions fall very far from the experimental ideal.[11] As Churchill might have said, cross-country regression is the worst possible research design for the study of institutions and governance, except for all the others. Indeed, we must judge the merits of any research design against those of other research designs that one might plausibly apply to the theoretical question at hand. Research should be theory-driven, not methodologically driven. We are drawn to the cross-country regression format not because we are besotted by this research design but rather because we see no better expedient.

Note, finally, that countries are inherently more difficult to study than individuals or small groups. Consequently, what we know about constitutional institutions will always be more uncertain than what we know about voting behavior or legislative committees. However, the uncertainty of our understanding of this subject is counterbalanced by its substantive importance. It is eminently useful to know what effect (if any) constitutional institutions have on the quality of governance in a democracy. The experience of the world's democracies over the past four decades provides critical evidence for use in testing these causal relationships, as we hope to have shown in the preceding chapters.

ESTIMATING CAUSAL EFFECTS

Assuming that centripetalism does have a causal effect on governance (i.e., that the correlation is not spurious), one might still wonder about

[11] Kittel (2006).

TABLE 7.1. *Estimated effects of centripetal democratic governance*

Dependent Variable	Effect of Full Centripetalism: After Twenty Years	After Fifty Years
Tax revenue (% of GDP)	3.06	6.64
Telephone mainlines[a] (per 1,000 people, ln)	10.9%	23.7%
Participation (voter turnout, % adult population)	5.57	12.09
Democratic volatility	−0.11	−0.24
Import duties (% of imports)	−2.55	−5.52
Trade[a] (% of GDP, ln)	7.6%	16.6%
GDP per capita[a] (1995 dollars, ln)	4.4%	9.5%
Infant mortality[a] (per 1,000 live births, ln)	−5.5%	−11.9%
Health expenditure (% of GDP)	0.34	0.74
Total schooling (avg. total years of schooling)	−0.27	−0.59

[a] Effects for logged dependent variables reflect the effect of the specified period of Centripetalism as a percentage change in the dependent variable. Units or scale of dependent variable are in parentheses. Estimates of the effects of fully centripetal institutions use statistically significant Centripetalism coefficients from full models (column 1) in Tables 6.1–6.11.

the strength of this relationship. How much *practical* impact do constitutional institutions have on governance outcomes? In order to gauge this question we employ the coefficients for Centripetalism from our full-model regression tests to measure the effects of twenty and fifty years of centripetal institutions immediately preceding the observation year on the ten governance outcomes where it attains statistical significance (i.e., excluding growth volatility). Table 7.1 displays the results.

With respect to political development, our results suggest that fifty years of full Centripetalism is associated with an increase of more than 6 percent of GDP in tax revenue, more than 23 percent more telephone mainlines, 12 percent greater voter turnout (as a percentage of the adult population), and a drop in the five-year sum of democratic volatility of 0.24 (roughly 0.16 of a standard deviation of the summed variable). In the area of economic development, we find a drop in import duties of more than 5 percent of imports, a greater than 16 percent (as a share of GDP) rise in trade, and nearly 10 percent higher per capita income. In human development, fifty years of fully centripetal institutions are associated with almost 12 percent fewer infant deaths, greater health expenditure amounting to just under three quarters of 1 percent of GDP, and just under a year less total average schooling.[12]

As might be expected, the practical effect of Centripetalism varies considerably across outcomes. While modest in some areas (e.g., democratic volatility, health expenditure, and total schooling), it is much more substantial in others (e.g., telephone mainlines, trade, GDP per capita, and IMR). Separate tests employing standardized beta coefficients (taking into account the different units used across variables in order to assess their relative empirical relationship with the dependent variable) show that Centripetalism has an empirical relationship with good governance on a par with many of the stronger control variables used in this analysis.[13]

To be sure, these estimates are far from exact. We offer them as a heuristic device, a way of indicating the importance of constitutional institutions relative to other important factors. Based on this exercise, the causal effects of centripetal institutions seem to be significant from a practical, or policy perspective.

Granted, the full significance of centripetal political institutions can be judged only against the backdrop of the much larger set of policies and policy outcomes that we have *not* considered here. It is important to bear in mind that the eleven variables considered in this book merely scratch the surface of all the outcomes and dimensions of good governance. We are severely constrained by space limitations and, more fundamentally, by the scarcity of adequate indicators of good governance. We argue in chapter six that in order to provide a valid empirical test of political-institutional impact, a governance indicator must have a fairly clear normative import; must be causally related to basic-level political institutions; must be spatially and temporally

[12] The coefficients for the logged dependent variables (telephone mainlines, trade openness, GDP per capita, and IMR) reported in Tables 6.1–6.11 measure the effect of a one-unit change in the independent variable on those outcomes as a proportional change in the dependent variable. Thus, a one-unit change in the independent variable results in a change in the dependent variable of $100*\beta$ percent (Wooldridge 2002).

[13] For the models in which it attains statistical significance in the expected direction, the standardized coefficient for Centripetalism falls at approximately the forty-second percentile when compared to other right-hand-side variables. That is to say, Centripetalism falls well within the upper half of independent variables in terms of its causal strength. Its substantive effect on governance is greater than most of the other factors considered here.

valid; and must provide adequate data coverage across countries and through time (preferably, at least several decades). Few indicators satisfy all, or even some, of these demanding criteria. Consequently, we regard the limited tests performed in this book as illustrative, rather than comprehensive. We expect that a more thorough test of a broader range of policies and policy outcomes would corroborate the findings presented here.

In sum, the most important question for us to consider is not whether constitutional factor X has a substantial causal effect on outcome Y, but rather whether the *cumulative* effect of constitutional factor X across *all* outcomes of theoretical and practical interest is significant. Indeed, it is the far-reaching nature of constitutional institutions that has motivated interest in constitutional structures from Aristotle to the present. The evidence compiled in this analysis suggests that centripetal institutions lead to modest improvements in governance across ten out of eleven dimensions of good governance. We infer – though we cannot prove – that this pattern of improved governance operates across a broader range of outcomes.

This inference rests upon two assumptions. First, we assume that different dimensions of good governance (not to mention different measures of the same dimension) are highly correlated. Good things often go together, as do bad things. Second, we assume that the causal mechanisms vetted in the first part of the book (chapters two, three, and four) apply across a broad range of policy areas. The generality of the theory gives us confidence in this assumption, though, as we have repeatedly stressed, it is not a provable assumption.

PART THREE

CONCLUSIONS

We began this book by contrasting two normative models of governance: decentralism and centripetalism (see Table 1.1). We argued that institutions combining centralized authority and popular inclusion are likely to lead to better governance overall. This is the theory of centripetalism. Three institutions are paramount to this theory, in terms of both their causal impact and their expected causal exogeneity: unitarism (the absence of federalism and bicameralism), parliamentarism (the absence of a directly elected executive with policy-making powers), and closed-list PR (defined in contrast to majoritarian and preferential-vote systems).

In the first part of the book, we attempted to trace the causal pathways that might plausibly connect centripetal constitutions with good governance outcomes across a range of policy areas. We argued that these causal mechanisms could be profitably (though not uniquely) reduced to three intermediate factors: party government, conflict mediation, and policy coordination. Figure 1.2 depicts the expected interrelationships among these concepts.

In the second part of the book, we generated specific research hypotheses and examined empirical results from a series of cross-national regressions employing a wide range of policy outcomes in the areas of political, economic, and human development. These showed strong correlations between centripetal institutions and measures of good governance, patterns that are robust to changes in model specification and measurement techniques. Table 6.12 summarizes the results.

In the concluding section, we comment briefly on the nature of this enterprise. What is the role of “grand theory” in the discipline of political science and in the practical arena of policy making? And what is its justification?

8

In Defense of Grand Theory

In recent years, a growing corpus of work within the disciplines of political science and economics has focused on the causal effect of political institutions on the quality of governance.[1] Having fallen into desuetude for nearly a century, the concerns of eighteenth- and nineteenth-century political commentators like Rousseau, Bentham, Bagehot, Bryce, Lowell, and Wilson – not to mention classical writers such as Aristotle – are once again front and center. This is driven in part by a renewed theoretical interest in the role of institutions in structuring behavior (the "new institutionalism"). But it is also motivated by a more specific question: what role might basic-level political institutions play in fostering political, economic, and human development? The general assumption, as framed by James Buchanan, is that "constitutions and constitutional structure are the instruments through which reforms must be effected if ultimate improvements in patterns of political outcomes are to be expected."[2]

Yet within this burgeoning literature there have been few attempts to systematically test, and theorize, the impact of democratic institutions

[1] Following is a very short list of works focused on *democratic* political institutions (the subject of this book): Bardhan and Mookherjee (2000), Bellamy (1996), Berggren et al. (2002), Brennan and Buchanan (1985/2000), Buchanan and Tullock (1962), Bellamy and Castiglione (1996), Congleton and Swedenborg (2006), Ferejohn et al. (2001), Finer et al. (1995), Mueller (1996), Mudambi et al. (2001), Persson and Tabellini (2003), Roller (2006), Sartori (1994), Scully (1992), Weingast (1993).

[2] Buchanan (2002: 1).

across a wide range of policies and policy outcomes. Usually, writers limit themselves to a single political institution and a single outcome – one X/Y relationship, with the usual ceteris paribus conditions. Thus, scholars might explore the role of electoral systems in structuring party systems[3] or trade policy outcomes,[4] but not both (much less a wider range of outcomes). And, whatever institutions and outcomes they might choose to explore, scholars home in on particular mechanisms – causal factors that lie close, in causal distance, to the object of explanation. Often the empirical scope is limited to a small sample of countries or a relatively narrow time period.[5] Recent work by Torsten Persson and Guido Tabellini is broader than most.[6] Even so, the authors make no attempt to provide a unified theory of good governance.

The narrow-angle, microanalytic approach to social phenomena is shared by scholars who practice a wide variety of methods, including case studies, experiments, formal models, and quantitative analysis. It also encompasses a wide variety of disciplinary backgrounds, including anthropology, economics, political science, and sociology.[7] The turn toward the microanalytic is historic, and perhaps unprecedented (albeit little-noticed). The academy has refocused its attention from Big Things – a la Freud, Marx, and Weber – to Little Things.

In contrast to most contemporary work on the problem of governance, our endeavor is ambitious, both theoretically and empirically. Note that centripetalism is an unusual sort of theory. It purports to explain a wide range of governance outcomes. It has an explicitly normative orientation (it is about good government, rather than government per se). It concerns distal ("structural"), rather than proximal, causal relationships. And it invokes a wide range of causal mechanisms, none of which are easily subjected to numerical reduction. As such, it harkens back to an earlier style of theorizing. Indeed, the centripetal model owes a strong theoretical debt to Woodrow Wilson and other theorists in the responsible party government mold (see chapter one).

[3] Taagepera and Shugart (1989).
[4] Rogowski (1987).
[5] For example, Weaver and Rockman (1993).
[6] Persson and Tabellini (2003).
[7] Achen (2002), Hedstrom and Swedberg (1998).

The question then arises: Is the theory of centripetalism *too* big? How general a theoretical frame is appropriate to the topic of good governance? The arguments presented in part one and the validity of the findings presented in part two depend upon the willingness of readers to contemplate a large theoretical frame. We have left it to the end to take up this cudgel because it is clearer, by now, what the fruits of such an inquiry might be.

Let us begin by stating the obvious: we have no quarrel with micro-foundational work. This is the style of most of our own prior work, and it will undoubtedly orient much of our work in the future. Moreover, micro- and macro-foundations need not be at odds with one another. Ideally, micro-processes fit neatly within macro-models, and macro-models incorporate and build upon the foundations of micro-theory. In our most hopeful moments, we imagine tracing a direct causal link through a series of identifiable, and measurable, intervening variables that stretch from basic-level political institutions to governance outcomes.

Sometimes this is possible. Usually, however, it is not. How, for example, would one demonstrate a unique causal chain connecting parliamentarism with lower infant mortality? Such arguments are necessarily highly speculative because the factors affecting IMR are myriad. At best, parliamentarism explains only a modest portion of the variance on such distal outcomes. And because the causal connections between X and Y run through multiple intermediate steps – none of which can be accurately measured – one is at pains to trace a determinate causal path.

Should this uncertainty lead us to conclude that basic-level institutions have *no* impact on distal policy outcomes? This conclusion seems unwarranted. At any rate, it can no more be assumed than its obverse. The general point here is that while one might be inclined to doubt an isolated finding such as the foregoing (parliamentary systems lead to lower infant mortality), one is forced to take this finding seriously *if* it is embedded in a larger pattern. Insofar as parliamentarism is correlated with better governance across a wide range of outcomes, the notion that parliamentarism saves babies no longer seems so far-fetched, even if we cannot trace a distinct causal path.

To be sure, there is no guarantee that a wide-ranging study of governance will find consistent causal relations between an institution and a set of policy outcomes. And the fairly consistent patterns uncovered in part two of the book may be challenged. But this misses the point. Even if *in*consistency is the rule of the day, we shall not discover this fact unless and until a consistent methodology is applied to a wide range of policy outcomes. Narrowly focused studies cannot answer wide-ranging questions because their methods and samples are, for the most part, quite distinct. As such, they do not cumulate well.

Our theoretical hubris is motivated by the need to build general theory from otherwise dissociated empirical findings. While governance in one form or another has been under investigation since roughly the beginning of time, there have been few integrative approaches to this time-honored subject. The theory of centripetalism, as elaborated in previous chapters, is an attempt to put the loose pieces of this vast puzzle together in a single framework. Whether the theory works is for the reader to decide. For the moment, we dwell on the utility of theorizing on a grand scale.

From a Popperian perspective, the grandness of a theory is not at all problematic. Ceteris paribus, the greater the breadth of a theory, the wider the range of its empirical implications and the more falsifiable it will be – so long, that is, as it generates specific causal predictions. On this score, Big Theory is preferable to Small Theory.

More problematic is the distance that inevitably separates structural causes from their distal outcomes and the corresponding complexity of the intervening causal processes, as discussed in part one of the book. Indeed, there are so many possible causal pathways that we hesitate to employ the term "causal chain," for the set of interacting variables is more complex than the chain metaphor allows. It is here that the theory of centripetal governance is most vulnerable. There are many things going on inside the box – many ways in which unitary, parliamentary, and closed-list PR institutions might structure political outcomes within a democratic framework. Moreover, one is at pains to specify precisely which causal mechanisms are at work on which outcomes, or how much weight each causal path bears (in a situation of multicausality). Indeed, we can barely distinguish among diverse causal pathways, which seem to merge seamlessly into one another. This is perhaps the most bothersome aspect of the theory: it sits atop a large and opaque black box. The inputs and outputs are clear, but what goes on inside is not.

Some of this theoretical ambiguity could be avoided if we approached the topic of governance with a finer lens – for example, by looking at a single institution and a smaller set of governance outcomes, as standard practice suggests. However, many fine-grained studies also wave a blithe hand over the question of causal mechanisms. Indeed, the most common explanatory tropes in the field of governance are concepts like accountability, public goods, competition, veto points, stationary bandits, credible commitment, and encompassing-ness. These sorts of explanations are hardly any clearer, or more falsifiable, when invoked in the context of a specific X/Y relationship. They remain unmeasurable, and hence highly speculative. This does not mean we should banish them from the social science lexicon. But it does mean that we might question the usual wisdom: that a narrower focus leads to clearer, and more operational, causal mechanisms.

Our defense of a broader theoretical brush is that it brings into focus elements of the political process that are left untouched by more narrowly focused studies. Recall that politics is a holistic enterprise. That which occurs in one institutional sphere, or policy sphere, is rarely limited to that particular sphere. Constitutional institutions have multiple effects, and these effects intermingle. The workings of a bureaucracy may be affected by unitarism, parliamentarism, and closed-list PR, to take just one example. And constitutional institutions affect the ways in which other constitutional institutions operate. In short, politics involves causal relationships that are properly understood as "systemic," that is, interdependent, holistic, and nested. A *system effect*, as defined by Robert Jervis, refers to a situation in which "a) a set of units or elements is interconnected so that changes in some elements or their relations produce changes in other parts of the system, and b) the entire system exhibits properties and behaviors that are different from those of the parts."[8] Polities are political systems. This means that any attempt to isolate a particular X and Y without examining surrounding causal factors is bound to involve considerable causal reductionism.

[8] Jervis (1997: 6). We place more emphasis on the first component of this definition than the second, but are otherwise in tune with Jervis's understanding of "system effects."

These observations are not intended to derogate the study of micro-foundations. They are merely intended to call attention to the fact that both micro- *and* macro-foundational work are subject to a species of causal reductionism. The forest-versus-trees debate is miscast insofar as writers imply that by narrowing the scope of our investigation we might, somehow, be getting down to the real (bare-bones, essential, micro-foundational) truth. In fact, a narrower focus may occlude the true nature of causal relationships at work in a polity. Both the trees and the forest induce their own sort of myopia.

It is our hope to have constructed a theory that is not only broad in reach, but also determinate and specific enough to be falsifiable. Note that writers in the public choice tradition have been constructing grand theories of political economy for nearly a century. Such work generally begins with an abstract model of institutional incentives based on a few a priori, and necessarily highly simplified, assumptions about political behavior.[9] This is then extended to explain a wide range of policy outcomes. The problem frequently encountered in this style of work is that the model, as constructed, is far removed from the realities of politics. This means that the writer is at pains to confirm the theory, that is, to distinguish its empirical claims from the claims of rival theories. It is not clear, for example, how Andrei Shleifer and Robert Vishny's theory of the "grabbing hand" might be falsified.[10] The same might be said for many theories in the rational choice genre, which are perhaps better regarded as theoretical *frameworks* rather than falsifiable propositions.[11]

Our final argument for a macro-theoretical approach is pragmatic. We are constrained to live with some set of constitutional institutions, if we wish to avoid anarchy. Definitionally speaking, there is no way around this. The relevant question is, which institutions shall we have? Since it seems likely that a particular institution such as

[9] Barro (1973), Barzel (2002), Bates et al. (1998), Baumol (1965), Becker (1976), Breton (1996), Buchanan and Musgrave (1999), Buchanan and Tullock (1962), Hammond and Miller (1987), Hardin (1997), Levi (1988, 1997), Mueller (1997), Musgrave and Peacock (1958), Niskanen (1971, 1994), Oates (1972), Peltzman (1976), Posner (1974), Scully (1992), Shleifer and Vishny (1998), Stigler (1972), Tiebout (1956), Weingast (1993), Wittman (1995).

[10] Shleifer and Vishny (1998).

[11] Green and Shapiro (1994).

parliamentarism affects a wide range of policies, it seems logical to investigate a broad assortment of these policies, rather than just one or two. Highly disaggregated studies run the risk of missing the big picture, and this, as it happens, is the most policy-relevant part of the problem. For we cannot switch institutions on a whim to suit different policy needs.

Consider the skeptic's counterargument when faced with structural causes, distal outcomes, and difficult questions of causal assessment. Parliamentarism might influence infant mortality rates, but then again it might not. The skeptic may claim that we simply do not know, and by the nature of the evidence cannot know, the answer to this sort of question, at least not with any degree of certitude. The best approach when faced with an intractable empirical problem, according to the ultra cautious mode of scientific endeavor, is avoidance. Let us leave this matter for politicians, journalists, and amateur prognosticators. We thereby preserve the methodological purity of social science by addressing only those questions that can be settled in a more or less definitive manner. Indeed, some methodologists appear to recommend the abandonment of structural-level causal arguments altogether on account of their fuzziness and lack of determinacy.[12]

We feel that such a position privileges methodological purity over methodological utility. The choice of topics for investigation should be driven by their relevance, not by abstract considerations of method. The test of method and theory is not an absolute threshold but a sliding bar. It consists of adopting the best theory and method available to examine the empirical problem at hand.[13] We need to know whether constitutional political institutions affect the governance process, and if so, what those effects might be – even if the results of such an investigation are necessarily somewhat speculative, as they are in this study. Naturally, it is important to emphasize the high degree of uncertainty that accompanies any answers at which we arrive. But the assignment of uncertainty should not doom the enterprise. Worse than uncertain knowledge is soothsaying, and this is what we are reduced to if we refuse to investigate the basic constitutional question that faces all policy makers and concerned citizens. In this quest, exclusive attention

[12] Achen (2002).

[13] Dewey (1938), Gerring (2001: epilogue).

to micro-foundations will not suffice; we must also assemble those micro-foundations into a macro-argument. Otherwise, practical questions, as well as theoretical advances, are stymied. If this requires some degree of speculation, and a continual acknowledgement of causal complexity, then so be it. This is the entry price of doing useful social science.

APPENDIX A

Defining Good Governance

This book purports to describe the political-institutional foundations of good governance within democratic polities. We operationalize this ineffable concept across three policy areas – political development, economic development, and human development – each of which we capture with several empirical indicators (see chapter six). We believe that each of these indicators has a fairly clear normative valence: it is good, or bad, for governance. Yet the reader may wonder how we arrived at this determination. What is "good governance," anyway? Does it mean anything at all? Or worse, is it simply a misleading label for a particular ideological agenda?

Arguably, the concept of good governance functions as a rhetorical mask for views propounded by international financial institutions (e.g., the World Bank, the IMF, the WTO), economists, the United States, and a crop of neoliberal reformers around the world. Indeed, the term's rise in popularity coincides suspiciously with the rise of the "Washington Consensus" policy model in the late 1980s and 1990s. There is, in short, ample reason for skepticism when approaching this vexed term.[1]

If there is no current consensus over what good governance means (in policy- and outcome-specific terms), and if no such consensus is likely to be forthcoming, then any choice of policies and policy outcomes must be viewed as highly arbitrary, and all causal arguments

[1] Hewitt de Alcantara (1998), Weyland (2003).

based upon those outcomes will have no clear normative implications, or will be tied to problematic assumptions about the role of government. That is to say, centripetal institutions might be associated with a particular set of policies and policy outcomes, as demonstrated in chapter six. However, if we cannot identify those policies as preferable to others, then we cannot conclude that centripetal institutions are actually superior to decentralized institutions. The results would be ambiguous from a programmatic perspective.

It is therefore incumbent upon us to identify a set of policies and policy outcomes that can be classified as desirable or undesirable. We must be able to distinguish among the good, the bad, and the indifferent in order to identify a meaningful set of dependent variables.

Of course, we could sidestep this question entirely by stating that our conclusions are contingent upon certain normative assumptions that lie beyond the scope of our investigation, and leave it at that. However, insofar as one wishes to craft a coherent argument, rather than one that is simply stipulative, one must explain the grounds upon which some policies were included on this list and others excluded, and the procedures through which the included measures were judged good or bad. This involves not only practical criteria such as data availability but also normative criteria: namely, what constitutes good governance? Chapter six explains our basic rationale for selecting the variables and indicators that we use in this study. Our intention in this appendix is not to justify those specific choices further, but rather to delineate a series of criteria that might guide further work in the field of governance studies. Here, we argue against the narrow focus of most governance studies and for a broader moral-philosophical ground that we label "deliberative."

NARROW NORMATIVE FRAMEWORKS

Conventionally, good governance has been grounded upon a consideration of preferences, Pareto optimality, efficiency, public goods, the market, and/or rent. Since these six visions of good governance are closely related, the following discussion contains a good deal of unavoidable overlap. Nonetheless, these normative frameworks are logically and conceptually distinct, and thus deserve separate treatment.

Preferences. Perhaps the most straightforward method of specifying good and bad governance is by reference to existing preferences among the general public. From this perspective, good governance is what people say it is. This might be understood as majority preference or the preference of the median voter, and may or may not include weightings for issue salience.[2] These are minor, though not unimportant, technical issues. The bigger problem is that, as Mencken was fond of pointing out, what the public wants at any given point in time is not always what the public deserves. Indeed, the job of a responsible public servant is sometimes to resist the pressures of public opinion when such opinions might damage the public's long-run interests. Insulation, as well as responsiveness, characterizes good government. Distinguishing between them is a matter of determining which course of action is in the public interest. In short, the public interest should not be equated with the public's preferences at any given point in time, though preferences must certainly be taken into account.

The conveyor belt vision of governance (preferences → policies) becomes even more unsatisfactory when one considers the role of elites in *creating* preferences. Schumpeter points out that "the will of the people is the product, not the motive power of the political process."[3] If governments shape public opinion, as much research on this topic suggests, then preferences cannot form a solid foundation for the consideration of good governance.[4] The notion of a public interest, to some extent independent of public opinion, seems essential.

Pareto Optimality. A second way to define good governance rests on the concept of Pareto optimality. A Pareto-optimal policy is one that cannot be changed without harming at least one person. Similarly, a Pareto improvement is one that helps at least one person but hurts no one, a pure gain (in utilitarian terms).[5] This minimalist goal is unobjectionable; we are aware of no political philosophy that would dismiss a

[2] Colomer (2001), Powell (2000).

[3] Schumpeter (1942/1950: 263).

[4] Rothstein and Steinmo (2002: chapter one), Steinmo (2001).

[5] This may be restated in terms of preferences. "A policy is Pareto efficient," state Hammond and Miller (1987: 1170) "if there exists no other policy unanimously preferred to it."

Pareto-superior outcome on conceptual grounds. Yet Pareto optimality has an exceedingly narrow scope of application. Indeed, we cannot think of a single public policy that is truly Pareto optimal, strictly construed. A Paretian vision of good governance would amount to no governance at all, since all political actions impose costs on someone. There is at least one person opposed to every hanging, it has been observed. By this logic, Paretian criteria would preclude criminal justice. Of course, no one interprets Pareto optimality so restrictively. However, if one interprets Pareto optimality loosely, it becomes difficult to distinguish it from garden variety utilitarianism.

Efficiency. A third baseline for specifying good governance is found in the concept of efficiency, which may be defined as "the production of a commodity at the minimum possible cost in terms of the resources used."[6] If a government provides a service or good that could be provided at lower cost in some other fashion (either by the free market or by some alternate organization of public provision), then we might reasonably consider this as an example of bad governance.

But efficiency is not the sum total of good governance. For example, an efficiently designed program to discriminate against a minority group should not be considered an example of good government. One must contemplate both means and ends when making such judgments. Thus, however useful the notion of efficiency might be, it provides only a partial basis on which to judge the complex matter of good governance.

Public Goods. A fourth approach to governance identifies goodness in governance with the provision of public goods.[7] A public good is conventionally defined as a good that is (a) joint (nonrival) and (b) nonexcludable. One person's enjoyment of a good does not impinge

[6] Le Grand (1991: 425–6) differentiates several broader definitions of efficiency, including allocative efficiency ("whether the commodity concerned meets the wants of its consumers as effectively as possible") and dynamic efficiency ("the capacity of firms to innovate and thereby to lower their costs of production or to find better ways of meeting the wants of consumers," or, in the context of the nation-state, "the rate of economic growth"). For further discussion of this protean term, see Breton (1996: 17–24).

[7] Barro (1973), Colomer (2001), Samuelson (1954).

upon another's enjoyment of the same good, and no one can be prevented from consuming that good. In such circumstances, actors have incentives to free-ride on the efforts of others, generating collective action problems. As such, a free (unregulated) market generally underprovides public goods.

This seems clear enough at first blush. But a second glance at this concept reveals a central ambiguity. Virtually any policy currently undertaken by governments might be defended as a public good. This is presumably true of all environmental and conservation programs, energy programs, and defense programs. It could also be argued that it is true of agricultural subsidies (which help provide the public good of food self-sufficiency and family farms and which do not exclude anyone who might become a farmer), investment tax credits, and antitrust policies (which help provide the public good of economic competition and are nonexclusive in the sense of benefiting directly all those who might choose to invest their capital, as well as consumers). One could go on. While carrying a strong intellectual appeal, the distinction between public and private goods is difficult to operationalize.

Perhaps a stricter reading of "public goods" can save the concept from such troubling ambiguities. Clearly, proponents of this concept have a more limited role for government in mind. Let us imagine a restrictive interpretation of "public goods" that includes only those goods enjoyed by all members of a polity at some point in their lives. This would presumably include defense, clean air, law and order, and so forth. Even so, such a definition of the concept would have nothing to say about how large the defense budget should be, how clean the air, water, and soil should be, or how these goods might be prioritized. The theory of public goods tells us nothing about how to discern the relative goodness of goods (or about what even qualifies as a "good"). All public goods are treated equally.

A second problem is that few public goods are enjoyed equally by all members of a polity. Indeed, some members may not gain any benefit at all from the provision of a (so-called) public good. Money spent cleaning up a toxic dump benefits those who live in the immediate vicinity but has no demonstrable effect on others. Money spent for parks benefits those who enjoy the outdoors. Crime is more severe in some areas than in others, requiring an uneven pattern of spending.

Indeed, many goods that are plausibly public in nature can be provided only when services, benefits, or sanctions are concentrated – for example, on a geographic area where a military base is located, on the poor, the unemployed, criminals, minorities, the rich, offshore oil explorers, banks, and so forth. The universality test of public goods does not restore precision to this highly ambiguous concept.

The Market. The test of the marketplace, closely associated with the concept of a public good, may help to clarify things. Arguably, if a market produces a good or could potentially produce a good, the government should not. This litmus test seems to offer a simple criterion for evaluating the goodness of governance across a range of policy contexts (and it is of course quite similar to the public/private good distinction).

Yet governments produce some private goods more efficiently than private markets do. One thinks of health care, where the OECD's most statist system, the United Kingdom's, is also one of the most efficient, and the most market-based system, that of the United States, is perhaps the least efficient. Private markets can provide many public goods, but only at the cost of excluding those who cannot pay, or providing services of differential quality (high quality for the rich, low quality for the poor). Still others, like utilities, transportation, and communication, are often considered natural monopolies and require, at the very least, governmental regulation, thus occupying an intermediate position in this state/market dichotomy. To hold that government should not be in the business of producing goods that would otherwise be produced by the free exchange of goods and services begs the question of which mode of production is more efficient and effective, *given some public interest goal.* Free markets provide jobs, but not for everyone. Does this then constitute a government responsibility? Is it a public or private good? The stylized contrast between private and public goods is useful as a first cut but does not go far enough in resolving specific policy questions.

Rent. Closely related to the foregoing approaches is the concept of rent, or directly unproductive (DUP) activities. Hector Schamis defines rent as "that part of the payment to an owner of resources above the alternative earning power of those resources, that is, as a receipt in excess of opportunity cost. Rents are profits, but the 'in excess' clause indicates that those kinds of profits are realized in activities where freedom of entry is curtailed."[8]

The concept of rent seeking, like that of public goods, is often difficult to operationalize. This is largely because the assignment of a rent is contingent on a variety of metrics that are themselves difficult to operationalize – for example, a "true" free market or open-entry cost, a "first-best solution," overall "productivity," or a "conventional utility function."[9] When applied to the operation of governments, the notion of rent seems fairly useful in cases where a government service might be provided, or is already provided, by the private sector and where the efficiency of this service is amenable to quantitative measures. If a private mail carrier can deliver a letter from point A to point B for half the cost of the government service, then one might reasonably label the excess cost demanded by the government provider as rent. But in most instances of government activity such comparisons are difficult to draw. Indeed, the notion of a public good presumes the existence of a large class of goods that have no "true" (market) value. Here, our only recourse is to evaluate what level of service a government might provide under different circumstances, and at what cost. This is a useful thought experiment. But here the concept of rent seems no different from standard notions of efficiency, which we have already discussed. Moreover, certain (so-called) rents may stimulate economic development or help achieve other socially desirable outcomes. Tax-free export-promotion zones, temporary tariffs levied in order to protect "sunrise" industries, selective credit allocation focused on export industries, special treatment for less-developed regions, affirmative action policies, copyright and patent protection, subsidies to businesses and individuals who use and/or produce environmentally

[8] Schamis (2002: 9). For a long list of alternative definitions of rent seeking, see Samuels and Mercuro (1984: 55–6). DUP activities have been defined as those that "yield pecuniary returns but produce no goods or services that enter a conventional utility function directly or indirectly" (Bhagwati et al. 1984: 18). From this perspective, rent seeking is a subset of DUP activities. For other work on these interrelated subjects, see Ades and Di Tella (1999), Beck and Connolly (1996), Bhagwati (1982), Buchanan et al. (1980), Colander (1984), Krueger (1974), Lambsdorff (2001), Murphy et al. (1993), and Scully (1991).

[9] Bhagwati et al. (1984: 18), Khan and Jomo K.S. (2000), Lambsdorff (2002), Tullock (1980: 17).

friendly technologies, bailouts to strategically important industries or industries affected by unforeseen (and temporary) global or climactic shocks: all might be viewed, at least in certain circumstances, as justifiable rents.[10] In short, the concept of rent is not very clear; to the extent that it is clear, it is not equivalent to good governance.[11]

A DELIBERATIVE FRAMEWORK

In contrast to these rather narrow frameworks, we argue for the adoption of a broader framework captured in the concept of *deliberation.* The best way to resolve the normative question of governance (what are "good" and "bad" policy outcomes?) is to deliberate in a disinterested fashion upon the public interest. The public interest refers to actions and states of affairs that we, hypothetical citizens in a hypothetical state, could agree upon during the course of an unconstrained process of deliberation.[12] Colloquially, good governance refers to what is (truly) in the public interest, an idea one can trace back at least as far as the Roman Republic (*salus populi suprema lex esto*).[13]

[10] Khan (2000).

[11] For similar criticisms of "rent" as an analytic device, see Lambsdorff (2002).

[12] This formulation follows closely Walter Lippmann (1955: 42), who writes of the public interest as "what men would choose if they saw clearly, thought rationally, acted disinterestedly and benevolently." Our approach builds on a growing body of work devoted to deliberation by James Bohman, Joshua Cohen, Jon Elster, James Fishkin, Archon Fung, and many others. There are, of course, quite a number of ways of conceptualizing or simulating this process of deliberation, for example, an "original position" (Rawls 1971), a "reflective equilibrium" (Rawls 1971), an "ideal-speech situation" (Habermas 1984), a "dialectical" method (Gewirth 1978: 43), or a "veil of uncertainty" (Brennan and Buchanan 1985/2000: 35). These heuristic devices have similar goals. All seek to strip away from the process of deliberation any aspect deemed arbitrary, and hence inappropriate. But rather than rest at a theoretical or procedural level, or at the level of "basic institutions," we attempt in this study to identify specific policies and policy outcomes that would be agreed upon in a fully deliberative process. Thus, our argument begins where existing work on deliberation and political philosophy leaves off. For work on the concept of the public interest that runs parallel to our arguments, see Barry (1962), Colm (1962), and Pennock (1962). Robert Dahl (quoted in Colm 1962: 116–17) provides a contrasting view of the public interest by arguing that "[i]f one rejects the notion that public interest is some sort of amalgamation of private interests, there is little philosophical mileage to be gained from using the term at all."

[13] This phrase is drawn from the Twelve Tables, which served as a sort of constitution for the original Roman Republic. Loosely translated, it means "the welfare of the people must be the supreme law" (Gordon 1999: 14).

To be sure, deliberation does not exclude any of the criteria introduced thus far (preferences, Pareto optimality, efficiency, public goods, the market, and rent). Nor does it exclude more abstract concepts such as justice and the general welfare. We assume that deliberation draws upon the entire range of our moral and empirical vocabulary. Our argument is quite simple. Because none of the narrower concepts just reviewed provides a determinate and convincing yardstick for good governance, we must seek to resolve this question in a different way.

To invoke the model of deliberation is to imply something more than deep thinking.[14] A deliberative approach presumes, first, that all persons within a political community have equal moral worth. Each should count for one and none for more than one, in Bentham's well-worn phrase. It presumes, second, that deliberation focuses on the needs and desires of the whole community, rather than on particularistic interests or ideologies. The important point is that whatever goal or set of goals is identified as a basis for deliberation should be general in purview, not targeted to a particular perspective or interest.

It presumes, third, that a wide variety of goals may be relevant to the consideration of any particular policy issue. These goals will have to be weighed according to their intrinsic importance and their bearing on the issue at hand. Deliberation is rarely a hierarchical calculus in which each value can be placed neatly within another and assigned a particular weight. It demands, rather, a balancing of ultimate and midlevel values and goals so as to achieve the most satisfactory resolution possible for a society as a whole. The concept of public interest deliberation is a convenient way of calling attention to this delicate process of weighing and estimating, with an eye toward taking everyone's interests into account.[15]

It presumes, fourth, that the process of consideration is truly deliberative – that is, logical (not internally contradictory), evidence-based (wherever relevant), and disinterested (not merely a reflection of one's own interests). The work of social science is integral to any deliberative process focused on political subjects, even though, we hasten to add, social science cannot answer all questions.

[14] The following discussion builds on Bohman (1996), Chambers (2003), Elster (1998), Fishkin (1991), and Fung (2005).

[15] This conforms to a "pluralistic" vision of moral philosophy, as adumbrated by William Galston, Stuart Hampshire, Thomas Nagel, and Bernard Williams (see Galston 2002: 5).

It presumes, finally, that the process of deliberation is oriented toward a consideration of consequences. Only by contemplating alternative outcomes can we hope to reach agreement on how to prioritize, and hence choose among, alternative courses of action. Any cost-benefit analysis, even where concrete numbers are not assignable to specific courses of action, rests on a consideration of counterfactuals. In the language of economists, we must consider each alternative's opportunity costs. What else might one do under the circumstances, and what would the results of this alternative course of action be? Consequentialism renders concrete the otherwise nebulous notion of a public interest.

IS DELIBERATION PRACTICAL?

We argue that political processes, policies, and policy outcomes that pass this deliberative test should be considered beneficial, and hence good for governance. Of course, this is a hypothetical test. We cannot conduct societywide studies of deliberative reason in action to determine what the general public would consider to be in the public interest on a range of public policies.[16] Even so, we imagine that on most issues, where evidence and moral considerations are both fairly straightforward, consensus could be reached on a societywide level. In other words, we presume that the results of our own deliberative process are not unlike conclusions that others might reach, given sufficient time, attention, knowledge, and public spirit. We can reason about the public interest even if it is not practical to engage all citizens in such deliberations for all public policies. Our selection procedures thus serve as a microcosm of that public debate. In this sense, our approach enlists Kant in the service of Habermas. Universal reason and actual ("real-life") deliberation are complementary processes.

Indeed, despite the prevalence of sharp partisan conflict and interest-based behavior in most political arenas today, there is remarkable agreement on the goodness and badness of specific policy outcomes. Most citizens prefer a government that dispatches business efficiently, encourages economic growth, avoids war (while defending national

[16] Fishkin (1991).

borders), maintains order, preserves civil liberties, and helps those in need. A government that achieves these goals would, in most parts of the world, be perceived as serving the public interest. This, in the simplest of terms, constitutes good governance.

Politics, from this perspective, is a pragmatic debate over the most efficacious means to achieve mutually agreed-upon ends. Political conservatives characteristically believe that the best way to help the poor is by stimulating economic growth through the market. Liberals believe that growth does not always trickle down and that, consequently, the expansion of social welfare programs is necessary to alleviate poverty. This classic argument is thus reducible to an essentially empirical question, not a question of moral fundamentals. Here, as elsewhere, partisan strife often hides a good deal of cross-partisan agreement.

This consensus is probably broader today than it was a century ago. At the present time, fundamental debates over the viability of a market-based economy – capitalism versus socialism – have given way to more refined debates over the viability of particular policy instruments in alleviating generally acknowledged social ills. (Will an increase in the minimum wage help the working class by raising wages, or hurt the working class by raising unemployment?) This is not to say that political ideologies have disappeared; indeed, they continue to play a central role in all political communities.[17] Yet partisans on the left and right appear to recognize more common ground than they did in the early twentieth century. This area of consensus allows for judgments about good governance that transcend partisan politics.

Note that deliberation relies on *public* statements for and against public policies. This is important because statements made publicly, in full view of all members of a community, are more likely to reflect the general interests of that community than statements uttered in private conversation or in small groups of like-minded individuals. This is because claims based on self-interest or narrow, particularistic interests have little appeal and little public legitimacy. Thus, although the

[17] By "ideology" we mean a relatively coherent, differentiated, and enduring set of values, ideas, and policies. On the concept of ideology, see Gerring (1997). On the role of ideology in the United States, see Gerring (1998), where it is argued that in the United States, somewhat contrary to the pattern in other Anglo-European countries, there has not been a significant diminution in partisan ideologies (see also Thomas 1975, 1979).

well-off are usually leery of redistribution, they tend not to oppose such policies publicly on grounds of self-interest or personal privilege. There are no generally accepted rights adhering to social class. (Even in India, the prerogatives of caste are rarely openly asserted.) Rather, opposition to redistribution takes the form of appealing to consensual goals such as economic growth or the alleviation of poverty. If property is forcibly redistributed, it may be argued, all will suffer; if market mechanisms are respected, all will gain. This is a public interest argument. Moreover, it is amenable to empirical analysis. Pending a resolution of this empirical question, and pending a truly deliberative process, we can imagine reaching societywide consensus on the matter.

Thus, in claiming that a given policy is in the public interest we are not declaring that it is uncontested or even that a majority of citizens favor it. We are certainly not declaring that it is in everyone's interest. Achieving the public interest does not entail a pursuit of Pareto optimality. It simply calls attention to a range of policies about which existing disagreements are primarily instrumental rather than substantive, a matter of means rather than ends. With *this* set of policies consensus is possible, at least in principle, across ideological, class, ethnic, and other cleavages.

Consensus is thus partly a matter of fact, insofar as citizens do agree on the desirability of a wide range of policies and policy outcomes, and partly a useful fiction, insofar as we imagine that they might agree under circumstances of full deliberation. Of course, we cannot specify a precise threshold of consensus (actual or potential) above which a policy might become a matter of "public interest." It is a question of degree. Some policies have the potential to call forth greater consensus than others.

Issues such as the death penalty, abortion, and the regulation of recreational drugs are, in many polities, hotly contested. Here it is the outcomes themselves, not just the means of their achievement, that are disputed. Yet even here deliberation is well advised. Indeed, we can imagine no other method of reaching a just consensus on these charged issues. However, it is clearly more difficult to achieve. This genre of fundamentally contested issues therefore lies outside the scope of the present investigation.

The question of who is included in this consensus must also remain somewhat ambiguous. To suppose that agreement may be reached among citizens of the same polity, who presumably share similar moral principles and principles of moral reasoning, sounds plausible. It is somewhat more problematic when one presumes that the public interest extends across cultural boundaries, as we do here. Even so, we suspect that most of the conclusions that we draw in this study are not culturally specific to any particular nation or group of nations.[18] Thus, we set no bounds on the scope of this investigation or the scope of its applicability except to say that it is predicated on contemporary perspectives.[19]

We are cognizant of the fact that there is an important ceteris paribus qualification to any policy consensus. We hesitate to recommend a policy or policy outcome, no matter how beneficial, if it has strongly deleterious effects on other policies or policy outcomes that are held to be desirable. Social equality, for example, is universally acclaimed, but only if all other things (or most other things) are equal. Wherever measures to achieve equality may conflict with other goals, such as prosperity, one may question the goal of equality. In order to address the ceteris paribus difficulty we limit the purview of this study to governance policies and outcomes that are expected to have positive or neutral effects on other good governance outcomes. They are positive-sum. In considering redistributional policies, for example, we focus on those that are generally considered to be cost-effective and market-friendly.

The goals of politics are manifold, and thus not easily contained within a single philosophical system. Yet this diversity need not impair

[18] This must remain a matter of conjecture; we are aware of no cross-cultural experiments in moral reasoning pertaining to matters of public policy.

[19] The fact that this investigation is historically situated (in the early twenty-first century) does not undermine its validity. Social science, to the extent that it addresses problems that people care about, is always constrained by the knowledge and perspectives of a particular era. This project is no different from any other in this regard. We might also observe that consensus on matters of governance has waxed and waned through human history. During the medieval period, an "Aristotelian" consensus held sway among the educated classes of Europe. Questions of governance were understood within Aristotelian categories and judged accordingly. Thus framed, it was possible to speak of good and bad governance without striking a partisan pose. We are in a similar situation today, except that the consensus is more or less global in scope and extends beyond the literati. Whether this set of shared perspectives will increase in breadth and consensus, or decompose into some new partisan/philosophical/epistemological cleavage(s), cannot be foreseen.

the attainment of consensus on many specific policies and policy outcomes. Such consensus is possible because an outcome like urban sanitation can be grounded in many moral systems and arrived at by many deliberative routes. It is virtually everybody's reflective equilibrium. This is perhaps what is meant by the old saw that there is no Democratic or Republican method of cleaning city streets.

APPENDIX B

Alternative Theories Revisited

A theory is convincing only to the extent that it outpaces its rivals. Thus, in order to fully evaluate the success of centripetalism in accounting for good governance we must balance its successes and failures against the successes and failures of contending paradigms. In this appendix we return to the primary foil of the narrative, the decentralist model of good government, first introduced in chapter one.

We begin with a reconsideration of the general theory of decentralism, according to which democratic government works best when power is deconcentrated from the center. This theory, we argue, suffers from two major conceptual difficulties. First, it is not clear how decentralized a polity should be (or in what respects) in order to maximize good governance. Second, insofar as the theory rests on an implicit comparison between the operation of politics and markets, it is not clear whether (or in what respects) decentralized polities reproduce the virtues of a free market.

From thence, we proceed to a more focused explication of one influential exemplar of the decentralist ideal. Up to this point we have treated decentralism as if it were a unified theory. Readers conversant with the voluminous literature cited in chapter one are well aware that the label glosses over a great deal of variation. Indeed, some might prefer to call decentralism an orientation, rather than a theory. We are agnostic on this point. Before concluding this book, in any case, we want to explore one influential tradition of decentralist work in greater detail: the *veto points* model, as elaborated by Philip Keefer and Witold Henisz.

In the concluding section, we discuss the *consensus* model developed by Arend Lijphart and associates. This model, which stimulated our own thinking (to an extent that is difficult to clarify after many years), defies easy categorization. It is neither wholeheartedly decentralist nor wholeheartedly centripetalist. Even so, it stands as the most influential general theoretical statement about the functioning of democratic polities. As such, it demands close attention.

A CENTRAL AMBIGUITY

In order to be convincing, a normative theory of government should be capable of identifying institutions that produce good government without a great deal of backing and filling. There should be minimal slippage between theory and operationalization. The theory must be falsifiable.

Yet one finds that the most basic institutional questions associated with the theory of decentralism go begging. How many formally independent political bodies should be formed? How independent should they be? How many offices should be elective? How many different election cycles should be created? How long should elective tenures be? What number of consecutive terms should be allowed? Are direct referenda (presumably a decentralizing institution) conducive to good governance? If not, why not? The list goes on.

There is considerable disagreement among writers we have labeled "decentralist" on these details. Of course, they are not mere details; they are, in fact, integral to any theory of governance. Decentralist logic implies that smaller constituent units will be superior to larger units, ceteris paribus. Yet no one seems to favor a return to sovereign city-states or villages. Thus, decentralist theory is caught in a paradox. Smaller is better, but only to a point, and the theory is ambiguous on the question of when or how this point might be achieved. Indeed, from a theoretical standpoint decentralism is difficult to distinguish from anarchism or libertarianism (and these theories too are fraught with ambiguity). It is unstable – indeed, it makes no sense – without some set of supplementary principles, to which we now turn.

THE MARKET MODEL

One way of supplementing the decentralist vision is to say that institutions should be constructed in such a way as to maximize efficiency. But this provokes the obvious question: which institutions *are* most efficient (and how do we determine "efficiency")? An institutional theory of government cannot fall back on an ex post evaluation of efficiency or utility.

Another way of resolving the problem of theoretical ambiguity is by recourse to the metaphor of the free market. Indeed, advocates of decentralized political institutions often view the marketplace as a normative model of politics. To William Baumol, Gary Becker, James Buchanan, Charles Tiebout, Gordon Tullock, and their followers, government is good to the extent that it exemplifies the virtues of the market, that is, open competition. Although government is, by definition, a monopoly (at the very least, it possesses a monopoly on the use of physical force), these writers have argued that it can be structured in such a way as to maximize competitive forces. Increased competition translates into enhanced accountability and, ultimately, improved provision of public goods.[1] Becker explains:

> An ideal democracy is defined as *an institutional arrangement for arriving at political decisions in which individuals endeavor to acquire political office through perfectly free competition for the votes of a broadly based electorate*.... In an ideal political democracy competition is free in the sense that no appreciable costs or artificial barriers prevent an individual from running for office, and from putting a platform before the electorate. The transfer of activities from the market to the state in a political democracy does not necessarily reduce the amount of competition, but does change its form from competition by enterprises to competition by parties. Indeed, perfect competition is as necessary to an ideal political democracy as it is to an ideal free

[1] Bac (2001), Barro (1973), Baumol (1965), Beck and Connolly (1996), Becker (1968, 1976, 1983), Becker and Stigler (1974), Breton (1996), Buchanan and Musgrave (1999), Buchanan and Tullock (1962), Buchanan et al. (1980), De Haan et al. (1999), Goel and Nelson (1998), Hardin (1997), Holsey and Borcherding (1997), Lake and Baum (2001), Levi (1988, 1997), Niskanen (1971, 1994), Oates (1972), Ostrom (1983), Palda (1999), Peltzman (1976), Posner (1974), Rasmusen and Ramseyer (1992), Schwartz (1994), Scully (1991, 1992), Shleifer and Vishny (1993), Stigler (1972), Tiebout (1956). For overviews of this literature, see Becker (1976), Mueller (1997), Musgrave and Peacock (1958), and Wittman (1995). For critical discussion of the market model and its application to politics, see Pierson (2004: chapter one).

> enterprise system. This suggests that the analysis of the workings of a free enterprise economy can be used to understand the workings of a political democracy.[2]

So constructed, "[a]n ideal political democracy would be perfectly responsive to the 'will' of the people."[3]

There are several difficulties with this model of politics (understood as a normative model). First, the issue of competition, while fairly clear in a market setting, is more opaque in a political setting. What is a competitive relationship in politics, and how might it be enhanced (or diminished)? Competition among whom? Does competition refer to relationships (a) among candidates within parties, (b) among candidates across parties, (c) among parties, (d) among governing institutions, or (e) among some combination of the foregoing? With respect to all these questions we must add the inevitable follow-up question: to what degree is competition desirable? Competition among candidates could be increased to the point that elections occur monthly, or even weekly, with no barriers to nomination or election, and low campaign costs. Yet few writers would advocate such an institutional design. Moreover, competition at one level may impede competition at another, forcing one to decide where to encourage and where to suppress competitive forces. To take one example, enhancing competition among candidates within a party detracts from the competition that might otherwise exist among parties, for they are no longer unitary bodies. Intra- and interparty competition are inversely related.[4] Thus, although competition in a democratic polity is undoubtedly an important ingredient of good governance (and indeed plays a central role in the theory of centripetalism), it is insufficient by itself to specify the shape of good institutions. It is by no means a complete theory.

More broadly, theories that view politics through an economic lens must grapple with the question of how far the economic model of human behavior can be extended. Consider Douglass North's model of the state:

> First, the state trades a group of services, which we shall call protection and justice, for revenue.... Second, the state attempts to act like a discriminating

[2] Becker (1976: 34).

[3] Ibid., 35.

[4] Schattschneider (1942).

monopolist, separating each group of constituents and devising property rights for each so as to maximize state revenue. Third, the state is constrained by the opportunity cost of its constituents since there always exist potential rivals to provide the same set of services.[5]

The question is: does this view of the state, and of politics more generally, accurately describe the motives and behavior of politicians and citizens?

Note that although economic models are useful for elucidating certain relatively constrained situations of strategic choice (such as buying and selling), they may offer a misleading picture of political situations where options are much more fluid, where there are no overwhelming material incentives, or where the analyst wishes to understand long-term institutional developments rather than short-term individual behavior. Politics at an aggregate level – that is to say, at the level of a nation-state – involves the actions of a multitude of actors at both the elite and the mass level. It is characterized by an extreme indeterminacy such that it is often difficult to say what one's "self-interest" consists of in any particular situation. To the extent that interests can be calculated, they are often multiple and cross-cutting. As such, human motivations and behavior may be as influenced by ideas and identities as by interests. Or, to put the matter somewhat differently, the former cannot easily be reduced to the latter. Indeed, interests may be defined by ideas and identities.

We do not mean to dismiss the importance of interests; indeed, some of our own prior work has put interests at the explanatory forefront. We wish merely to point out that the application of "interests" to the question of good governance is often less tractable than these models imply. All models simplify reality, but market-based models sometimes extend the analogy beyond its usefulness. Politics is like a market, *kinda sorta*.

VETO-POINTS MODELS

In recent years, the decentralist paradigm has come to be understood by many scholars in terms of *veto points*. Veto points (or players), are "individual or collective actors whose agreement is necessary for a change of the status quo. It follows that a change in the status quo

[5] North (1981: 23). See also Alt and Shepsle (1990), Becker (1976), and Mueller (1997).

requires a unanimous decision of all veto players."[6] The veto-points architecture allows one to conceptualize a wide variety of institutions, including political parties, the legislature, the executive, the judiciary, and subnational units, within a single conceptual framework. It also offers a unified explanation for the interrelationships found among a diverse set of institutions.

Naturally, there are many ways to operationalize the notion of a veto point in a polity.[7] The *Checks* indices (Checks1 and Checks2), developed by Thorsten Beck, George Clarke, Alberto Groff, Philip Keefer, and Patrick Walsh as part of the Database of Political Institutions (DPI), "count the number of veto players in a political system, adjusting for whether these veto players are independent of each other, as determined by the level of electoral competitiveness in a system, their respective party affiliations, and the electoral rules."[8]

The *Political Constraints* indices developed by Witold Henisz comprise three separate measures, each of which is operationalized in a somewhat different fashion.[9] "PolConV," the most fully articulated, is described as the feasibility of policy change (the extent to which a change in the preferences of any one actor may lead to a change in government policy) in a political system, and is measured by (a) the independence of five possible veto points (the executive, the lower and upper legislative chambers, subfederal units, and the judiciary), (b) party alignment among the branches, and (c) party alignment within the legislature(s).[10] (The three parts receive equal weight.)

The composite nature of these indices raises a great many aggregation problems. Why do Beck and associates choose to include the legislature but not the judiciary (as in the Henisz index)? Why are electoral systems excluded from the Henisz index? Weighting schemes are also problematic, and one wonders on what basis authors have arrived at their (quite different) choices.

One might also raise questions regarding the measurement of various components employed in these indices. One wonders, for example,

[6] Tsebelis (2002: 19).
[7] Jochem (2003).
[8] Beck et al. (2000: 28). The precise coding of the index is not readily accessible to the uninitiated (see ibid. and explanations offered on Philip Keefer's web site: http://econ.worldbank.org/staff/pkeefer/).
[9] Henisz (2000).
[10] Ibid.

TABLE B.1. *Correlation matrix: veto points indices and democracy*

	Checks2	PCIII	PCV	PCVJ	Political Rights
Checks1	.974	.396	.406	.298	.396
Checks2		.408	.422	.310	.398
Political Constraints III			.884	.839	.789
Political Constraints V				.880	.836
Political Constraints VJ					.694

All variables represent values for the mid-1990s. N varies from 130 to 173. All correlations significant at the 0.01 level (two-tailed). Sources: *Checks* (Beck et al. 2000); *Political Constraints* (Henisz 2000); *Political Rights* (www.freedomhouse.org)

whether it is possible to gauge (quantitatively) the independence of the judiciary across so many country-cases (a crucial component of two of the Political Constraints indices). Henisz relies on a qualitative measure of law and order drawn from PRS/ICRG (a consulting group) to score this measure in one index and employs a measure of judicial tenure for another. Neither is a very close approximation of the concept of judicial independence, however.

Questions of variable choice, weighting, and measurement result in a set of indices that vary within a single work and among the works of different writers. Correlations between the Checks and Political Constraints indicators range from 0.3 to just over 0.4, as shown in Table B.1.[11]

A final question concerns the interpretation of veto-points indices relative to the concept of democracy. Is democracy a facet of veto points, or is it an independent dimension of governance? As we can see in Table B.1, Henisz's indicators are highly correlated with democracy, as measured by the Freedom House indicator of Political Rights (R = 0.69–0.84). The Checks indicators are also correlated with democracy (and statistically significant), though not as strongly. It could be that the positive associations that these scholars have found between veto points and good governance simply reflect the positive association between democracy and good governance. In other words, the existence of divided party control in a government (such as occurs

[11] Beck and associates (2000: 24) note that their coding of the same fourteen countries differs appreciably from the Index of Political Cohesion developed by Roubini and Sachs (1989), such that the correlation between these two indices is only .53, even though the two indices (Checks and the Index of Political Cohesion) aim at very similar underlying concepts.

with great regularity in the United States and in many other separate-powers systems) may reflect the fact that these countries are democracies, for it is difficult to imagine different parties controlling different branches in an authoritarian regime. Highly aggregated indices such as these, when tested across good governance outcomes, should *not* be interpreted to mean that democracies function better when control of the legislature and the executive is divided among several parties. This would require a more disaggregated measure of institutional arrangements.

Of course, there is no reason not to subsume democracy within the concept of veto points if it is theoretically derivative. This is a difficult question to resolve.[12] But surely, such a demonstration must begin by disaggregating the veto-points index into its component parts so as to determine if all of these parts, or only some of them, have positive governance effects. As constructed by the Keefer and Henisz teams, the veto-points indices are large and unwieldy instruments. It is impossible to determine empirically which aspects of the indices are exerting which effects.

Perhaps the most important objection to the veto-points model is theoretical, however. It is the same difficulty that we have already noted with respect to other decentralist models. There is no strong theoretical reason to surmise that more veto points per se will translate into better governance outcomes. George Tsebelis, whose work provides the theoretical touchstone for the veto-points model, clarifies his own position vis-à-vis those of some of his more enthusiastic followers. Veto points, Tsebelis concludes, explain why polities have more or less capacity to change course (i.e., to alter policy from the status quo); the existence of a greater number of veto points will usually mean a more stable policy environment. The point is, "sometimes policy stability is desirable; at other times policy change is necessary."[13] In his view, and in ours, there is no reason a priori to prefer either stability or change. One's stance must depend on the policy in question. Sometimes reform is required; sometimes a defense of the status quo is warranted.

[12] What is clear is that the claim deserves more attention than it has received thus far by scholars of veto points.

[13] Tsebelis (2000: 443).

We are not convinced that a veto-points elaboration of the decentralist ideal provides strong theoretical or empirical support for the proposition that good governance is achieved by fragmenting political power.

THE CONSENSUS MODEL

Of all the work reviewed in chapter one and in this appendix, the centripetal model owes its greatest debt to Arend Lijphart's seminal work over the past four decades. Although we demur from some of his theoretical assertions and expand on the scope of his empirical tests, there is a close kinship between this project and that undertaken in *The Politics of Accommodation* (1968), *Democracy in Plural Societies* (1977), *Democracies* (1984), and *Patterns of Democracy* (1999), as well as in numerous articles by Lijphart and others.[14]

Lijphart conceptualizes political systems along a single spectrum running from *majoritarian* to *consensus*. A polity is majoritarian to the extent that a single group is able to rule through simple majority or plurality. A polity is consensual to the extent that leaders find it necessary to rule through super-majorities, which is interpreted as a move toward greater consensus.[15]

Ten specific institutions matter in this determination: (1) the effective number of parliamentary parties (two-party versus multiparty systems), (2) minimal winning one-party cabinets (concentration of executive power in single-party majority cabinets versus executive power sharing in broad multiparty coalitions), (3) executive dominance (executive-legislative relationships in which the executive is dominant versus executive-legislative balance of power), (4) electoral disproportionality (majoritarian and disproportional electoral systems versus proportional representation), (5) interest group organization (pluralist interest group systems with free-for-all competition among groups versus coordinated, "corporatist" interest group systems aimed at compromise and concertation), (6) federalism/decentralization

[14] Crepaz et al. (2000), Lijphart (1968, 1977, 1984b, 1999), Powell (2000).

[15] The consensus model opens up decision making to "as many people as possible" (Lijphart 1999: 2). It "tries to share, disperse, and limit power in a variety of ways" (ibid.).

(unitary and centralized government versus federal and decentralized government), (7) bicameralism (concentration of legislative power in a unicameral legislature versus division of legislative power between two equally strong but differently constituted houses), (8) constitutional rigidity (flexible constitutions that can be amended by simple majorities versus rigid constitutions that can be changed only by extraordinary majorities), (9) judicial review (systems in which legislatures have the final word on the constitutionality of their own legislation versus systems in which laws are subject to a judicial review of their constitutionality by supreme or constitutional courts), and (10) central bank independence (central banks that are dependent on the executive versus independent central banks).[16]

The first element listed parenthetically along each of these ten dimensions is the majoritarian ideal; the second is the consensus ideal. Thus, a country exemplifying a multiparty system, executive power sharing in broad multiparty coalitions, an executive-legislative balance of power, proportional representation, coordinated ("corporatist") interest group systems aimed at compromise and concertation, federal and decentralized government, bicameralism (division of legislative power between two equally strong but differently constituted houses), a rigid constitution that can be changed only by extraordinary majorities, judicial review, and central bank independence is the purest case of consensus. Switzerland is the best extant example.

According to Lijphart, better governance across a range of outcomes should emanate from consensus institutions. Readers will notice that this set of institutions bears more than a casual resemblance to the veto-points model discussed earlier.[17] However, Lijphart's discussion of these issues, and some of his choices of operationalization, mark key departures from the decentralist ideal. Indeed, they foreshadow our arguments for centripetalism.

A key issue concerns whether decentralized institutions lead to mutual vetoes (i.e., defection) or power sharing (i.e., cooperation). If it is the latter, Lijphart and his colleagues reason, better policies are

[16] Headings and numbering are drawn from Lijphart (1999: 246) and parenthetical explanations from Lijphart (1999: 3–4). All are direct quotations from the text. For further commentary, see Birchfield and Crepaz (1998), Crepaz (1996, 1998), Crepaz et al. (2000), Crepaz and Moser (2002), Lijphart (1984b), and Powell (2000).

[17] Lijphart (1999: 302) refers specifically to "divided-power institutions."

likely to result.[18] This is quite similar to our reasoning; indeed, it is the very heart of the idea of centripetalism. However, the point is lightly theorized in Lijphart's main theoretical work and is not integrated into the ten-part typology set forth here.

Lijphart's empirical strategy is to factor-analyze the ten institutional factors and then conduct tests on various outcome measures of good governance using the two underlying dimensions that account for most of the variance. In this fashion, Lijphart distinguishes between an *executive-parties* dimension (comprising the first five variables just listed) and a *federal-unitary* dimension (comprising the latter five variables). As it happens, only the first dimension shows a consistent relationship to good governance across Lijphart's chosen sample of thirty-six long-term democracies.[19] Since the first dimension closely resembles the centripetal model, our results, across a much larger sample, may be viewed as providing corroborating evidence – but only for the first dimension of the consensus model.

Perhaps the greatest difference between the consensus and centripetal models is that they identify *different institutions* as key causal variables in the governance process. Of the ten features of consensus, only two, federalism and bicameralism, correspond to core features of the centripetal model. We would argue that many of the defining variables in the consensus model have only weak or ambivalent effects on the overall quality of governance. The rigid nature of a constitution, for example, seems much less important than other features of constitutional design. Other features of Lijphart's schema seem likely to be endogenous relative to other features of the polity. For example, power sharing in the executive usually occurs when parliamentarism is combined with a PR electoral system; in this sense it is not really an exogenous institutional feature of polities. At the same time, Lijphart ignores or downplays certain additional causal mechanisms that we believe to be central to the achievement of good governance, for example, strong political parties and institutions that effectively coordinate policy choices.

A theoretical difficulty with the consensus model is its high level of aggregation. In this respect, the tests introduced by Lijphart suffer

[18] Birchfield and Crepaz (1998) contrast "competitive" and "collective" veto points. See also Crepaz and Moser (2002), and Goodin (1996).

[19] Lijphart (1999: chapters 15–16).

from the same conceptual ambiguity as the tests conducted by Keefer and Henisz. Lijphart combines five elements in each of the two latent variables, as described earlier; none are tested independently. Lijphart might counter that the choice of variables is secondary to the overall theory: since all the variables belong to a single argument (consensus), and since it is this argument that is of theoretical and empirical interest, one rightly focuses on the overall theory rather than on its component parts. This is true as far as it goes, and is similar to our approach in combining Centripetalism's three subcomponents into a single aggregate indicator (though our empirical analysis also breaks them out separately).

Questions can be raised, however, about the conceptual unity of Lijphart's model. For example, why is interest group pluralism – the diffusion of interest group representation – classified as a feature of majoritarianism rather than of consensus? It would seem that the multiplication of groups in civil society should be classified in much the same way as the multiplication of groups in government: if multiparty systems are a feature of consensus, why not multi–interest group systems? Moreover, why is a feature of civil society grouped together with a typology in which all the other elements are political institutions? And why are some political institutions, such as parliamentarism/presidentialism, left untheorized and untested?

Of course, every far-reaching model of governance generates a degree of ambiguity. Conciseness and comprehensiveness impose predictable costs. In this respect, Lijphart's consensus model is no different from the veto-points model – or the centripetal model, whose ambiguities we explored in chapter eight.

We are grateful to have benefited from Lijphart's expansive and insightful work and from his remarkable capacity to integrate the normative and empirical elements of political science, a vision that we hope to have moved forward in this book. The question of whether the present work is best viewed as a refinement of Lijphart's consensus model, or as a fundamental reconceptualization, need not detain us. We would be delighted with either formulation.

Sources

Aberbach, Joel D., Robert Putnam, and Bert A. Rockman. 1981. *Bureaucrats and Politicians in Western Democracies*. Cambridge, MA: Harvard University Press.

Aberbach, Joel D., and Bert A. Rockman. 1991. "Mandates or Mandarins? Control and Discretion in the Modern Administrative State." In James P. Pfiffner (ed.), *The Managerial Presidency* (Pacific Grove, CA: Brooks/Cole), 162–74.

Acemoglu, Daron. 2005. "Constitutions, Politics, and Economics: A Review Essay on Persson and Tabellini's *The Economic Effects of Constitutions*." *Journal of Economic Literature* 43:4 (December), 1025–48.

Acemoglu, Daron, Simon Johnson, and James A. Robinson. 2003. "An African Success Story: Botswana." In Dani Rodrik (ed.), *In Search of Prosperity: Analytic Narratives on Economic Growth* (Princeton, NJ: Princeton University Press), 80–122.

Achen, Christopher H. 2002. "Toward a New Political Methodology: Microfoundations and ART." *Annual Review of Political Science* 5, 423–50.

Ades, Alberto, and Rafael Di Tella. 1999. "Rents, Competition and Corruption." *American Economic Review* 89:4, 982–94.

Adetunji, Jacob Ayo. 1995. "Infant Mortality Levels in Africa: Does Method of Estimation Matter?" Working Paper Series Number 95.01, Harvard Center for Population and Development Studies (June).

Aghion, Philippe, Alberto Alesina, and Francesco Trebbi. 2004. "Endogenous Political Institutions." *Quarterly Journal of Economics* 119:2 (May), 565–611.

Aldrich, John H. 1995. *Why Parties? The Origin and Transformation of Party Politics in America*. Chicago: University of Chicago Press.

Alesina, Alberto, Arnaud Devleeschauwer, William Easterly, Sergio Kurlat, and Romain Wacziarg. 2003. "Fractionalization." *Journal of Economic Growth* 8:2, 155–94.

Alt, James E., and Kenneth A. Shepsle (eds.). 1990. *Perspectives on Positive Political Economy*. Cambridge: Cambridge University Press.

Alvarez, Mike, Jose Antonio Cheibub, Fernando Limongi, and Adam Przeworski. 1999. ACLP political and economic database and ACLP political and economic database codebook (May).

American Political Science Association. 1950. *Toward a More Responsible Two-Party System*. New York: Holt, Rinehart.

Amorim Neto, Octávio, and Fabiano Santos. 2001. "The Executive Connection: Presidentially-Defined Factions and Party Discipline in Brazil." *Party Politics* 7:2, 213–34.

Anand, Sudhir, and Martin Ravallion. 1993. "Human Development in Poor Countries: On the Role of Private Incomes and Public Services." *Journal of Economic Perspectives* 7:1 (Winter), 133–50.

Andeweg, Rudy B. 1988. "Centrifugal Forces and Collective Decision Making: The Case of the Dutch Cabinet." *European Journal of Political Research* 19, 125–51.

Andeweg, Rudy B. 2000. "Consociational Democracy." *Annual Review of Political Science* 3, 509–36.

Bac, Mehmet. 2001. "Corruption, Connections and Transparency." *Public Choice* 107 (April), 87–96.

Bachtiger, Andre, Markus Sporndli, and Jurg Steiner. 2002. "The Consociational Theory and Deliberative Politics: A Conceptual Framework for a Cross-National Analysis." In Stephen Brooks (ed.), *Conflict and Compromise in Pluralist Democracies* (Westport, CT: Praeger).

Bagehot, Walter. 1867/1963. *The English Constitution*. Ithaca, NY: Cornell University Press.

Bailyn, Bernard. 1967. *The Ideological Origins of the American Revolution*. Cambridge, MA: The Belknap Press of Harvard University Press.

Bailyn, Bernard. 1968. *The Origins of American Politics*. New York: Vintage Books.

Baldassare, Mark. 1998. *When Government Fails: The Orange County Bankruptcy*. Berkeley: University of California Press.

Banfield, Edward C. 1975. "Corruption as a Feature of Governmental Organization." *Journal of Law and Economics* 18:3, 587–605.

Banks, Arthur S. 1994. "Cross-National Time-Series Data Archive." Center for Social Analysis, State University of New York at Binghamton. Binghamton, New York.

Barber, Kathleen L. 1995. *Proportional Representation and Election Reform in Ohio*. Columbus: Ohio State University Press.

Bardach, Eugene. 1977. *The Implementation Game: What Happens after a Bill Becomes a Law*. Cambridge, MA: MIT Press.

Bardhan, Pranab, and Dilip Mookherjee. 2000. "Capture and Governance at Local and National Levels." *American Economic Review* 90:2 (May), 135–9.

Barlow, Robin, and Bilkis Vissandjee. 1999. "Determinants of National Life Expectancy." *Canadian Journal of Development Studies* 20:1, 9–29.

Baron, David P., and Daniel Diermeier. 2001. "Elections, Governments, and Parliaments in Proportional Representation Systems." *Quarterly Journal of Economics* 116:3, 933–67.

Barro, Robert J. 1973. "The Control of Politicians: An Economic Model." *Public Choice* 14, 19–42.

Barro, Robert J., and Jong-Wha Lee. 2000. "International Data on Educational Attainment: Updates and Implications." Working Paper 7911. Cambridge, MA: National Bureau of Economic Research.

Barry, Brian M. 1962. "The Use and Abuse of 'The Public Interest.'" In Carl J. Friedrich (ed.), *Nomos V: The Public Interest* (New York: Atherton), 191–204.

Barth, Fredrik. 1969. *Ethnic Groups and Boundaries: The Social Organization of Cultural Differences*. Boston: Little, Brown.

Barzel, Yoram. 2002. *A Theory of the State: Economic Rights, Legal Rights, and the Scope of the State*. Cambridge: Cambridge University Press.

Bates, Robert H., Avner Greif, Margaret Levi, Jean-Laurent Rosenthal, and Barry Weingast. 1998. *Analytic Narratives*. Princeton, NJ: Princeton University Press.

Baumol, William J. 1965. *Welfare Economics and the Theory of the State*. London: G. Bell and Sons.

Beck, Nathaniel. 2001. "Time-Series Cross-Section Data: What Have We Learned in the Last Few Years?" *Annual Review of Political Science* 4, 271–93.

Beck, Nathaniel, and Jonathan N. Katz. 2001. "Throwing the Baby Out with the Bathwater: A Comment on Green, Kim, and Yoon." *International Organization* 55: 2, 487–95.

Beck, R. L., and J. M. Connolly. 1996. "Some Empirical Evidence on Rent-Seeking." *Public Choice* 87:1–2, 19–33.

Beck, Thorsten, George Clarke, Alberto Groff, Philip Keefer, and Patrick Walsh. 2000. "New Tools and New Tests in Comparative Political Economy: The Database of Political Institutions." Policy Research Working Paper 2283. Washington: World Bank, Development Research Group. For further information, see: personal website, <http//www.worldbank.org/research/bios/pkeefer.htm>; research group website, <http//econ.worldbank.org>.

Becker, Gary S. 1968. "Crime and Punishment: An Economic Approach." *Journal of Political Economy* 76 (March–April), 169–217.

Becker, Gary S. 1976. *The Economic Approach to Human Behavior*. Chicago: University of Chicago Press.

Becker, Gary S. 1983. "A Theory of Competition among Pressure Groups for Political Influence." *Quarterly Journal of Economics* 98, 371–400.

Becker, Gary S., and George J. Stigler. 1974. "Law Enforcement, Malfeasance, and the Compensation of Enforcers." *Journal of Legal Studies* 3, 1–19.

Beer, Samuel H. 1993. *To Make a Nation: The Rediscovery of American Federalism*. Cambridge, MA: Harvard University Press.

Bellamy, Richard (ed.). 1996. *Constitutionalism, Democracy and Sovereignty: American and European Perspectives*. Aldershot, UK: Avebury.

Bellamy, Richard, and Dario Castiglione (eds.). 1996. *Constitutionalism in Transformation: European and Theoretical Perspectives*. Oxford: Blackwell.

Belloni, Frank P., and Dennis C. Beller (eds.). 1978. *Faction Politics: Political Parties and Factionalism in Comparative Perspective*. Santa Barbara, CA: ABC-Clio Press.

Bensel, Richard Franklin. 1984. *Sectionalism and American Political Development 1880–1980*. Madison: University of Wisconsin Press.

Bentley, Arthur. 1908/1967. *The Process of Government*. Cambridge, MA: Harvard University Press.

Berggren, Niclas, Nils Karlson, and Jokim Nergelius (eds.). 2002. *Why Constitutions Matter*. New Brunswick, NJ: Transaction.

Bermeo, Nancy. 2004. "Conclusion: The Merits of Federalism." In Ugo M. Amoretti and Nancydr Bermeo (eds.), *Federalism and Territorial Cleavages* (Baltimore: Johns Hopkins University Press), 457–82.

Bhagwati, Jagdish N. 1982. "Directly Unproductive, Profit-seeking (DUP) Activities." *Journal of Political Economy* 90, 988–1002.

Bhagwati, Jagdish N. 1998. *A Stream of Windows*. Cambridge, MA: MIT Press.

Bhagwati, Jagdish N., Richard A. Brecher, and T. N. Srinivasan. 1984. "DUP Activities and Economic Theory." In David Colander (ed.), *Neoclassical Political Economy: The Analysis of Rent-seeking and DUP Activities* (Cambridge, MA: Ballinger), 17–32.

Bidani, Benu, and Martin Ravallion. 1997. "Decomposing Social Indicators Using Distributional Data." *Journal of Econometrics* 77, 125–39.

Bilodeau, Antoine, and André Blais. 2005. "Le vote obligatoire exerce-t-il un effet de socialisation politique?" Paper presented to the International Colloquium on Mandatory Voting, Institut d'Études Politiques de Lille, October 20–21.

Birchfield, Vicki, and Marcus L. Crepaz. 1998. "The Impact of Constitutional Structures and Collective and Competitive Veto Points: On Income Inequality in Industrialized Democracies." *European Journal of Political Research* 34:2 (October), 175–200.

Bird, Richard, and Francois Vaillancourt (eds.). 1998. *Fiscal Decentralization in Developing Countries*. Cambridge: Cambridge University Press.

Blackstone, William. 1862. *Commentaries on the Laws of England, Volume 1: Of the Rights of Persons*, 3rd ed., ed. Robert Malcolm Kerr. London: John Murray.

Blanchard, Olivier, and Andrei Shleifer. 2000. "Federalism with and without Political Centralization: China versus Russia." NBER Working Paper 7616, National Bureau of Economic Research, Cambridge, MA.

Blondel, Jean, and Nick Manning. 2002. "Do Members of Government Do What They Say? Ministerial Unreliability, Collegial and Hierarchical Governments." *Political Studies* 50:3, 455–76.

Blondel, Jean, and Ferdinand Muller-Rommel (eds.). 1993. *Governing Together: The Extent and Limits of Joint Decision Making in Western European Cabinets*. New York: St. Martin's.

Blondel, Jean, and Ferdinand Muller-Rommel. 1997. *Cabinets in Western Europe*. Houndsmiths, Basingstoke: Palgrave.

Bogaards, Matthijs. 2000. "The Uneasy Relationship between Empirical and Normative Types in Consociational Theory." *Journal of Theoretical Politics* 12:4, 395–423.

Bohman, James. 1996. *Public Deliberation: Pluralism, Complexity, and Democracy*. Cambridge, MA: MIT Press.

Bohn, David E. 1980. "Consociational Democracy and the Case of Switzerland." *Journal of Politics* 42, 165–79.

Bollen, Kenneth A. 1993. "Liberal Democracy: Validity and Method Factors in Cross-National Measures." *American Journal of Political Science* 37, 1207–30.

Bos, Eduard, My Vu, and Patience Stephens. 1992. "*Sources of World Bank Estimates of Current Mortality Rates.*" World Bank Working Paper Series 851. Washington, DC: World Bank.

Bowler, Shaun, and David Farrell. 1991. "Voter Behavior under STV-PR: Solving the Puzzle of the Irish Party System." *Political Behavior* 13, 303–20.

Bowler, Shaun, David M. Farrell, and Richard S. Katz (eds.). 1999. *Party Discipline and Parliamentary Government*. Columbus: Ohio State University Press.

Bowler, Shaun, and Bernard Grofman (eds.). 2000. *Elections in Australia, Ireland and Malta under the Single-Transferable Vote: Reflections on an Embedded Institution*. Ann Arbor: University of Michigan Press.

Brancati, Dawn. 2006. "Decentralization: Fueling the Fire or Dampening the Flames of Ethnic Conflict?" *International Organization* 60:3 (July), 651–85.

Brancati, Dawn. 2007. "The Origins of Regional Parties." *British Journal of Political Science* (forthcoming).

Braun, Dietmar. 1999. "Interests or Ideas? An Overview of Ideational Concepts in Public Policy Research." In Dietmar Braun and Andreas Busch (eds.), *Public Policy and Political Ideas* (Cheltenham, UK: Edward Elgar), 11–29.

Braun, Dietmar, Anne-Beatrice Buillinger, and Sonja Walti. 2002. "The Influence of Federalism on Fiscal Policy Making." *European Journal of Political Research* 41:1 (January), 115–45.

Brautigam, Deborah. 1997. "Institutions, Economic Reform, and Democratic Consolidation in Mauritius." *Comparative Politics* 30:1 (October), 45–62.

Brennan, H. Geoffrey, and James M. Buchanan. 1985/2000. *The Reason of Rules: Constitutional Political Economy*. Republished in *The Collected Works of James M. Buchanan*, vol. 10. Indianapolis: Liberty Fund.

Brennan, H. Geoffrey, and Alan Hamlin. 1994. "A Revisionist View of the Separation of Powers." *Journal of Theoretical Politics* 6:3 (July), 345–68.

Breton, Albert. 1996. *Competitive Governments: An Economic Theory of Politics and Public Finance*. Cambridge: Cambridge University Press.

Brewer, John. 1976. *Party Ideology and Popular Politics at the Accession of George III*. Cambridge: Cambridge University Press.

Brown, Michael E. 2000. "The Causes of Internal Conflict: An Overview." In Michael E. Brown, Owen R. Cote, Jr., Sean M. Lynn-Jones, and Steven E. Miller (eds.), *Nationalism and Ethnic Conflict* (Cambridge, MA: MIT Press), 3–25.

Bryce, James. 1905. *Constitutions*. New York: Oxford University Press.

Buchanan, James M. 1980. "Reform in the Rent-Seeking Society." In James M. Buchanan, Robert Tollison, and Gordon Tullock (eds.), *Toward a Theory of the Rent-Seeking Society* (College Station: Texas A& M University Press), 359–67.

Buchanan, James M. 2002. "Why Do Constitutions Matter?" In Niclas Berggren, Nils Karlson, and Jokim Nergelius (eds.), *Why Constitutions Matter* (New Brunswick, NJ: Transaction), 1–16.

Buchanan, James M., and Richard A. Musgrave. 1999. *Public Finance and Public Choice: Two Contrasting Visions of the State*. Cambridge, MA: MIT Press.

Buchanan, James M., Robert Tollison, and Gordon Tullock (eds.). 1980. *Toward a Theory of the Rent-Seeking Society*. College Station: Texas A&M University Press.

Buchanan, James M., and Gordon Tullock. 1962. *The Calculus of Consent: Logical Foundations of Constitutional Democracy*. Ann Arbor: University of Michigan Press.

Bunce, Valerie. 2004. "Federalism, Nationalism, and Secession." In Ugo M. Amoretti and Nancy Bermeo (eds.), *Federalism and Territorial Cleavages* (Baltimore: Johns Hopkins University Press), 417–40.

Bunce, Valerie. 2005. "Promoting Democracy in Divided Societies." Unpublished manuscript.

Bunce, Valerie, and Stephen Watts. 2005. "Managing Diversity and Sustaining Democracy: Ethnofederal versus Unitary States in the Postsocialist World." In Philip Roeder and Donald Rothchild (eds.), *Sustainable Peace: Democracy and Power-dividing Institutions after Civil Wars* (Ithaca, NY: Cornell University Press), 133–58.

Burki, Shahid Javed, Guillermo E. Perry, and William Dillinger. 1999. *Beyond the Center: Decentralizing the State*. Washington, DC: World Bank.

Burns, James McGregor. 1963. *The Deadlock of Democracy*. Englewood Cliffs, NJ: Prentice-Hall.

Cairns, Alain C. 1988. *Constitution, Government, and Society in Canada*. Toronto: McClelland and Stewart.

Caldwell, John C. 1986. "Routes to Low Mortality in Poor Countries." *Population and Development Review* 12:2 (June), 171–220.

Campbell, Colin. 1983. *Governments under Stress: Political Executives and Key Bureaucrats in Washington, London and Ottawa*. Toronto: University of Toronto Press.

Canning, David, and Marianne Fay. 1993. "The Effect of Transportation Networks on Economic Growth." Discussion Paper Series, Columbia University, Department of Economics.

Carey, John M. 2002. "Getting Their Way, or Getting in the Way? Presidents and Party Unity in Legislative Voting." Paper presented at the annual meeting of the American Political Science Association, Boston, MA (August).

Carey, John M., and Matthew Soberg Shugart. 1995. "Incentives to Cultivate a Personal Vote: A Rank Ordering of Electoral Formulas." *Electoral Studies* 14:4, 417–39.

Carlsson, Sten. 1987. "From Four Estates to Two Chambers: The Riksdag in a Period of Transition, 1809–1921." In Michael F. Metcalf (ed.), *The Riksdag: A History of the Swedish Parliament* (New York: St. Martin's), 165–222.

Carroll, Barbara Wake, and Terrance Carroll. 1997. "State and Ethnicity in Botswana and Mauritius: A Democratic Route to Development?" *Journal of Development Studies* 33:4, 464–86.

Carroll, Barbara Wake, and S. K. Jaypaul. 1993. "The Mauritian Senior Public Service since Independence: Some Lessons for Developing and Developed Nations." *International Review of Administrative Sciences* 59:3, 423–40.

Carstairs, A. M. 1980. *A Short History of Electoral Systems in Western Europe*. London: Allen and Unwin.

Casper, Gerhard. 1989. "An Essay in Separation of Powers: Some Early Versions and Practices." *William and Mary Law Review* 30, 260–1.

Castles, Francis G., Franz Lehner, and Manfred G. Schmidt et al. (eds.). 1988. *The Future of Party Government. Volume III: Managing Mixed Economies*. Berlin: de Gruyter.

Castles, Frances G., and Rudolf Wildenmann (eds.). 1986. *The Future of Party Government. Volume I: Visions and Realities of Party Government*. Berlin: de Gruyter.

Chambers, Simone. 2003. "Deliberative Democratic Theory." *Annual Review of Political Science* 6, 307–26.

Chandler, William. 1987. "Federalism and Political Parties." In Herman Bakvis and William M. Chandler (eds.), *Federalism and the Role of the State* (Toronto: University of Toronto Press), 149–70.

Charlton, Roger. 1991. "Bureaucrats and Politicians in Botswana's Policy Making Process." *Journal of Commonwealth and Comparative Politics* 29:3, 265–82.

Cheibub, José Antonio. 1998. "Political Regimes and the Extractive Capacity of Governments: Taxation in Democracies and Dictatorships." *World Politics* 50:3 (April), 349–76.

Cheibub, José Antonio. 2007. *Presidentialism, Parliamentarism, and Democracy*. Cambridge: Cambridge University Press.

Chhibber, Pradeep K. 1999. *Democracy without Associations: Transformation of the Party System and Social Cleavages in India*. Ann Arbor: University of Michigan Press.

Church, Clive H. 2000. "Switzerland: A Paradigm in Evolution." *Parliamentary Affairs* 53:1 (January), 96–113.

Citrin, Jack, and Donald Philip Green. 1990. "The Self-Interest Motive in American Public Opinion." *Research in Micropolitics* 3, 1–27.

Cohen, Frank S. 1997. "Proportional versus Majoritarian Ethnic Conflict Management in Democracies." *Comparative Political Studies* 30:5, 607–30.

Cohen, Joshua, and Charles Sabel. 1997. "Directly-Deliberative Polyarchy." *European Law Journal* 3:4 (December), 313–42.

Colander, David (ed.). 1984. *Neoclassical Political Economy: The Analysis of Rent-seeking and DUP Activities*. Cambridge, MA: Ballinger.

Collier, Paul. 2001. "Ethnic Diversity: An Economic Analysis." *Economic Policy* 32 (April), 129–66.

Collier, Ruth Berins, and David Collier. 1991. *Shaping the Political Arena: Critical Junctures, the Labor Movement, and Regime Dynamics in Latin America*. Princeton, NJ: Princeton University Press.

Colm, Gerhard. 1962. "The Public Interest: Essential Key to Public Policy." In Carl J. Friedrich (ed.), *Nomos V: The Public Interest* (New York: Atherton), 115–28.

Colomer, Josep Maria. 2001. *Political Institutions: Democracy and Social Choice*. Oxford: Oxford University Press.

Commons, John R. 1907. *Proportional Representation*, 2nd ed. New York: Macmillan.

Congleton, Roger D., and Birgita Swedenborg (eds.). 2006. *Democratic Constitutional Design and Public Policy: Analysis and Evidence*. Cambridge, MA: MIT Press.

Coppedge, Michael. 1994. *Strong Parties and Lame Ducks: Presidential Partyarchy and Factionalism in Venezuela*. Stanford, CA: Stanford University Press.

Cornelius, Wayne A., Todd A. Eisenstadt, and Jane Hindley (eds.). 1999. *Subnational Politics and Democratization in Mexico*. La Jolla, CA: Center for U.S-Mexican Studies, University of California, San Diego.

Cornell, Svante E. 2002. "Autonomy as a Source of Conflict: Caucasian Conflicts in Theoretical Perspective." *World Politics* 54 (January), 245–76.

Cox, Gary W. 1987. *The Efficient Secret: The Cabinet and the Development of Political Parties in Victorian England*. Cambridge: Cambridge University Press.

Cox, Gary W. 1990. "Centripetal and Centrifugal Incentives in Electoral Systems." *American Journal of Political Science* 34, 903–35.

Cox, Gary W., and Mathew D. McCubbins. 1993. *Legislative Leviathan: Party Government in the House*. Berkeley: University of California Press.

Cox, Gary W., and Matthew Soberg Shugart. 1996. "Strategic Voting under Proportional Representation." *Journal of Law, Economics, and Organization* 12:2, 299–324.

Crabb, Cecil Van Meter. 1992. *Invitation to Struggle: Congress, the President, and Foreign Policy*. Washington, DC: Congressional Quarterly.

Cremieux, P. Y., P. Ouellette, and C. Pilon. 1999. "Health Care Spending as Determinants of Health Outcomes." *Health Economics* 8:7 (November), 627–39.

Crepaz, Markus M. L. 1996. "Consensus vs. Majoritarian Democracy: Political Institutions and Their Impact on Macroeconomic Performance and Industrial Disputes." *Comparative Political Studies* 29:1 (February), 4–26.

Crepaz, Marcus M. L. 1998. "Inclusion versus Exclusion: Political Institutions and Welfare Expenditures." *Comparative Politics* 31:1, 61–80.

Crepaz, Marcus M. L., and Vicki Birchfield. 2000. "Global Economics, Local Politics: Lijphart's Theory of Consensus Democracy and the Politics of Inclusion." In Markus M. L. Crepaz, Thomas A. Koelble, and David Wilsford (eds.), *Democracy and Institutions: The Life Work of Arend Lijphart* (Ann Arbor: University of Michigan Press), 197–224.

Crepaz, Markus M. L., Thomas A. Koelble, and David Wilsford (eds.). 2000. *Democracy and Institutions: The Life Work of Arend Lijphart*. Ann Arbor: University of Michigan Press.

Crepaz, Markus M. L., and Ann Moser. 2002. "The Impact of Collective and Competitive Veto Points on Redistribution in the Global Age." School of Public and International Affairs, University of Georgia.

Crepaz, Markus M.L., and Ann Moser. 2004. "The Impact of Collective and Competitive Veto Points on Public Expenditures in the Global Age." *Comparative Political Studies* 37:3, 259–85.

Cronin, Thomas E. 1975. " 'Everybody Believes in Democracy until He Gets to the White House . . .': An Examination of White House–Departmental Relations." In Aaron Wildavsky (ed.), *Perspectives on the Presidency* (Boston: Little, Brown), 362–92.

Crozier, Michael J., Samuel P. Huntington, and Joji Watanuki. 1975. *The Crisis of Democracy*. New York: New York University Press.

Daalder, Hans. 1974. "The Consociational Democracy Theme." *World Politics* 26, 604–21.

Dahl, Robert A. 1956. *Preface to Democratic Theory*. Chicago: University of Chicago Press.

Dahl, Robert A. 1961. *Who Governs? Democracy and Power in an American City*. New Haven, CT: Yale University Press.

Dahl, Robert A. 1967. *Pluralist Democracy in the United States*. Chicago: Rand McNally.

Davis, J. Rufus. 1978. *The Federal Principle: A Journey through Time in Quest of Meaning*. Berkeley: University of California Press.

De Haan, Jakob, Jan-Egbert Sturm, and Geert Beekhuis. 1999. "The Weak Government Thesis: Some New Evidence." *Public Choice* 101:3–4 (December), 163–76.

Delury, George E. (ed.). 1999. *World Encyclopedia of Political Systems and Parties*, 3 vols. New York: Facts on File.

Dent, Martin. 2000. "Nigeria: Federalism and Ethnic Rivalry." *Parliamentary Affairs* 53:1 (January), 157–68.

Derbyshire, J. Denis, and Ian Derbyshire. 1996. *Political Systems of the World*. New York: St. Martin's.

Dewey, John. 1938. *Logic: The Theory of Inquiry*. New York: Henry Holt.

Diamond, Larry. 1999. *Developing Democracy: Toward Consolidation*. Baltimore: John Hopkins University Press.

Dikshit, Ramesh Dutta. 1975. *The Political Geography of Federalism: An Inquiry into Origins and Stability*. Delhi: Macmillan Company of India.

Dimitrov, Martin. 2003. "Federalism and the Enforcement of Intellectual Property Rights (IPR) Laws." Unpublished manuscript, Stanford University.

Dogan, Mattei (ed.). 1975. *The Mandarins of Western Europe: The Political Role of Top Civil Servants*. New York: Wiley.

Dominguez, Jorge. 1998. *Democratic Politics in Latin America and the Caribbean*. Baltimore: Johns Hopkins University Press.

Downs, Anthony. 1957. *An Economic Theory of Democracy*. New York: Harper and Row.

Dreze, Jean, and Amartya Sen. 1989. *Hunger and Public Action*. Oxford: Clarendon Press.

Droop, Henry Richmond. 1869. "On the Political and Social Effects of Different Methods of Electing Representatives." Pamphlets on the History of England in the 19th Century 50.

du Toit, Pierre. 1995. *State Building and Democracy in Southern Africa: Botswana, Zimbabwe, and South Africa*. Washington, DC: United States Institute of Peace.

Easterly, William, and Ross Levine. 1997. "Africa's Growth Tragedy: Policies and Ethnic Divisions." *Quarterly Journal of Economics* 112, 1203–50.

Eaton, Kent. 2000. "Parliamentarism versus Presidentialism in the Policy Arena." *Comparative Politics* 32:3 (October), 355–76.

Eaton, Kent. 2002. *Politicians and Economic Reform in New Democracies*. University Park: Pennsylvania State University Press.

Eaton, Kent. 2006. "Menem and the Governors: Intergovernmental Relations in the 1990s." In Steven Levitsky and M. Victoria Murillo (eds.), *Argentine Democracy: The Politics of Institutional Weakness* (University Park: Pennsylvania State University Press).

Economist, The. 2002. "Finance and Economics: Thirteen into One Won't Go; Canada's Securities Markets." July 13: 69.

Economist, The. 2003. "A Survey of Brazil: Fixing the Finances." Februrary 22: 6–13.

Edwards, Sebastian. 1989. "Trade Orientation, Distortions and Growth in Developing Countries." *Journal of Development Economics* 39:1, 31–57.

Elazar, Daniel J. 1972. *American Federalism: A View from the States*, 2d ed. New York: Crowell.

Elazar, Daniel J. (ed.). 1991. *Federal Systems of the World: A Handbook of Federal, Confederal and Autonomy Arrangements*. Detroit: Gale Research.

Elbadawi, Ibrahim, and Nicholas Sambanis. 2000. "Why Are There So Many Civil Wars in Africa? Understanding and Preventing Violent Conflict." *Journal of African Economies* 9:3, 244–69.

Elgie, Robert. 1997. "Models of Executive Politics: A Framework for the Study of Executive Power Relations in Parliamentary and Semi-presidential Regimes." *Political Studies* 45, 217–31.

Elgie, Robert (ed.). 1999. *Semi-presidentialism in Europe*. Oxford: Oxford University Press.

Elster, Jon (ed.). 1998. *Deliberative Democracy*. Cambridge: Cambridge University Press.

Epstein, Leon D. 1964. "A Comparative Study of Canadian Parties." *American Political Science Review* 58, 46–59.

Epstein, Leon D. 1967/1980. *Political Parties in Western Democracies*. New Brunswick, NJ: Transaction.

Esman, Milton J. 1993. *Ethnic Politics*. Ithaca, NY: Cornell University Press.

Evans, Gord, and Nick Manning. 2002. "Helping Governments Keep Their Promises: Making Ministers and Governments More Reliable through Improved Policy Management." Unpublished manuscript.

Evans, Peter B., Dietrich Rueschemeyer, and Theda Skocpol (eds.). 1985. *Bringing the State Back In*. Cambridge: Cambridge University Press.

Farrell, David M. 2001. *Electoral Systems: A Comparative Introduction*. Houndmills, Basingstoke, Hampshire, UK: Palgrave.

Feigenbaum, Harvey, Richard Samuels, and R. Kent Weaver. 1993. "Innovation, Coordination, and Implementation in Energy Policy." In R. Kent Weaver and Bert A. Rockman (eds.), *Do Institutions Matter? Government Capabilities in the United States and Abroad* (Washington, DC: Brookings Institution), 42–43.

Feldman, Stanley. 1982. "Economic Self-Interest and Political Behavior." *American Journal of Political Science* 26:3 (August), 446–66.

Ferejohn, John, Jack N. Rakove, and Jonathan Riley (eds.). 2001. *Constitutional Culture and Democratic Rule*. Cambridge: Cambridge University Press.

Filmer, Deon, Jeffrey S. Hammer, and Lant H. Pritchett. 2000. "Weak Links in the Chain: A Diagnosis of Health Policies in Poor Countries." *World Bank Research Observer* 15:2 (August), 199–224.

Filmer, Deon, and Lant Pritchett. 1999. "The Impact of Public Spending on Health: Does Money Matter?" *Social Science and Medicine* 49:10 (November), 1309–23.

Finer, Samuel E. (ed.). 1975. *Adversary Politics and Electoral Reform*. London: Anthony Wigram.

Finer, Samuel E., Vernon Bogdanor, and Bernard Rudden. 1995. *Comparing Constitutions*. Oxford: Oxford University Press.

Fiorina, Morris. 1977. *Congress: Keystone of the Washington Establishment*. New Haven, CT: Yale University Press.

Fiorina, Morris. 1980. "The Decline of Collective Responsibility in American Politics." *Daedalus* 109:3, 25–46.

Fisher, Louis. 1985. *Constitutional Conflicts between Congress and the President*. Princeton, NJ: Princeton University Press.

Fishkin, James S. 1991. *Democracy and Deliberation: New Directions for Democratic Reform*. New Haven, CT: Yale University Press.

Fisman, Raymond, and Roberta Gatti. 2002. "Decentralization and Corruption: Evidence across Countries." *Journal of Public Economics* 83:3 (March), 325–45.

Foord, Archibald. 1964. *His Majesty's Opposition, 1714–1830*. Oxford: Clarendon Press.

Ford, Henry Jones. 1898/1967. *The Rise and Growth of American Politics*. New York: Da Capo.

Ford, Henry Jones. 1904/1974. "Municipal Corruption: A Comment on Lincoln Steffens." In John A. Gardiner and David J. Olson (eds.), *Theft of the City: Readings on Corruption in Urban America* (Bloomington: Indiana University Press), 396–408.

Forrest, Alan. 1988. "Federalism." In Colin Lucas (ed.), *The French Revolution and the Creation of Modern Political Culture. Volume 2: The Political Culture of the French Revolution* (Oxford: Pergamon Press), 309–28.

Frankel, Jeffrey A., and David Romer. 1999. "Does Trade Cause Growth?" *American Economic Review* 89:3, 379–98.

Franks, C. E. S. 1987. *The Parliament of Canada*. Toronto: University of Toronto Press.

Freeden, Michael. 1978. *The New Liberalism: An Ideology of Social Reform*. Oxford: Clarendon Press.

Freedman, David A. 1991. "Statistical Models and Shoe Leather." *Sociological Methodology* 21, 291–313.

Friedman, Milton. 1962/1982. *Capitalism and Freedom*. Chicago: University of Chicago Press.

Fung, Archon. 2005. "Deliberation before the Revolution: Toward an Ethics of Deliberative Democracy in an Unjust World." *Political Theory* 33:2 (June), 397–419.

Galanter, Marc. 1984. *Competing Equalities: Law and the Backward Classes in India*. Berkeley: University of California Press.

Gallagher, Michael. 1988. "Conclusion." In Michael Gallagher and Michael Marsh (eds.), *Candidate Selection in Comparative Perspective: The Secret Garden of Politics* (London: Sage), 236–83.

Galston, William. 2002. *Liberal Pluralism: The Implications of Value Pluralism for Political Theory and Practice*. Cambridge: Cambridge University Press.

Gastil, Raymond D. (ed.). [Various years]. *Freedom in the World*. Westport, CT: Greenwood Press.

Geddes, Barbara, and Allyson Benton. 1997. "Federalism and Party System." Paper prepared for the conference The Transformation of Argentina: Democratic Consolidation, Economic Reforms and Institutional Design, Universidad de San Andres.

Gerring, John. 1997. "Ideology: A Definitional Analysis." *Political Research Quarterly* 50:4 (December), 957–94.

Gerring, John. 1998. *Party Ideologies in America, 1828–1996*. Cambridge: Cambridge University Press.

Gerring, John. 2001. *Social Science Methodology: A Criterial Framework*. Cambridge: Cambridge University Press.

Gerring, John. 2004. "What Is a Case Study and What Is It Good For?" *American Political Science Review* 98:2 (May), 341–54.
Gerring, John. 2005. "Minor Parties in Plurality Electoral Systems." *Party Politics* 11:1, 79–107.
Gerring, John. 2007. *Case Study Research: Principles and Practices*. Cambridge: Cambridge University Press.
Gerring, John, Philip Bond, William Barndt, and Carola Moreno. 2005. "Democracy and Growth: A Historical Perspective." *World Politics* 57:3 (April), 323–64.
Gerring, John, and Strom C. Thacker. 2004. "Political Institutions and Corruption: The Role of Unitarism and Parliamentarism." *British Journal of Political Science* 34:2 (April), 295–330.
Gerring, John, and Strom C. Thacker. 2006. "Do Neoliberal Policies Kill or Save Lives?" Unpublished manuscript, Boston University.
Gerring, John, Strom C. Thacker, and Rodrigo Alfaro. 2006. "Democracy and Human Development." Unpublished manuscript, Boston University.
Gerring, John, Strom C. Thacker, and Carola Moreno. 2005. "Centripetal Democratic Governance: A Theory and Global Inquiry." *American Political Science Review* 99:4 (November), 567–81.
Gewirth, Alan. 1978. *Reason and Morality*. Chicago: University of Chicago Press.
Ghai, Dharam (ed.). 2000. *Social Development and Public Policy: Some Lessons from Successful Experiences*. London: St. Martin's.
Gibson, Edward L. 1997. "The Populist Road to Market Reform: Policy and Electoral Coalitions in Mexico and Argentina." *World Politics* 49 (April), 339–70.
Goel, Rajeev K. and Michael A. Nelson. 1998. "Corruption and Government Size: A Disaggregated Analysis." *Public Choice* 97, 107–120.
Golden, Marissa Martino. 2000. *What Motivates Bureaucrats?* New York: Columbia University Press.
Golden, Miriam A., and Eric C. C. Chang. 2000. "Competitive Corruption: Factional Conflict and Political Malfeasance in Postwar Italian Christian Democracy." *World Politics* 53:4 (July), 588–622.
Golder, Matt. 2005. "Democratic Electoral Systems around the World, 1946–2000." *Electoral Studies* 24, 103–21.
Goldstein, Judith, and Robert O. Keohane (eds.). 1993. *Ideas and Foreign Policy: Beliefs, Institutions, and Political Change*. Ithaca, NY: Cornell University Press.
Good, Kenneth. 1994. "Corruption and Mismanagement in Botswana: A Best-Case Example?" *Journal of Modern African Studies* 32, 499–521.
Goodin, Robert E. 1996. "Institutionalizing the Public Interest: The Defense of Deadlock and Beyond." *American Political Science Review* 90:2 (June), 331–43.
Goodnow, Frank J. 1900. *Politics and Administration*. New York: Macmillan.
Gordon, Scott. 1999. *Controlling the State: Constitutionalism from Ancient Athens to Today*. Cambridge, MA: Harvard University Press.

Green, Donald P., and Ian Shapiro. 1994. *Pathologies of Rational Choice Theory: A Critique of Applications in Political Science*. New Haven, CT: Yale University Press.

Grey-Johnson, Crispin. 1994. "Capacity Building, Strengthening, and Retention for Socio-economic Development in Africa: Lessons from Mauritius and Madagascar." *African Journal of Public Administration and Management* 3:2.

Grofman, Bernard, Sung-Chull Lee, and Edwin A. Winckler (eds.). 1999. *Elections in Japan, Korea, and Taiwan under the Single Non-Transferable Vote: The Comparative Study of an Embedded Institution*. Ann Arbor: University of Michigan Press.

Gunn, J. A. W. 1969. *Politics and the Public Interest in the Seventeenth Century*. London: Routledge and Kegan Paul.

Gunther, Richard, and Anthony Mughan. 1993. "Political Institutions and Cleavage Management." In R. Kent Weaver and Bert A. Rockman (eds.), *Do Institutions Matter? Government Capabilities in the United States and Abroad* (Washington, DC: Brookings Institution), 272–302.

Gurr, Ted Robert. 2000. *Peoples versus States: Minorities at Risk in the New Century*. Washington, DC: United States Institute of Peace Press.

Gwyn, W. B. 1965. *Meaning of the Separation of Powers: An Analysis of the Doctrine from Its Origin to the Adoption of the United States Constitution*. New Orleans: Tulane University Press.

Habermas, Jurgen. 1984. *The Theory of Communicative Action*. Boston: Beacon Press.

Hackett, Steven, Edella Schlager, and James M. Walker. 1994. "The Role of Communication in Resolving Commons Dilemmas: Experimental Evidence with Heterogeneous Appropriators." *Journal of Environmental Economics and Management* 27, 99–126.

Haggard, Stephan, and Mathew D. McCubbins (eds.). 2001. *Presidents, Parliaments, and Policy*. Cambridge: Cambridge University Press.

Halpern, Sue M. 1986. "The Disorderly Universe of Consociational Democracy." *West European Politics* 9, 161–97.

Halstead, Scott B., Julia A. Walsh, and Kenneth S. Warren (eds.). 1985. *Good Health at Low Cost: A Conference Report*. New York: The Rockefeller Foundation.

Hamilton, Alexander, James Madison, and John Jay. 1787–88/1992. *The Federalist*, ed. William R. Brock. London: Everyman/J. M. Dent.

Hammond, Thomas H., and Gary J. Miller. 1987. "The Core of the Constitution." *American Political Science Review* 81, 1155–74.

Hardgrave, Robert, Jr. 1994. "India: The Dilemmas of Diversity." In Larry Diamond and Marc F. Plattner (eds.), *Nationalism, Ethnic Conflict and Democracy* (Baltimore: Johns Hopkins University Press), 71–85.

Hardin, Charles M. 1989. *Constitutional Reform in America: Essays on the Separation of Powers*. Ames: Iowa State University Press.

Hardin, Russell. 1982. *Collective Action*. Baltimore: Johns Hopkins University Press.

Hardin, Russell. 1997. "Economic Theories of the State." In Dennis C. Mueller (ed.), *Perspectives on Public Choice: A Handbook* (Cambridge: Cambridge University Press), 21–34.

Hardin, Russell. 1999. *Liberalism, Constitutionalism, and Democracy*. Oxford: Oxford University Press.

Harrison, Brian. 1996. *The Transformation of British Politics, 1860–1995*. New York: Oxford University Press.

Hart, Jenifer. 1992. *Proportional Representation: Critics of the British Electoral System, 1820–1945*. Oxford: Oxford University Press.

Haspel, Moshe, Thomas F. Remington, and Steven S. Smith. 1998. "Electoral Institutions and Party Cohesion in the Russian Duma." *Journal of Politics* 60, 417–39.

Hayek, Friedrich A. 1944. *The Road to Serfdom*. Chicago: University of Chicago Press.

Healey, John. 1995. "Multi-party Electoral Politics: Comparative Experience and Conclusions." In John Healey and William Tordoff (eds.), *Votes and Budgets: Comparative Studies in Accountable Governance in the South* (Houndsmills, Basingstoke, Hampshire, UK: Macmillan), 237–55.

Heclo, Hugh. 1974. *Modern Social Policies in Britain and Sweden: From Relief to Income Maintenance*. New Haven, CT: Yale University Press.

Heclo, Hugh. 1977. *A Government of Strangers: Executive Politics in Washington*. Washington, DC: Brookings.

Heclo, Hugh. 1986. "The Political Foundations of Antipoverty Policy." In Sheldon H. Danziger and Daniel H. Weinberg (eds.), *Fighting Poverty: What Works and What Doesn't* (Cambridge, MA: Harvard University Press), 312–40.

Hedstrom, Peter, and Richard Swedberg (eds.). 1998. *Social Mechanisms: An Analytical Approach to Social Theory*. Cambridge: Cambridge University Press.

Heitshusen, Valerie, Garry Young, and David M. Wood. 2002. "MP Constituency Activity in Westminster-Style Parliaments: Australia, Canada, Ireland, New Zealand, and the UK." Paper presented at the annual meeting of the American Political Science Association, Boston, August–September.

Henisz, Witold J. 2000. "The Institutional Environment for Economic Growth." *Economics and Politics* 12:1, 1–32.

Henisz, Witold J. 2002. "The Institutional Environment for Infrastructure Investment." *Industrial and Corporate Change* 11:2, 355–89.

Herring, Pendleton. 1940. *The Politics of Democracy: American Parties in Action*. New York: Norton.

Hess, Stephen. 1976. *Organizing the Presidency*. Washington, DC: Brookings.

Heston, Alan, Robert Summers, and Bettina Aten. 2002. *Penn World Tables Version 6.1*. Center for International Comparisons at the University of Pennsylvania (CICUP).

Hewitt de Alcantara, Cynthia. 1998. "Uses and Abuses of the Concept of Governance." *International Social Science Journal* 50:155 (March), 105–13.

Hicken, Allen D., and Yuko Kasuya. 2001. "A Guide to the Constitutional Structures and Electoral Systems of East, South, and Southeast Asia." *Electoral Studies* 22, 121–51.

Hill, Kenneth. 1991. "Approaches in the Measurement of Childhood Mortality: A Comparative Review." *Population Index* 57:3 (Fall), 368–82.

Hill, Kenneth, Rohini Pande, Mary Mahy, and Gareth Jones. 1999. *Trends in Child Mortality in the Developing World: 1960 to 1996*. New York: UNICEF.

Hine, David. 1982. "Factionalism in West European Parties: A Framework for Analysis." *West European Politics* 5, 36–52.

Hirst, Paul Q. (ed.). 1989. *The Pluralist Theory of the State: Selected Writings of G. D. H. Cole, J. N. Figgis, and H. J. Laski*. New York: Routledge.

Hojnacki, William P. 1996. "Politicization as a Civil Service Dilemma." In Hans A. G. M. Bekke et al. (eds.), *Civil Service Systems in Comparative Perspective* (Bloomington: Indiana University Press), 137–64.

Holm, John D. 1994. "Botswana: One African Success Story." *Current History* 93:583 (May), 198–202.

Holm, John D. 2000. "Curbing Corruption through Democratic Accountability: Lessons from Botswana." In Ronald Kepme Hope, Sr., and Bornwell C. Chikulo (eds.), *Corruption and Development in Africa* (Houndsmills, Basingstoke, UK: Macmillan), 288–304.

Holm, John D., and Patrick Molutsi (eds.). 1989. *Democracy in Botswana*. Athens: Ohio University Press.

Holsey, Cheryl M., and Thomas E. Borcherding. 1997. "Why Does Government's Share of National Income Grow? An Assessment of the Recent Literature on the U.S Experience." In Dennis C. Mueller (ed.), *Perspectives on Public Choice: A Handbook* (Cambridge: Cambridge University Press), 562–90.

Horowitz, Donald L. 1985. *Ethnic Groups in Conflict*. Berkeley: University of California Press.

Horowitz, Donald L. 1991. *A Democratic South Africa? Constitutional Engineering in a Divided Society*. Berkeley: University of California Press.

Huber, Evelyne. 1995. "Assessments of State Strength." In Peter H. Smith (ed.), *Latin America in Comparative Perspective: New Approaches to Methods and Analysis* (Boulder, CO: Westview), 163–194.

Humphreys, Macartan. 2005. "Natural Resources, Conflict, and Conflict Resolution: Uncovering the Mechanisms." *Journal of Conflict Resolution* 49:4, 508–37.

Huntington, Samuel P. 1968. *Political Order in Changing Societies*. New Haven, CT: Yale University Press.

Huntington, Samuel P. 1981. *American Politics: The Promise of Disharmony*. Cambridge, MA: Harvard University Press.

Huther, Jeff, and Anwar Shah. 1998. "Applying a Simple Measure of Good Governance to the Debate on Fiscal Decentralization." World Bank Operations Evaluation Department Policy Research Working Paper No. 1894. Washington, DC: World Bank.

Immergut, Ellen M. 1992. *Health Politics: Interests and Institutions in Western Europe*. Cambridge: Cambridge University Press.

International Year Book and Statesmen's Who's Who, 48th ed. 2001. East Grinstead, West Sussex, UK: Bowker, Saur.

Janda, Kenneth. 1992. "The American Constitutional Framework and the Structure of American Political Parties." In Peter F. Nardulli (ed.), *The Constitution and American Political Development: An Institutional Perspective* (Urbana: University of Illinois Press), 179–206.

Jasanoff, Sheila. 1997. "American Exceptionalism and the Political Acknowledgement of Risk." In Edward Burger (ed.), *Risk* (Ann Arbor: University of Michigan Press), 61–82.

Jasper, James M. 1990. *Nuclear Politics: Energy and the State in the United States, Sweden, and France*. Princeton, NJ: Princeton University Press.

Jervis, Robert. 1997. *System Effects: Complexity in Political and Social Life*. Princeton, NJ: Princeton University Press.

Jochem, Sven. 2003. "Veto Players or Veto Points? The Politics of Welfare State Reforms in Europe." Paper presented at the annual meeting of the American Political Science Association, Philadelphia (August).

Johnstone, Patrick. 1993. *Operation World*. Grand Rapids, MI: Zondervan.

Jones, Charles I. 1997. "On the Evolution of the World Income Distribution." *Journal of Economic Perspectives* 11:3 (Summer), 19–36.

Jones, Mark P. 1995. *Electoral Laws and the Survival of Presidential Democracies*. Notre Dame, IN: University of Notre Dame Press.

Jones, Mark P., Pablo Sanguinetti, and Mariano Tommasi. 2000. "Politics, Institutions and Fiscal Performance in a Federal System: An Analysis of the Argentine Provinces." *Journal of Development Economics* 61:2, 305–33.

Kagan, Robert A. 1995. "Adversarial Legalism and American Government." In Marc K. Landy and Martin A. Levin (eds.), *The New Politics of Public Policy* (Baltimore: Johns Hopkins University Press), 88–120.

Kagan, Robert A. 2001. *Adversarial Legalism: The American Way of Law*. Cambridge, MA: Harvard University Press.

Kagan, Robert A., and Lee Axelrad. 1997. "Adversarial Legalism: An International Perspective." In Pietro S. Nivola (ed.), *Comparative Disadvantages? Social Regulations and the Global Economy* (Washington, DC: Brookings), 146–81.

Karvonen, Lauri. 2004. "Preferential Voting." *International Political Science Review* 25:2, 203–26.

Katz, Richard S. 1980. *A Theory of Parties and Electoral Systems*. Baltimore: Johns Hopkins University Press.

Katz, Richard S. 1986. "Intraparty Preference Voting." In Bernard Grofman and Arend Lijphart (eds.), *Electoral Laws and Their Political Consequences* (New York: Agathon Press), 85–103.

Katz, Richard S. (ed.). 1987. *The Future of Party Government. Volume I: Party Governments: European and American Experiences*. Berlin: Walter de Gruyter.

Katz, Richard S., and Peter Mair (eds.). 1992. *Party Organizations: A Data Handbook*. Newbury Park, CA: Sage.

Katz, Richard S., and Peter Mair. 1995. "Changing Models of Party Organization and Party Democracy: The Emergence of the Cartel Party." *Party Politics* 1:1, 5–28.

Katzenstein, Peter J. (ed.). 1978. *Between Power and Plenty: Foreign Economic Policies of Advanced Industrial States*. Madison: University of Wisconsin Press.

Kaufman, Chaim. 1996. "Possible and Impossible Solutions to Ethnic Civil Wars." *International Security* 20:4, 133–75.

Keefer, Philip, and David Stasavage. 2002. "Checks and Balances, Private Information, and the Credibility of Monetary Commitments." *International Organization* 56:4 (Autumn), 751–74.

Kelman, Steven. 1981. *Regulating America, Regulating Sweden: A Comparative Study of Occupational Safety and Health Policy*. Cambridge, MA: MIT Press.

Kelman, Steven. 1990. *Procurement and Public Management: The Fear of Discretion and the Quality of Government Performance*. Washington, DC: AEI Press.

Keman, Hans (ed.). 1997. *Politics of Problem-Solving in Postwar Democracies: Institutionalizing Conflict and Consensus*. Basingstoke, Hampshire, UK: Palgrave.

Key, V. O., Jr. 1949. *Southern Politics in State and Nation*. New York: Vintage.

Khan, Mushtaq. 2000. "Rents, Efficiency, and Growth." In Mushtaq H. Khan and Jomo K.S. (eds.), *Rents, Rent-Seeking and Economic Development* (Cambridge: Cambridge University Press), 21–69.

Khan, Mushtaq H., and Jomo K.S. (eds.). 2000. *Rents, Rent-Seeking and Economic Development*. Cambridge: Cambridge University Press.

Kim, Kwangkee, and Philip M. Moody. 1992. "More Resources Better Health? A Cross-National Perspective." *Social Science and Medicine* 34:8 (April), 837–42.

King, Anthony (ed.). 1983. *Both Ends of the Avenue*. Washington, DC: American Enterprise Institute.

Kingdon, John W. 1993. "Politicians, Self-Interest, and Ideas." In George E. Marcus and Russell L. Hanson (eds.), *Reconsidering the Democratic Public* (University Park: Pennsylvania State University Press), 73–89.

Kitschelt, Herbert. 2000. "Citizens, Politicians, and Party Cartelization: Political Representation and State Failure in Post-industrial Democracies." *European Journal of Political Research* 37:2 (March), 149–79.

Kittel, Bernhard. 2006. "A Crazy Methodology? On the Limits of Macro-quantitative Social Science Research." *International Sociology* 21, 647–77.

Knack, Stephen, and Philip Keefer. 1995. "Institutions and Economic Performance: Cross-Country Tests Using Alternative Institutional Measures." *Economics and Politics* 7:3, 207–27.

Kramnick, Isaac. 1968. *Bolingbroke and His Circle: The Politics of Nostalgia in the Age of Walpole*. Cambridge, MA: Harvard University Press.

Krasner, Stephen D. 1978. *Defending the National Interest: Raw Materials Investments and U.S Foreign Policy*. Princeton, NJ: Princeton University Press.

Krause, George A. 1999. *A Two-Way Street: The Institutional Dynamics of the Modern Administrative State*. Pittsburgh: University of Pittsburgh Press.

Krueger, Anne O. 1974. "The Political Economy of the Rent-Seeking Society." *The American Economic Review* 64:3 (June), 291–303.

Krueger, Anne O. 1997. "Trade Policy and Economic Development: How We Learn." *American Economic Review* 87:1, 1–22.

Kymlicka, Will. 1998. "Is Federalism a Viable Alternative to Secessionism?" In Percy B. Lehning (ed.), *Theories of Secession* (New York: Routledge), 111–50.

Lake, David A., and Matthew A. Baum. 2001. "The Invisible Hand of Democracy: Political Control and the Provision of Public Services." *Comparative Political Studies* 34:6 (August), 587–621.

Lake, David A., and Donald Rothchild. 1997. "Containing Fear: The Origins and Management of Ethnic Conflict." In Michael E. Brown, Owen R. Cote, Jr., Sean M. Lynn-Jones, and Steven E. Miller (eds.) *Nationalism and Ethnic Conflict* (Cambridge, MA: MIT Press), 126–62.

Lal, Brij V., and Peter Larmour (eds.). 1997. *Electoral Systems in Divided Societies: The Fiji Constitution Review*. Canberra: National Centre for Development Studies, Research School of Pacific and Asian Studies, The Australian National University.

Lambsdorff, Johann Graf. 2002. "Corruption and Rent-Seeking." *Public Choice* 113, 97–125.

Lancaster, Thomas D. 1986. "Electoral Structures and Pork Barrel Politics." *International Political Science Review* 7 (January), 67–81.

Lande, Carl H. 1965. *Leaders, Factions and Parties: The Structure of Philippine Politics*. Monograph Series No. 6. New Haven, CT: Yale University Southeast Asian Studies.

Laski, Harold J. 1917. *Studies in the Problem of Sovereignty*. New Haven, CT: Yale University Press.

Laski, Harold J. 1919. *Authority in the Modern State*. New Haven, CT: Yale University Press.

Laski, Harold J. 1921. *Foundations of Sovereignty and Other Essays*. New York: Harcourt, Brace.

Laver, Michael, and Kenneth A. Shepsle (eds.). 1994. *Cabinet Ministers and Parliamentary Government*. Cambridge: Cambridge University Press.

Lawson, Chappell, and Strom C. Thacker. 2003. "Democracy? In *Iraq*?" *Hoover Digest* no. 3: 24–33.

Le Grand, Julian. 1991. "The Theory of Government Failure." *British Journal of Political Science* 21, 423–42.

Leff, Carol Skalnik. 1999. "Democratization and Disintegration in Multinational States: The Breakup of the Communist Federations." *World Politics* 51:2, 205–35.

Lehmbruch, Gerhard. 1993. "Consociational Democracy and Corporatism in Switzerland." *Publius: The Journal of Federalism* 23 (Spring), 43–60.

Levi, Margaret. 1988. *Of Rule and Revenue*. Berkeley: University of California Press.

Levi, Margaret. 1997. *Consent, Dissent and Patriotism*. Cambridge: Cambridge University Press.

Levitsky, Steven. 2003. *Transforming Labor-Based Parties in Latin America: Argentine Peronism in Comparative Perspective*. Cambridge: Cambridge University Press.

Levy, Leonard W. 1988. *Original Intent and the Framers' Constitution*. New York: Macmillan.

Lewin, Leif. 1991. *Self-Interest and Public Interest in Western Politics*. Oxford: Oxford University Press.

Lieberman, Evan S. 2002. "Taxation Data as Indicators of State-Society Relations: Possibilities and Pitfalls in Cross-National Research." *Studies in Comparative International Development* 36:4 (Winter), 89–115.

Lijphart, Arend. 1968. *The Politics of Accommodation: Pluralism and Democracy in the Netherlands*. Berkeley: University of California Press.

Lijphart, Arend. 1977. *Democracy in Plural Societies*. New Haven, CT: Yale University Press.

Lijphart, Arend. 1984a. "A Note on the Meaning of Cabinet Durability: A Conceptual and Empirical Evaluation." *Comparative Political Studies* 17:2, 265–79.

Lijphart, Arend. 1984b. *Democracies: Patterns of Majoritarian and Consensus Government in Twenty-One Countries*. New Haven, CT: Yale University Press.

Lijphart, Arend. 1999. *Patterns of Democracy: Government Forms and Performance in Thirty-Six Countries*. New Haven, CT: Yale University Press.

Lijphart, Arend (ed.). 1992. *Parliamentary versus Presidential Government*. New York: Oxford University Press.

Linz, Juan. 1990. "The Perils of Presidentialism." *Journal of Democracy* 1, 51–69.

Linz, Juan. 1994. "Presidential or Parliamentary Democracy: Does It Make a Difference?" In Juan J. Linz and Arturo Valenzuela (eds.), *The Failure of Presidential Democracy* (Baltimore: Johns Hopkins University Press), 3–90.

Linz, Juan J., and Alfred Stepan (eds.). 1978. *The Breakdown of Democratic Regimes: Crisis, Breakdown, and Reequilibration*. Baltimore: Johns Hopkins University Press.

Lippmann, Walter. 1955. *The Public Philosophy*. New York: Little, Brown.

Lowell, A. Lawrence. 1889. *Essays on Government*. Boston: Houghton Mifflin.

Lowi, Theodore. 1969. *The End of Liberalism*. New York: Norton.

Lustick, Ian S. 1979. "Stability in Deeply Divided Societies: Consociationalism versus Control." *World Politics* 31:3 (April), 325–44.

Lustick, Ian S. 1997. "Lijphart, Lakatos, and Consociationalism." *World Politics* 50, 88–117.

Luther, Kurt Richard, and Kris Deschouwer (eds.). 1999. *Party Elites in Divided Societies: Political Parties in Consociational Democracy*. London: Routledge.

MacIntyre, Andrew. 2003. *Power of Institutions: Political Architecture and Governance*. Ithaca, NY: Cornell University Press.

Mackintosh, John P. 1962. *The British Cabinet*, 2nd ed. London: Methuen.

Madison, James. 1973. *The Mind of the Founder: Sources of the Political Thought of James Madison*, ed. Marvin Meyers. Indianapolis: Bobbs-Merrill.

Mainwaring, Scott P., and David Samuels. 2004. "Strong Federalism, Constraints on the Central Government, and Economic Reform in Democratic Brazil." In Edward L. Gibson (ed.), *Federalism and Democracy in Latin America* (Baltimore: Johns Hopkins University Press), 85–130.

Mainwaring, Scott, and Timothy Scully (eds.). 1995. *Building Democratic Institutions: Party Systems in Latin America*. Stanford, CA: Stanford University Press.

Mainwaring, Scott P., and Matthew J. Shugart (eds.). 1997. *Presidentialism and Democracy in Latin America*. Cambridge: Cambridge University Press.

Manning, Nick, Naazneen Barma, Jean Blondel, Elsa Pilichowski, and Vincent Wright. 1999. *Strategic Decisionmaking in Cabinet Government: Institutional Underpinnings and Obstacles*. Washington, DC: World Bank.

Mansbridge, Jane. 1983. *Beyond Adversarial Democracy*. Chicago: University of Chicago Press.

Mansbridge, Jane (ed.). 1990. *Beyond Self-Interest*. Chicago: University of Chicago Press.

Marshall, Geoffrey. 1971. *Constitutional Theory*. Oxford: Clarendon Press.

Marshall, Monty. 1999. "Major Armed Conflicts and Conflict Regions, 1946–1997." Dataset from CIDCM, University of Maryland. Obtained via the State Failure Task Force dataset, <http://gking.harvard.edu/data.shtml>, accessed April 25, 2005.

Marshall, Monty G., and Keith Jaggers. 2002. "Polity IV Dataset Project: Political Regime Characteristics and Transitions, 1800–1999." <http://www.bsos.umd.edu/cidcm/polity>.

Martiniello, Marco. 1997. "The Dilemma of Separation versus Union: The New Dynamics of Nationalist Politics in Belgium." In H. R. Wicker (ed.), *Rethinking Nationalism and Ethnicity: The Struggle for Meaning and Order in Europe*. Oxford: Berg, 287–302.

Massicote, Louis, and Andre Blais. 1999. "Mixed Electoral Systems: A Conceptual and Empirical Survey." *Electoral Studies* 18:3 (September), 341–66.

Mathur, Raj. 1997a. "Parliamentary Representation of Minority Communities: The Mauritian Experience." *Africa Today* 44:1 (January–March), 61–82.

Mathur, Raj. 1997b. "Party Cooperation and the Electoral System in Mauritius." In Brij V. Lal and Peter Larmour (eds.), *Electoral Systems in Divided Societies: The Fiji Constitution Review* (Canberra: National Centre for

Development Studies, Research School of Pacific and Asian Studies, The Australian National University), 135–46.

McConnell, Grant. 1966. *Private Power and American Democracy*. New York: Alfred A. Knopf.

McGarry, John, and Brendan O'Leary (eds.). 1993. *The Politics of Ethnic Conflict Regulation*. London: Routledge.

McGuire, James W. "Politics, Policy, and Mortality Decline in East Asia and Latin America." Unpublished manuscript, Department of Government, Wesleyan University.

McHenry, Dean E. 1997. "Federalism in Africa: Is It a Solution to, or a Cause of, Ethnic Problems?" Paper presented at the annual meeting of the African Studies Association, Columbus, OH (November).

McKeown, Thomas. 1967. *The Role of Medicine: Dream, Mirage or Nemesis*. London: Nuffield Hospitals Trust.

McRae, K. D. (ed.). 1974. *Consociational Democracy: Political Accommodation in Segmented Societies*. Toronto: McClelland and Stewart.

Mecham, R. Quinn. 2004. "From the Ashes of Virtue, a Promise of Light: The Transformation of Political Islam in Turkey." *Third World Quarterly* 25:2 (March), 339–58.

Meerman, Jacob. 1979. *Public Expenditure in Malaysia: Who Benefits and Why*. New York: Oxford University Press.

Mehrotra, S., and Richard Jolly (eds.). 1997. *Development with a Human Face: Experiences in Social Achievement and Economic Growth*. Oxford: Clarendon.

Merriam, Charles E. 1900. *History of the Theory of Sovereignty since Rousseau*. New York: Columbia University Press.

Mill, John Stuart. 1865/1958. *Considerations on Representative Government*, 3d ed., ed. Curren V. Shields. Indianapolis: Bobbs-Merrill.

Mitchell, J., and B. Seyd. 1999. "Fragmentation in the Party and Political System." In R. Hazell (ed.), *Constitutional Futures* (Oxford: Oxford University Press), 86–110.

Moe, Terry M. 1989. "The Politics of Bureaucratic Structure." In John E. Chubb and Paul E. Peterson (eds.), *Can the Government Govern?* (Washington, DC: Brookings), 267–329.

Moe, Terry M. 1990a. "Political Institutions: The Neglected Side of the Story." *Journal of Law, Economics, and Organization* 6, 213–53.

Moe, Terry M. 1990b. "The Politics of Structural Choice: Towards a Theory of Public Bureaucracy." In Oliver Williamson (ed.), *Organization Theory: From Chester Barnard to the Present and Beyond* (New York: Oxford University Press), 116–53

Moe, Terry M. 1991. "The Politicized Presidency." In James P. Pfiffner (ed.), *The Managerial Presidency* (Pacific Grove, CA: Brooks/Cole), 135–57.

Moe, Terry M., and Michael Caldwell. 1994. "The Institutional Foundations of Democratic Government: A Comparison of Presidential and Parliamentary Systems." *Journal of Institutional and Theoretical Economics* 150, 171–95.

Mogi, Sobei. 1931. *The Problem of Federalism,* 2 vols. London: Allen and Unwin.

Moon, Bruce E. 1991. *The Political Economy of Basic Human Needs.* Ithaca, NY: Cornell University Press.

Moreno, Erika, Brian F. Crisp, and Matthew Soberg Shugart. 2003. "The Accountability Deficit in Latin America." In Scott Mainwaring and Christopher Welna (eds.), *Democratic Accountability in Latin America* (Oxford: Oxford University Press), 79–131.

Moser, Robert G. 2001. *Unexpected Outcomes: Electoral Systems, Political Parties, and Representation in Russia.* Pittsburgh: University of Pittsburgh Press.

Mudambi, Ram, Petro Navarra, and Giuseppe Sobbrio (eds.). 2001. *Rules and Reason: Perspectives on Constitutional Political Economy.* Cambridge: Cambridge University Press.

Mueller, Dennis C. 1996. *Constitutional Democracy.* New York: Oxford University Press.

Mueller, Dennis C. (ed.). 1997. *Perspectives on Public Choice: A Handbook.* Cambridge: Cambridge University Press.

Muhuri, Pradip K. 1995. "Health Programs, Maternal Education, and Differential Child Mortality in Matlab, Bangladesh." *Population and Development Review* 21:4 (December), 813–34.

Muller, Wolfgang C. 2000. "Political Parties in Parliamentary Democracies: Making Delegation and Accountability Work." *European Journal of Political Research* 37, 309–33.

Murphy, Kevin M., Andrei Shleifer, and Robert W. Vishny. 1993. "Why Is Rent-Seeking So Costly to Growth?" *American Economic Review* 83:2, 409–14.

Musgrave, Richard A., and Alan T. Peacock (eds.). 1958. *Classics in the Theory of Public Finance.* London: Macmillan.

Musgrove, Philip. 1996. "Public and Private Roles in Health: Theory and Financing Patterns." World Bank Discussion Paper No. 339. Washington, DC: World Bank.

Myrdal, Gunnar. 1968. *Asian Drama: An Inquiry into the Poverty of Nations,* 3 vols. New York: Pantheon.

Nathan, Richard P. 1983. *The Administrative Presidency.* New York: Wiley.

Neustadt, Richard E. 1980. *Presidential Power: The Politics of Leadership from FDR to Carter.* New York: Wiley.

Newey, Whitney K., and Kenneth D. West. 1987. "A Simple, Positive Semi-Definite, Heteroskedasticity and Autocorrelation Consistent Covariance Matrix." *Econometrica* 55:3 (May), 703–8.

Niskanen, William. 1971. *Bureaucracy and Representative Government.* Chicago: Aldine.

Niskanen, William. 1994. *Bureaucracy and Public Economics.* Aldershot, UK: Edward Elgar.

Nohlen, Dieter, Florian Grotz, and Christof Harmann (eds.). 2002. *Elections in Asia and the Pacific: A Data Handbook,* 2 vols. New York: Oxford University Press.

Nohlen, Dieter, Michael Krennerich, and Berhard Thibaut (eds.). 1999. *Elections in Africa: A Data Handbook*. Oxford: Oxford University Press.

Noiret, Serge (ed.). 1990. *Political Strategies and Electoral Reforms: Origins of Voting Systems in Europe in the 19th and 20th Centuries*. Baden-Baden: Nomos.

Noll, Roger G., and Frances M. Rosenbluth. 1995. "Telecommunications Policy: Structure, Process, Outcomes." In Peter F. Cowhey and Mathew D. McCubbins (eds.), *Structure and Policy in Japan and the United States* (Cambridge: Cambridge University Press), 119–76.

Nordlinger, Eric. 1972. *Conflict Regulation in Divided Societies*. Cambridge, MA: Harvard University Center for International Affairs.

Norris, Pippa. 2002. "Ballots Not Bullets: Testing Consociational Theories of Ethnic Conflict, Electoral Systems and Democratization." In Andrew Reynolds (ed.), *The Architecture of Democracy* (New York: Oxford University Press), 206–47.

Norris, Pippa. 2004. *Electoral Engineering: Voting Rules and Political Behavior*. Cambridge: Cambridge University Press.

North, Douglass C. 1981. *Structure and Change in Economic History*. New York: Norton.

North, Douglass C. 1993. "Institutions and Credible Commitment." *Journal of Institutional and Theoretical Economics* 149:1, 11–23.

North, Douglass C., and Barry R. Weingast. 1989. "Constitutions and Commitment: The Evolution of Institutions Governing Public Choice in Seventeenth-Century England." *Journal of Economic History* 49, 803–32.

Nousiainen, Jaakko. 1988. "Bureaucratic Tradition, Semi-Presidential Rule and Parliamentary Government: The Case of Finland." *European Journal of Political Research* 16 (March), 229–49.

Nousiainen, Jaakko. 2001. "From Semi-Presidentialism to Parliamentary Government: Political and Constitutional Developments in Finland." *Scandinavian Political Studies* 24, 95–109.

Ockey, James. 1994. "Political Parties, Factions, and Corruption in Thailand." *Modern Asian Studies* 28:2, 251–77.

O'Donnell, Guillermo. 1999. "Horizontal Accountability in New Democracies." In Andreas Schedler, Larry Diamond, and Marc F. Plattner (eds.), *The Self-Restraining State: Power and Accountability in New Democracies* (Boulder, CO: Lynne Rienner), 29–52.

O'Duffy, Brendan. 1993. "Containment or Regulation? The British Approach to Ethnic Conflict in Northern Ireland." In John McGarry and Brendan O'Leary (eds.), *The Politics of Ethnic Conflict Regulation* (London: Routledge), 128–150.

O'Neill, Michael. 2000. "Belgium: Language, Ethnicity and Nationality." *Parliamentary Affairs* 53:1 (January), 114–34.

Oates, Wallace E. 1972. *Fiscal Federalism*. New York: Harcourt, Brace, Jovanovich.

Oates, Wallace E. 1999. "An Essay on Fiscal Federalism." *Journal of Economic Literature* 37:3, 1120–49.

Olson, Mancur. 1965. *The Logic of Collective Action: Public Goods and the Theory of Goods*. Cambridge, MA: Harvard University Press.
Olson, Mancur. 1982. *The Rise and Decline of Nations*. New Haven, CT: Yale University Press.
Olson, Mancur. 1986. "A Theory of the Incentives Facing Political Organizations: Neo-corporatism and the Hegemonic State." *International Political Science Review* 7, 165–89.
Ordeshook, Peter. 1996. "Russia's Party System: Is Russian Federalism Viable?" *Post-Soviet Affairs* 12:3, 195–217.
Ostrom, Elinor. 1983. "A Public Choice Approach to Metropolitan Institutions: Structure, Incentives, and Performance." *Social Science Journal* 20, 79–96.
Ostrom, Elinor. 1990. *Governing the Commons: The Evolution of Institutions for Collective Action*. Cambridge: Cambridge University Press.
Ostrom, Elinor, and James Walker. 1997. "Neither Markets nor States: Linking Transformation Processes in Collective Action Arenas." In Dennis C. Mueller (ed.), *Perspectives on Public Choice: A Handbook* (Cambridge: Cambridge University Press), 35–72.
Ostrom, Vincent. 1973. *The Intellectual Crisis of Public Administration*. Tuscaloosa: University of Alabama Press.
Ozbudun, Ergun. 1970. *Party Cohesion in Western Democracies: A Causal Analysis*. Beverly Hills, CA: Sage.
Page, Edward C., and Vincent Wright (eds.). 2000. *Bureaucratic Elites in Western European States*. Oxford: Oxford University Press.
Paine, Thomas. 1776/1953. "Common Sense." In *Common Sense and Other Political Writings* (New York: Macmillan).
Palda, Filip. 1999. "Property Rights vs. Redistribution: Which Path to National Wealth?" *Public Choice* 101:1–2, 129–45.
Pascal, Blaise. 1958. *Pascal's Pensees*. New York: E. P. Dutton.
Patterson, Samuel C., and Anthony Mughan (eds.). 1999. *Senates: Bicameralism in the Contemporary World*. Columbus: Ohio State University Press.
Patzelt, Werner J. 2000. "What Can an Individual MP Do in German Parliamentary Politics?" In Lawrence D. Longley and Reuven Y. Hazan (eds.), *The Uneasy Relationships between Parliamentary Members and Leaders* (London: Frank Cass), 23–52.
Peltzman, Sam. 1976. "Towards a More General Theory of Regulation." *Journal of Law and Economics* 20, 322–40.
Pempel, T. J. (ed.). 1990. *Uncommon Democracies: The One-Party Dominant Regimes*. Ithaca, NY: Cornell University Press.
Penfold-Becerra, Michael. 2004. "Federalism and Institutional Change in Venezuela." In Edward L. Gibson (ed.), *Federalism and Democracy in Latin America* (Baltimore: Johns Hopkins University Press), 197–225.
Pennock, J. Roland. 1962. "Responsible Government, Separated Powers, and Special Interests: Agricultural Subsidies in Britain and America." *American Political Science Review* 56 (September), 621–33.

Persson, Torsten, Gerard Roland, and Guido Tabellini. 1997. "Separation of Powers and Political Accountability." *Quarterly Journal of Economics* 112, 1163–202.

Persson, Torsten, and Guido Tabellini. 2003. *The Economic Effects of Constitutions: What Do the Data Say?* Cambridge, MA: MIT Press.

Peters, B. Guy. 1997. "The Separation of Powers in Parliamentary Systems." In Kurt von Mettenheim (ed.), *Presidential Institutions and Democratic Politics: Comparing Regional and National Contexts* (Baltimore: Johns Hopkins University Press), 67–83.

Peterson, Paul E., and Mark C. Rom. 1990. *Welfare Magnets: A New Case for a National Standard.* Washington, DC: Brookings Institution.

Pierson, Paul. 2004. *Politics in Time.* Princeton, NJ: Princeton University Press.

Pitkin, Hanna Fenichel. 1967. *The Concept of Representation.* Berkeley: University of California Press.

Pocock, J. G. A. 1957/1987. *The Ancient Constitution and the Feudal Law: A Study of English Historical Thought in the Seventeenth Century.* Cambridge: Cambridge University Press.

Pocock, J. G. A. 1975. *The Machiavellian Moment: Florentine Political Thought and the Atlantic Republican Tradition.* Princeton, NJ: Princeton University Press.

Poikolainen, Kari, and Juhani Eskola. 1988. "Health Services Resources and Their Relation to Mortality from Causes Amenable to Health Care: A Cross-National Study." *International Journal of Epidemiology* 17, 86–9.

Pole, J. R. 1966. *Political Representation in England and the Origins of the American Republic.* Berkeley: University of California Press.

Posner, Richard A. 1974. "Theories of Economic Regulation." *Bell Journal of Economics and Management* 5:2, 335–58.

Powell, G. Bingham. 2000. *Elections as Instruments of Democracy: Majoritarian and Proportional Visions.* New Haven, CT: Yale University Press.

Pressman, Jeffrey L., and Aaron Wildavsky. 1973. *Implementation.* Berkeley: University of California Press.

Pritchett, Lant, and L. H. Summers. 1996. "Wealthier Is Healthier." *Journal of Human Resources* 31:4 (Fall), 841–68.

Prud'homme, Remy. 1995. "The Dangers of Decentralization." *World Bank Research Observer* 10:2 (August), 201–20.

Przeworski, Adam. 2003. *States and Markets: A Primer in Political Economy.* Cambridge: Cambridge University Press.

Rae, Nicol C. 1994. *Southern Democrats.* New York: Oxford University Press.

Ranis, Gustav, and Frances Stewart. 2000. "Strategies for Success in Human Development." *Journal of Human Development* 1:1, 49–70.

Ranis, Gustav, Frances Stewart, and Alejandro Ramirez. 2000. "Economic Growth and Human Development." *World Development* 28:2 (February), 197–219.

Ranney, Austin. 1962. *The Doctrine of Responsible Party Government: Its Origins and Present State.* Urbana: University of Illinois Press.

Ranney, Austin. 1965. *Pathways to Parliament: Candidate Selection in Britain.* Madison: University of Wisconsin Press.

Rasmusen, Eric, and J. Mark Ramseyer. 1992. "Cheap Bribes and the Corruption Ban: A Coordination Game among Rational Legislators." *Public Choice* 78, 305–27.

Ravallion, Martin. 1997. "Good and Bad Growth: The Human Development Reports." *World Development* 25, 631–8.

Rawls, John. 1971. *A Theory of Justice.* Cambridge, MA: Harvard University Press.

Ray, Amal. 1987. "Federalism and Political Development in India: Past Trends and Present Issues." In Tarun Chandra Bose (ed.), *Indian Federalism: Problems and Issues* (Calcutta: K. P. Bagchi).

Reilly, Ben. 2001. *Democracy in Divided Societies.* Cambridge: Cambridge University Press.

Reiss, Julian. 2003. "Practice Ahead of Theory: Instrumental Variables, Natural Experiments and Inductivism in Econometrics." Unpublished manuscript, Centre for Philosophy of Natural and Social Science, London School of Economics.

Remmer, Karen L., and Erik Wibbels. 2000. "The Subnational Politics of Economic Adjustment: Provincial Politics and Fiscal Performance in Argentina." *Comparative Political Studies* 33 (May), 419–51.

Reynolds, Andrew, and Ben Reilly. 1997. *The International IDEA Handbook of Electoral System Design.* Stockholm: Information Services, International IDEA.

Rhodes, R. A. W., and Patrick Dunleavy (eds.). 1995. *Prime Minister: Cabinet and Core Executive.* London: Palgrave Macmillan.

Riggs, Fred W. 1994. "Bureaucracy: A Profound Perplexity for Presidentialism." In Ali Farazmand (ed.), *Handbook on Bureaucracy* (New York: Marcel Dekker), 97–148.

Riggs, Fred W. 1997. "Presidentialism versus Parliamentarism: Implications for Representativeness and Legitimacy." *International Political Science Review* 18:3, 253–78.

Riker, William H. 1964. *Federalism: Origin, Operation, Significance.* Boston: Little, Brown.

Riker, William H. 1982. *Liberalism against Populism: A Confrontation between the Theory of Democracy and the Theory of Social Choice.* San Francisco: W. H. Freeman.

Riley, James C. 2001. *Rising Life Expectancy: A Global History.* Cambridge: Cambridge University Press.

Robbins, Caroline. 1959/1968. *The Eighteenth-Century Commonwealthman: Studies in the Transmission, Development, and Circumstances of English Liberal Thought from the Restoration of Charles II until the War with the Thirteen Colonies.* New York: Atheneum.

Robertson, David Brian. 1989. "The Bias of American Federalism: The Limits of Welfare-State Development in the Progressive Era." *Journal of Policy History* 1:3, 261–91.

Rockman, Bert A. 1981. "America's Departments of State: Irregular and Regular Syndromes of Policy Making." *American Political Science Review* 75, 911–27.

Rodden, Jonathan, and Gunnar S. Eskeland. 2003. "Lessons and Conclusions." In Jonathan Rodden, Gunnar Eskeland, and Jennie Litvack (eds.), *Fiscal Decentralization and the Challenge of Hard Budget Constraints* (Cambridge, MA: MIT Press), 431–66.

Rodden, Jonathan, Gunnar Eskeland, and Jennie Litvack (eds.). 2003. *Fiscal Decentralization and the Challenge of Hard Budget Constraints.* Cambridge, MA: MIT Press.

Rodriguez, Francisco, and Dani Rodrik. 2001. "Trade Policy and Economic Growth: A Skeptic's Guide to Cross-National Evidence." In Ben Bernanke and Ken Rogoff (eds.), *NBER Macroeconomics Annual 2000* (Cambridge, MA: MIT Press), 261–324.

Rodrik, Dani. 1997. *Has Globalization Gone Too Far?* Washington, DC: Institute for International Economics.

Rodrik, Dani. 1999. *Making Openness Work: The New Global Economy and the Developing Countries.* Washington, DC: The Overseas Development Council.

Roeder, Phillip G. 1991. "Soviet Federalism and Ethnic Mobilization." *World Politics* 43:2, 196–232.

Rogers, R. G., and S. Wofford. 1989. "Life Expectancy in Less Developed Countries: Socioeconomic Development or Public Health?" *Journal of Biosocial Science* 21:2 (April), 245–52.

Rogowski, Ronald. 1987. "Trade and the Variety of Democratic Institutions." *International Organization* 41:2 (Spring), 203–23.

Roller, Edeltraud. 2006. *The Performance of Democracies: Political Institutions and Public Policy.* Oxford: Oxford University Press.

Ross, Marc Howard. 1993. *The Culture of Conflict: Interpretations and Interests in Comparative Perspective.* New Haven, CT: Yale University Press.

Rothstein, Bo, and Sven Steinmo (eds.). 2002. *Restructuring the Welfare State: Political Institutions and Policy Change.* New York: Palgrave.

Roubini, Nouriel, and Jeffrey Sachs. 1989. "Government Spending and Budget Deficits in the Industrial Countries." *Economic Policy* 8 (April), 100–32.

Rourke, Francis. 1991. "Presidentializing the Bureaucracy: From Kennedy to Reagan." In James P. Pfiffner (ed.), *The Managerial Presidency* (Pacific Grove, CA: Brooks/Cole), 123–34.

Rubin, Jeffrey W. 1996. "Decentering the Regime: Culture and Regional Politics in Mexico." *Latin American Research Review* 31, 85–126.

Rustow, Dankwart A. 1955. *The Politics of Compromise: A Study of Parties and Cabinet Government in Sweden.* Princeton, NJ: Princeton University Press.

Sachs, Jeffrey D., and Andrew Warner. 1995. "Economic Reform and the Process of Global Integration." *Brookings Papers on Economic Activity* 95:1, 1–118.

Sagar, Ambuj D., and Adil Najam. 1998. "The Human Development Index: A Critical Review." *Ecological Economics* 25, 249–64.

Saideman, Stephen M., David J. Lanoue, M. Campenni, and S. Stanton. 2002. "Democratization, Political Institutions, and Ethnic Conflict: A Pooled Time-Series Analysis, 1985–1998." *Comparative Political Studies* 35, 103–29.

Samuels, David J. 2000a. "Concurrent Elections, Discordant Results: Presidentialism, Federalism, and Governance in Brazil." *Comparative Politics* 33:1 (October), 1–20.

Samuels, David J. 2000b. "The Gubernatorial Coattails Effect: Federalism and Congressional Elections in Brazil." *Journal of Politics* 62:1 (February), 240–53.

Samuels, David J. 2003. *Ambition, Federalism, and Legislative Politics in Brazil*. Cambridge: Cambridge University Press.

Samuels, David J. 2007. "Separation of Powers." In Carles Boix and Susan Stokes (eds.), *Oxford Handbook of Comparative Politics* (Oxford: Oxford University Press), 703–26.

Samuels, Warren, and Nicholas Mercuro. 1984. "A Critique of Rent-Seeking Theory." In David Colander (ed.), *Neoclassical Political Economy: The Analysis of Rent-seeking and DUP Activities* (Cambridge, MA: Ballinger), 55–70.

Samuelson, Paul A. 1954. "The Pure Theory of Public Expenditure." *Review of Economics and Statistics* 36, 387–9.

Sanyal, Bishwapriya, and Vinit Mukhija. 2001. "Institutional Pluralism and Housing Delivery: A Case of Unforeseen Conflicts in Mumbai, India." *World Development* 29:12 (December), 2043–57.

Sartori, Giovanni. 1976. *Parties and Party Systems: A Framework for Analysis*. Cambridge: Cambridge University Press.

Sartori, Giovanni. 1987. *The Theory of Democracy Revisited*. Chatham, NJ: Chatham House.

Sartori, Giovanni. 1994. *Comparative Constitutional Engineering: An Inquiry into Structures, Incentives and Outcomes*. New York: New York University Press.

Sawers, Larry. 1998. *The Other Argentina: The Interior and National Development*. Boulder, CO: Westview.

Schamis, Hector E. 2002. *Re-Forming the State: The Politics of Privatization in Latin America and Europe*. Ann Arbor: University of Michigan Press.

Schantz, Harvey L. 1996. "Sectionalism in Presidential Elections." In Harvey L. Schantz (ed.), *American Presidential Elections: Process, Policy, and Political Change* (Albany: State University of New York Press), 93–133.

Scharpf, Fritz W. 1988. "The Joint Decision Trap: Lessons from German Federalism and European Integration." *Public Administration* 66 (Autumn), 239–78.

Schattschneider, E. E. 1942. *Party Government*. New York: Rinehart.

Schattschneider, E. E. 1960. *The Semi-Sovereign People*. New York: Holt, Rinehart, and Winston.

Scheiber, Harry N. 1975. "Federalism and the American Economic Order, 1789–1910." *Law and Society Review* 10 (Fall), 57–118.

Schiavo-Campo, Salvatore, and Pachampet Sundaram. 2001. *To Serve and to Preserve: Improving Public Administration in a Competitive World.* Manila, Philippines: Asian Development Bank.

Schmidt, Steffen W., et al. (eds.). 1977. *Friends, Followers, and Factions: A Reader in Political Clientelism.* Berkeley: University of California Press.

Schneider, Ben Ross. 1993. "The Career Connection: A Comparative Analysis of Bureaucratic Preferences and Insulation." *Comparative Politics* 25:3, 331–50.

Schumpeter, Joseph A. 1942/1950. *Capitalism, Socialism and Democracy,* 3d ed. New York: Harper and Brothers.

Schwartz, Thomas. 1994. "Representation as Agency and the Pork Barrel Paradox." *Public Choice* 78, 3–21.

Scully, Gerald W. 1991. "Rent-seeking in U.S. Government Budgets, 1900–88." *Public Choice* 70, 99–106.

Scully, Gerald W. 1992. *Constitutional Environments and Economic Growth.* Princeton, NJ: Princeton University Press.

Sekhon, Jasjeet S. 2004. "Quality Meets Quantity: Case Studies, Conditional Probability and Counterfactuals." *Perspectives in Politics* 2:2 (June), 281–93.

Selowsky, Marcelo. 1979. *Who Benefits from Government Expenditure? A Case Study of Colombia.* New York: Oxford University Press.

Shalhope, Robert E. 1972. "Toward a Republican Synthesis: The Emergence of an Understanding of Republicanism in American Historiography." *William and Mary Quarterly* 29:1 (January), 49–80.

Shalhope, Robert E. 1982. "Republicanism and Early American Historiography." *William and Mary Quarterly* 39:2 (April), 334–56.

Shleifer, Andrei, and Robert W. Vishny. 1993. "Corruption." *Quarterly Journal of Economics* 108:3 (August), 599–617.

Shleifer, Andrei, and Robert W. Vishny. 1998. *The Grabbing Hand: Government Pathologies and Their Cures.* Cambridge, MA: Harvard University Press.

Shugart, Matthew Soberg, and John M. Carey. 1992. *Presidents and Assemblies: Constitutional Design and Electoral Dynamics.* New York: Cambridge University Press.

Shugart, Matthew Soberg, and Martin P. Wattenberg (eds.). 2001. *Mixed-Member Electoral Systems: The Best of Both Worlds?* Oxford: Oxford University Press.

Shvetsova, Olga. 1999. "A Survey of Post-Communist Electoral Institutions, 1990–1998." *Electoral Studies* 18, 397–409.

Sikkink, Kathryn. 1991. *Ideas and Institutions: Developmentalism in Brazil and Argentina.* Ithaca, NY: Cornell University Press.

Sisk, Timothy. 1995. *Democratization in South Africa: The Elusive Social Contract.* Princeton, NJ: Princeton University Press.

Skach, Cindy. 2006. *Borrowing Constitutional Designs: Constitutional Law in Weimar Germany and the French Fifth Republic*. Princeton, NJ: Princeton University Press.

Skocpol, Theda. 1985. "Bringing the State Back In: Strategies of Analysis in Current Research." In Peter B. Evans, Dietrichdr Rueschemeyer, and Theda Skocpol (eds.), *Bringing the State Back In* (Cambridge: Cambridge University Press), 3–37.

Smith, Adam. 1776/1939. *An Inquiry into the Nature and Causes of the Wealth of Nations*. New York: Modern Library.

Snyder, Jack L. 2000. *From Voting to Violence: Democratization and Nationalist Conflict*. New York: Norton.

Snyder, Richard. 2001. *Politics after Neoliberalism: Reregulation in Mexico*. Cambridge: Cambridge University Press.

Somide, Adegboyega. 2001. "Federalism, State Creation and Ethnic Management in Nigeria." In Bamidele A. Ojo (ed.), *Problems and Prospects of Sustaining Democracy in Nigeria* (Huntington, NY: Nova Science Publishers), 19–36.

Srinivasan, T. N. 1994. "Human Development: A New Paradigm or Reinvention of the Wheel?" *American Economic Review* 84:2 (May), 238–43.

Srinivasan, T. N., and Jagdish Bhagwati. 1999. "Outward-Orientation and Development: Are Revisionists Right?" Discussion Paper No. 806, Economic Growth Center, Yale University.

Steinberg, Jonathan. 1996. *Why Switzerland?*, 2nd ed. Cambridge: Cambridge University Press.

Steinmo, Sven. 1993. *Taxation and Democracy: Swedish, British and American Approaches to Financing the Modern State*. New Haven, CT: Yale University Press.

Steinmo, Sven. 2001. "Institutionalism." In *International Encyclopedia of the Social and Behavioral Sciences*, ed. Nelson Polsby (London: Elsevier Science), 7554–8.

Stepan, Alfred. 2004. "Toward a New Comparative Politics of Federalism, Multinationalism, and Democracy: Beyond Rikerian Federalism." In Edward L. Gibson (ed.), *Federalism and Democracy in Latin America* (Baltimore: Johns Hopkins University Press), 29–84.

Stepan, Alfred, and Cindy Skach. 1993. "Constitutional Frameworks and Democratic Consolidation: Parliamentarianism versus Presidentialism." *World Politics* 46, 1–22.

Stigler, George J. 1972. "Economic Competition and Political Competition." *Public Choice* 13, 91–106.

Stoker, Laura. 1992. "Interests and Ethics in Politics." *American Political Science Review* 86 (September), 369–80.

Stoner-Weiss, Kathryn. 2001. "The Limited Reach of Russia's Party System: Under-Institutionalization in Dual Transitions." *Politics and Society* 29:3 (September), 385–414.

Stratmann, Thomas, and Martin Baur. 2002. "Plurality Rule, Proportional Representation, and the German *Bundestag*: How Incentives to Pork-Barrel

Differ across Electoral Systems." *American Journal of Political Science* 46:3 (July), 506–14.

Strom, Kaare. 1990. *Minority Government and Majority Rule*. Cambridge: Cambridge University Press.

Suberu, Rotimi T. 2001. *Federalism and Ethnic Conflict in Nigeria*. Washington, DC: United States Institute of Peace.

Suleiman, Ezra N. (ed.). 1984. *Bureaucrats and Policy Making: A Comparative Overview*. New York: Holmes and Meier.

Susskind, Lawrence, and Jeffrey Cruikshank. 1987. *Breaking the Impasse: Consensual Approaches to Resolving Public Disputes*. New York: Basic Books.

Susskind, Lawrence, Sarah McKearnan, and Jennifer Thomas-Larmer. 1999. *The Consensus Building Handbook: A Comprehensive Guide to Reaching Agreement*. Beverly Hills, CA: Sage.

Taagepera, Rein, and Matthew S. Shugart. 1989. *Seats and Votes: The Effects and Determinants of Electoral Systems*. New Haven, CT: Yale University Press.

Taras, Ray (ed.). 1997. *Post-Communist Presidents*. Cambridge: Cambridge University Press.

Ter-Minassian, Teresa (ed.). 1997. *Fiscal Federalism in Theory and Practice*. Washington, DC: International Monetary Fund.

Thomas, John Clayton. 1975. *The Decline of Ideology in Western Political Parties: A Study of Changing Policy Orientations*. London: Sage.

Thomas, John Clayton. 1979. "The Changing Nature of Partisan Divisions in the West: Trends in Domestic Policy Orientations in Ten Party Systems." *European Journal of Political Research* 7, 397–413.

Tiebout, Charles M. 1956. "A Pure Theory of Local Government Expenditure." *Journal of Political Economy* 64, 416–24.

Tomkins, Adam. 2001. "Separations of Powers, Ancient and Modern." Unpublished manuscript, St. Catherine's College, Oxford.

Treisman, Daniel S. 1999. "Russia's Tax Crisis: Explaining Falling Revenues in a Transitional Economy." *Economics and Politics* 11, 145–69.

Treisman, Daniel S. 2003. "Political Decentralization: A Formal Analysis." Unpublished manuscript, Princeton University.

Truman, David B. 1951. *The Governmental Process*. New York: Alfred A. Knopf.

Truman, David B. 1955. "Federalism and the Party System." In Arthur W. MacMahon (ed.), *Federalism: Mature and Emergent* (New York: Columbia University Press), 115–36.

Tsebelis, George. 1990. "Elite Interaction and Constitution Building in Consociational Societies." *Journal of Theoretical Politics* 2:1, 5–29.

Tsebelis, George. 1995. "Decision Making in Political Systems: Veto Players in Presidentialism, Parliamentarism, Multicameralism and Multipartism." *British Journal of Political Science* 25:3, 289–326.

Tsebelis, George. 2000. "Veto Players in Institutional Analysis." *Governance* 13:4 (October), 441–74.

Tsebelis, George. 2002. *Veto Players: How Political Institutions Work*. Princeton, NJ: Princeton University Press.

Tsebelis, George, and Jeannette Money. 1997. *Bicameralism*. Cambridge: Cambridge University Press.

Tullock, Gordon. 1980. "Rent Seeking as a Negative-Sum Game." In James M. Buchanan, Robert Tollison, and Gordon Tullock (eds.), *Toward a Theory of the Rent-Seeking Society* (College Station: Texas A&M University Press), 16–38.

Turner, Frederick Jackson. 1932. *Sections in American History*. New York: Henry Holt.

United Nations. 1991. *Child Mortality in Developing Countries*. New York: United Nations.

United Nations. 1999. "*Guidelines on Tracking Child and Maternal Mortality.*" New York: United Nations Population Division, Department of Economic and Social Affairs.

Urwin, Derek W. 1982. "Germany: From Geographical Expression to Regional Accommodation." In Stein Rokkan and Derek Urwin (eds.), *The Politics of Territorial Identity* (Beverly Hills, CA: Sage), 165–250.

Vallin, Jacques, and Alan D. Lopez (eds.). 1985. *Health Policy, Social Policy, and Mortality Prospects*. Liege: International Union for the Scientific Study of Population.

Van de Walle, Dominique, and Kimberly Nead (eds.). 1995. *Public Spending and the Poor: Theory and Evidence*. Baltimore: Johns Hopkins University Press/World Bank.

Vanhanen, Tatu. 1990. *The Process of Democratization: A Comparative Study of 147 States, 1980–88*. New York: Crane Russak.

Vanhanen, Tatu. 2000. "A New Dataset for Measuring Democracy, 1810–1998." *Journal of Peace Research* 37:2, 251–65.

Vengroff, Richard. 1994. "The Impact of Electoral Systems on the Transition to Democracy in Africa: The Case of Mali." *Electoral Studies* 13, 29–37.

Vile, M. J. C. 1967/1998. *Constitutionalism and the Separation of Powers*. Indianapolis, IN: Liberty Fund.

Vogel, David J. 1986. *National Styles of Regulation*. Ithaca, NY: Cornell University Press.

von Mettenheim, Kurt (ed.). 1997. *Presidential Institutions and Democratic Politics: Comparing Regional and National Contexts*. Baltimore: Johns Hopkins University Press.

Wald, Kenneth D. 1987. *Religion and Politics in the United States*. New York: St Martin's.

Ward, Alan J. 1994. *The Irish Constitutional Tradition: Responsible Government and Modern Ireland, 1782–1992*. Washington, DC: Catholic University of America Press.

Ware, Alan. 1987. *Citizens, Parties and the State*. Cambridge, UK: Polity Press.

Watts, Ronald. 1997. *Comparing Federal Systems in the 1990s*. Montreal: McGill–Queen's University Press.

Weaver, R. Kent, and Bert A. Rockman (eds.). 1993. *Do Institutions Matter? Government Capabilities in the United States and Abroad.* Washington, DC: Brookings Institution.

Weber, Max. 1978. *Economy and Society: An Outline of Interpretive Sociology*, 2 vols., ed. Guenther Roth and Claus Wittich. Berkeley: University of California Press.

Weingast, Barry R. 1993. "Constitutions as Governance Structures: The Political Foundations of Secure Markets." *Journal of Institutional and Theoretical Economics* 149:1, 286–311.

Weingast, Barry R. 1995. "The Economic Role of Political Institutions: Market-Preserving Federalism and Economic Development." *Journal of Law, Economics, and Organization* 11:1, 1–31.

Weingast, Barry R. 2000. "A Comparative Theory of Federal Economic Performance." *APSA-CP: Newsletter of the Organized Section in Comparative Politics of the American Political Science Association* 11:1 (Winter) 6–11.

Wennemo, Irene. 1993. "Infant Mortality, Public Policy, and Inequality: A Comparison of 18 Industrialised Countries." *Sociology of Health and Illness* 15, 429–46.

Weyland, Kurt. 1996. *Democracy without Equity: The Failures of Reform in Brazil.* Pittsburgh: Pittsburgh University Press.

Weyland, Kurt. 2003. "'Good Governance' and Development: A Skeptical View." Unpublished manuscript, Department of Political Science, University of Texas at Austin.

Wheare, K. C. 1963. *Federal Government,* 4th ed. London: Oxford University Press.

Whitaker, Reginald. 1987. "Between Patronage and Bureaucracy: Democratic Politics in Transition." *Journal of Canadian Studies* 22, 55–71.

White, Leonard D. 1955. *Introduction to the Study of Public Administration.* New York: Macmillan.

Wibbels, Erik. 2000. "Federalism and the Politics of Macroeconomic Policy and Performance." *American Journal of Political Science* 44, 687–702.

Williamson, Oliver E. 1996. *Mechanisms of Governance.* Oxford: Oxford University Press.

Wilson, Bradford P., and Peter W. Schramm (eds.). 1994. *Separation of Powers and Good Government.* Lanham, MD: Rowman and Littlefield.

Wilson, James Q. 1989. *Bureaucracy: What Government Agencies Do and Why They Do It.* New York: Basic Books.

Wilson, James Q. 1992. *American Government: Institutions and Policies.* Boston: Houghton Mifflin.

Wilson, John. 1983. "On the Dangers of Bickering in a Federal State: Some Reflections on the Failure of the National Party System." In Allan Kornberg and Harold D. Clarke (eds.), *Political Support in Canada: The Crisis Years* (Durham, NC: Duke University Press), 171–224.

Wilson, Sven E., and Daniel M. Butler. 2003. "Too Good to Be True? The Promise and Peril of Panel Data in Political Science." Unpublished manuscript, Department of Political Science, Brigham Young University.

Wilson, Woodrow. 1879/1965. "Cabinet Government in the United States." *International Review* 7 (August). Reprinted in *The Political Thought of Woodrow Wilson*, ed. E. David Cronon (Indianapolis: Bobbs-Merrill), 29–53.

Wilson, Woodrow. 1885/1956. *Congressional Government*. Baltimore: Johns Hopkins University Press.

Wilson, Woodrow. 1887/1978. "The Study of Administration." *Political Science Quarterly* 2:1 (June). Reprinted in Jay M. Shafritz and Albert C. Hyde (eds.), *Classics of Public Administration* (Oak Park, IL: Moore Publishing Company), 3–16.

Wittman, Donald A. 1995. *The Myth of Democratic Failure: Why Political Institutions Are Efficient*. Chicago: University of Chicago Press.

Wood, Gordon S. 1969. *The Creation of the American Republic, 1776–1787*. Chapel Hill: University of North Carolina Press.

Wooldridge, Jeffrey. 2002. *Introductory Econometrics: A Modern Approach*. Cincinnati, OH: South-Western College Publishers.

World Bank. 2002. *World Bank World Development Indicators 2002*. CD-rom.

World Bank. 2003a. *World Bank World Development Indicators 2003*. CD-rom.

World Bank. 2003b. *World Development Report 2003: Sustainable Development in a Dynamic World: Transforming Institutions, Growth, and Quality of Life*. New York: Oxford University Press.

Yee, Albert S. 1996. "The Effects of Ideas on Policies." *International Organization* 50:1 (Winter), 69–111.

Zartman, William I. 1995. "Introduction: Posing the Problem of State Collapse." In William I. Zartman (ed.), *Collapsed States: The Disintegration and Restoration of Legitimate Authority* (Boulder, CO: Lynne Rienner), 1–14.

Zuckerman, Alan. 1979. *The Politics of Faction: Christian Democratic Rule in Italy*. New Haven, CT: Yale University Press.

Author Index

Subject Index